The Sea
Aboji
Father.

Had Overcome
as a First-Generation Korean-Japanese

Ri Heungseop

Translated by **Akiko Takemoto**

The Sea *Aboji* Had Overcome

as a First-Generation Korean-Japanese

The Sea *Aboji* Had Overcome:
as a First-Generation Korean-Japanese
Authored by Ri Heungseop
Translated by Akiko Takemoto

The original books are "アポジがこえた海—在日朝鮮人一世の証言" authored by Ri Heungseop, first published in 1987 by Ashi Shobō, ISBN978-4751201435, "続 アポジがこえた海—在日朝鮮人一世の戦後—" authored by Ri Heungseop, edited by Takuo Murota, first published in 2015 by Kaihō Shuppan-sha, ISBN978-4759262254.

This Edition Published by BIKOH Publishing, Takamatsu, Kagawa, Japan.
Printed in Japan, 2018
First Edition: August 2018
ISBN978-4-86387-089-5

The Sea *Aboji* Had Overcome:
as a First-Generation Korean-Japanese

ISBN 978-4-86387-089-5
2018年8月初版第1刷発行

原著者　李　興　燮
翻訳者　武本　明子
発行所　株式会社 美巧社
　　　　〒760-0063　香川県高松市多賀町1-8-10
　　　　〈電話〉087-833-5811

CONTENTS

From *Aboji* to Daughter

I . THE START OF THE LONG JOURNEY

ONE DAY IT CAME OUT OF THE BLUE

- In May, 1944 1
- Across the Dark Strait 4
- What Japan was like When I Saw it for the First Time 6
- What I have Remembered about the Land of my Ancestors:
  Goksan in Hwanghae-dō 9
- The First Day in Japan 13
- Being Trained in a Military Fashion 15
- Tunneling our Way through the Gallery 18
- A Scene of Beating up a Traitor 20

THE DAYS OF OUR COMPULSORY LABOR

- The Permission for me to Go out on the *Bon* Holiday was
  Suddenly Canceled 23
- My Determination to Take off 28
- I had been Branded as a Traitor 34
- Living in the Double Discrimination against the Koreans 41
- Those who had been out Returned 44
- We had Two More Watchmen at the Mess Hall 50
- The Three of us had Run Away 53
- What Happened at the Mess Hall 58

● Working in the Coal Mine 64

● Who was it that had Brought me the Package of the Burnt
Rice Ball? 69

● The Pieces of False Information Given by the Imperial
Headquarters 73

● My Thoughts on My Homeland 76

● The Packed Lunch 79

● The Hard Labor in the Coal Mine 82

● The First Salary I had Received 84

Ⅱ. AS FAR AS WHERE THE STRAIT WAS SEEN

● A Letter from Home 89

● Preparing for Running Away 92

● I had My Salary Raised from November on 97

● Our Plan to Run Away 102

● The Last Meal I had Taken *There* 108

● I Got the Permission to Go out 110

● The Decisive Action we Took 114

● In the Bus of our Destiny 120

● What I Thought in the Bus 124

Ⅲ. EMBRACING THE UNSEEN LAND OF MY ANCESTORS

THE ESCAPEE FROM THE COAL MINE

● In the Town of Karatsu 133

● We Found Ourselves at the Guard House 136

● Guided by the Note Handed by the Guard 143

● Our Encounter on the Bridge 149

● The White Rice and the Korean-Style Pickles 154

● We Entered our Accommodation 160

● A New Name Given to Me 167

I KEEP SURVIVING

● At an Unloading Port 176

● To a Small Fishing Village in Fukuoka Prefecture 182

● To Farther West 184

● The Young Men's School in Tatara 186

● My Third Flight 190

● What I Remember about the Pine Juice 193

● I was Employed at Itatsuki Air Port 195

● I Kept on Going Underground 200

● The Falls of Drum Cans 205

● The Train I Took for the First Time 209

● A Piece of Information I Obtained by Paying Three Hundred
  Yen 215

● What had been Done by the Government General of Korea ... 219

● The Atomic Bombings upon Hiroshima and Nagasaki 223

● Mr. Nakagawa, the Only Japanese among us 227

● The Broadcast of the Emperor's Announcement of Japan's
  Surrender 241

● Pondering over Korea, my Ancestral Land 245

● My Birthplace 248

● Japan's Unconditional Surrender 256

Ⅳ. OUR EXPECTATION TO GO HOME

● On the Morning of August 16 264

● Mr. Nakagawa's Talk 268

● Thinking about How to Go Home 277

- Mr. Umimoto's Way of Working 287
- Drinking *Doburoku* 291
- My Farewell Speech 295
- My First Step for Returning Home 299
- The Crowds of People at Hakata Harbor 301
- At the Harbor 304
- The Stable & the Harbor Police that had Remained Unburnt ... 307
- Our Miscalculation about Our Going Home 310
- Under the Staircase of the Harbor Police 314
- Heading for the Stable 322

From Daughter to *Aboji* 328

What was it that had led to Japan's Annexation of Korea?

In 1875, Japan tried to open diplomatic relations by means of military coercion and sent the gunboat *Un'yō* to the west coast of Korea. The action was of an intimidating nature. The Japanese gunboat was attacked at the island of Kanghwa by Korean coast guns, but the captain of the boat, Inoue Yoshika, returned the fire and occupied the fort. Then the Japanese government sent the envoy Kuroda Kiyotaka (1840-1900) to Korea, and the following year an amity treaty was concluded. Korea had to open the port of Pusan and grant consular jurisdiction. This marked the opening of Korea and the beginning of Japanese inroads into Korean territory.

—— *A DICTIONARY OF JAPANESE HISTORY*
By Joseph M. Goedertire, C.I.C.M. WALKER/WEATHERHILL, New York & Tokyo, 1968 (cf. P.92-93,P.221, P.247, P.256-258, P.260)

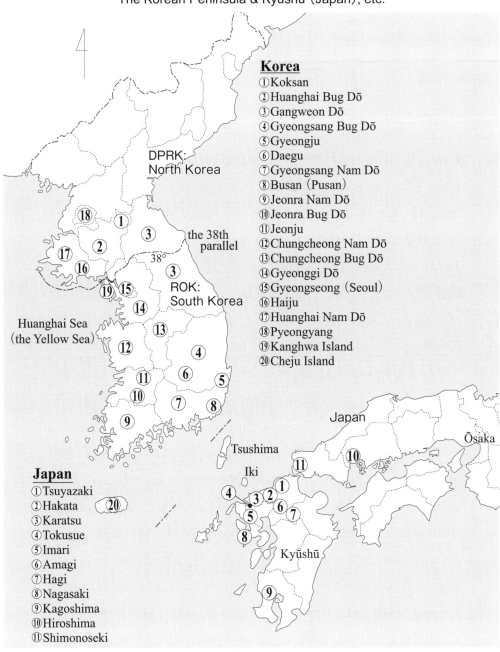

The Korean Peninsula & Kyūshū (Japan), etc.

Korea
① Koksan
② Huanghai Bug Dō
③ Gangweon Dō
④ Gyeongsang Bug Dō
⑤ Gyeongju
⑥ Daegu
⑦ Gyeongsang Nam Dō
⑧ Busan (Pusan)
⑨ Jeonra Nam Dō
⑩ Jeonra Bug Dō
⑪ Jeonju
⑫ Chungcheong Nam Dō
⑬ Chungcheong Bug Dō
⑭ Gyeonggi Dō
⑮ Gyeongseong (Seoul)
⑯ Haiju
⑰ Huanghai Nam Dō
⑱ Pyeongyang
⑲ Kanghwa Island
⑳ Cheju Island

DPRK:
North Korea

the 38th
parallel

38°

ROK:
South Korea

Huanghai Sea
(the Yellow Sea)

Japan

Ōsaka

Tsushima

Iki

Kyūshū

Japan
① Tsuyazaki
② Hakata
③ Karatsu
④ Tokusue
⑤ Imari
⑥ Amagi
⑦ Hagi
⑧ Nagasaki
⑨ Kagoshima
⑩ Hiroshima
⑪ Shimonoseki

From *Aboji* to Daughter

I am a Korean, born in 1928. Now in 1978, I am just fifty. So far I have lived in Japan for thirty-three years. It was in May, 1944, when I first stepped on the soil of Japan. Now I have you as my daughter, who is in the third year of a junior high school. I used to have one more daughter, but she was killed in a traffic accident in 1974. At present, I am living alone with my daughter mentioned first. Recently she has expressed her wish to write about what sort of life I have lived so far − or my personal history. That was why I had decided to talk about my own life so far.

I have often told about my life so far to those who have been familiar with me, but I have never told my own daughter a detailed story of my own life, because I felt it would be impossible for her to understand what I might tell her about it. That is, the era I used to live in before she was born and the present time we live in are so totally different from each other that I could not help doubting if she was able to understand me or believe me. In fact, it would be a great surprise to me, if the junior high school boys and girls today were able to understand what I am going to recount from now on. This does not mean I have lived such a specific life as might find a place in history. My life itself was a very modest one. I had not had any such admirable ambition nor any specific pleasure in my life, but it was not such a terrible life as to bring me close to death, either. To my mind, therefore, my life so far was by no means a specific one as a Korean who had to live in Japan.

It seems to me that different people have different ways of feeling pain, sorrow, pleasure and so on. Having heard me talk about my life so far, many of my acquaintances seem to take my life "a very hard one," but this simply makes me feel: different people have different ways of feelings, illusions, sufferings and so on, whether they were rich or poor.

Thirty-three years have passed since I was brought to Japan in May, 1944. I feel it would be impossible for my daughter still in the third year of the junior high school to write about everything I have experienced so far. So I should like to tell her only of those things I myself would like to keep in mind so that I might refresh my own thought. Now I should like to begin with what had brought me to Japan.

—— Ri Heungseop

I

THE START OF THE LONG JOURNEY

ONE DAY IT CAME OUT OF THE BLUE

● **In May, 1944**

Japan started the Sino-Japanese War (1937-45) and then the Pacific War (1941-45). Long before those actions of warfare took place, Japan had annexed (or colonized) Korea. So, it meant something to lead to the death for us Koreans to disobey the orders issued by the Government of the Imperialist Japan. When the Pacific War broke out (on December 8, 1941), what was called the conscription ordinance was applied to the Koreans, too. The conscription ordinance meant that: the male persons who had attained a certain age were forced to enter the armed forces. On the same line, there was what was called commandeering ordinance that forced the male persons who had attained a certain age to come to Japan to engage in compulsory labor. I myself had been made to come to Japan in this line, when I had just become seventeen.

Usually we Koreans were placed in a unit of one hundred men, just as my corps was. I soon found: three of our unit were still sixteen. At home, I had heard that: the boys to be drafted were above eighteen, but I soon found not a few of us were still seventeen or even sixteen. You may find it hard to understand why, but there were some tricks often employed on the side of invaders and colonialists.

You may say it is unbelievable, but I swear by the gods of heaven and earth that I shall be honest in saying: the government authorities in those days had arbitrarily changed our ages simply for their convenience. That was how hundreds of thousands of Korean boys were sent to Japan to engage in commandeering. We Koreans then used to describe that compulsory manner the Japanese authorities had adopted in bringing us to Japan as drafted workers in a certain metaphorical couplet which went as follows:

They've set a straw rope around our neck;
They've set fire upon our bottom…..

Recently I have been reminded of this couplet when I saw an American movie — *The Roots* — in which the hero was literally being pulled by a rope around his neck! In fact, that was not the way we were taken to Japan.

But, the humiliation we had to suffer then might have been greater. What had filled our heart then was the sorrow that: our ancestors had been so lacking in courage and vitality to keep their own off-springs safe and sound on the Korean Peninsula. What was it that had made our land so low as to be made a colony of Japan? I hope the readers of this book will find out *the* answer.

In May, 1944, when I was seventeen years old, I was working on the soybean farm with my father.

"It's almost lunch time, isn't it?" said my father.

Then, we saw the four men, including a village official, were approaching us in the farm. I saw the official hand my father a yellow envelope in total silence, before they turned back.

My father said; "Let's go home for lunch, though it's a little earlier than usual." Then we went home. But instead of having lunch at home, he took out a suit made of pure white cotton. By the way, I had been bereaved of my mother at thirteen, and this had led my father to live as a widower, taking care of us children. My father then urged me to put on the white cotton suit, and helped me do so. In my memory, this was the first time for me to have my father help me put on something. This led me to be convinced that I was about to be sent somewhere — as a drafted worker.

We had not been allowed to have any time to take lunch. Because we were expected to hurry as far as the bus stop at the edge of the village. On our way there, Father remained totally silent. It was fifteen or twenty minutes' walk there, I think. If we had wished to, we ought to have been able to exchange a considerable amount of conversation. But both of us simply remained silent. More precisely, I simply could neither tell what I should say to him nor what Father was feeling then.

The bus came, and I got on it. Then Father handed me a paper parcel that could be gripped in my hand, and a cotton bag with something in it. Later I found seventy *yen* in the paper parcel. As for the contents in the cotton bag, I then had simply left it as it was — even though it was to bring me a hard time later on.

By and by, we were brought to where the railroad ran and we were guided into the train. By that time, I had already been made a member of a corps consisting of youths who had been drafted as I was. The train ran and ran throughout the night and the next day. I simply could not tell where the train was heading for. On the third day, we were allowed to leave the train. Then we were told to get on board such a huge ship as I had never seen before, as if we were pigs driven into a slaughter house. This was how we left our native land of Korea behind — before we reached somewhere in Japan.

● **Across the Dark Strait**

I still remember how it looked like in the ship we were made to stay until we stepped out on to the soil of Japan. After having been driven into the ship like animals driven into the slaughter house, we were pushed down into the room at the bottom of the ship — to see a scene unbelievable for a moment. I felt as if I were seeing a raft of sleeping cranes. They were several groups of men who had already arrived there before us.

But while gazing at them for a while, I came to notice that their gazing was pointless or aimless. Their eyes appeared to me as if they were trying to tell their own fortune whether it was of sorrows or of pains. This sight made us stand still for a moment at the foot of the staircase. Then there came shouting from the watchmen standing on both sides of the staircase. We could not understand what had made them give that shouting. But their gesture had told us to sit down somewhere there.

This led us to go and take the empty seats one by one. Then there came a disgusting groaning as if from the bottom of the earth. Another shout of reproach did suppress it at once.

I think it was early in the morning, when we got on board the ship. Then we felt the ship begin to pitch and roll. As the time went on, the pitching and rolling got so worse that many of us began to vomit. But there came neither doctor to attend them nor anyone to give them any medicine. I myself had remained in agony, my face unusually flushed, keeping a towel on my mouth.

I could not tell how many hours had passed. I had never been on board such a large ship nor had I experienced so mush swaying that I vomited all that I had eaten. I felt a terrible pain in my stomach as if it was being bored with a drill. I was feeling as if I had been staying there for ten days or even twenty days, but now I think it was a seven or eight hour voyage.

About three hundred of us Koreans in the same boat were suffering the same kind of pain. The scene might have been compared to that of the Hell. But those who had actually been there could not afford to think anything like that. In due course of time, we found the ship's swaying growing less and less until it stopped still. I felt as if I had had my eyes sunken one *sun* (ca. 3cm) deep. All my energy had subsided so much so that I felt as if I had become totally weightless even to such an extent as I might be able to float or fly in the air, if I were equipped with a pair of wings.

Then I was driven back to a reality by a harsh voice of an angry shout of "Stand up!" We stood up in silence according to the jesture given by the man standing at the entrance at the bottom of the staircase. I felt something in my head turning round and round. I had never felt my body so heavy as that. "So we are finally at our destination," said I to myself. Then we were told to leave the ship.

● **What Japan was like When I Saw it for the First Time**

I left the boat, feeling as if I were stepping on the land for the first time after a long voyage that seemed to have lasted for as long as dozens of years. We were led to something like a palace dignified with the marble pillars. Its inside, however, was dark and sooty. We were told to come to our own party and to stand in rows so that the number of us could be counted. Then we had a round number ticket fixed upon our breast, beginning with the one who stood at the front. Then we were told to sit down on the concrete floor — no chair was seen — before we each received a couple of white rice balls, each of which was as large as a closed fist of a boy fourteen or fifteen years old.

At home, I had been told that the draftees were all made to starve to death, so those white rice balls were really surprising to me. This led me to imagine that the white rice might be the only food they could obtain in this land — a land totally strange to me. In fact, I felt as if the hardship I had been suffering during the voyage might have been a dream. Every one of us had eaten these rice balls in no time. In fact, I had never eaten anything so delicious as those rice balls. At home, I lived on the rice farm, but most of the rice we produced was expected to make obligatory supply to Japan as our suzerain state, and the boiled rice was served to us only on the New Year holidays and the *Bon* Festival holidays or the Buddhist All Souls Day

After having eaten those palatable rice balls, each of us was offered three cigarettes. This was something surprising to us, too. I had never smoked before, but I never refused to receive them. The smokers appeared happy to have one between their lips. But even before they finished consuming the first one, we were told to get on the train.

Several hours had passed. The night had already fallen, Once in a while, we saw small lights passing away. No one having worn a wrist watch, we could not tell any exact time. Then our train stopped and we were told to leave the train to walk somewhere. About half an hour's walk brought us to what seemed to be an athletic field. We were told to stand in a row to be made sure of the number on the number ticket fixed on our breast, before we were taken to what seemed to be our final destination.

Then we — what seemed to be three hundred of us in three units — were divided into three. As for my group, we were led to the entrance of the board fence, three meters high, and were guided into a long house with about ten rooms in it — each room with six *tatami* mats in it was for five of us. There was an unfloored space before each room, about 30cm wide and about 30m long.

Six full days and a half had passed before I sat down in this room — after having been taken away from that soybean field of my father's. Still I remained totally ignorant of what sort of life I should lead here. It was not long before the rice balls were again brought to us — two for each. What had attracted my attention was that: the rice balls here or in Japan were of palm-sized triangle. At home, rice balls were egg-shaped. Now the triangular one, I found, tasted as good as the ones I had eaten after having left the ship. Something new to me then was pickled radish, yellow in color! To myself the radish always remained white. This did add to my puzzlement.

Now I had five roommates. The oldest of us was an old man whose head was full of gray hairs. The youngest was one year younger than I. After the rice balls, we were served with hot water, which was also yellow in color! It tasted bitter and we all stopped drinking it after tasting a little bit of it, because we had wondered if it might be a sort of poison. By and by, however, we came to find what the tea was like if made in a Japanese fashion. The yellow radish was also found a sort of pickles — since it was pickled in a fermented mixture of rice bran and brine. At home in Korea, all kinds of pickles were white, excepting cucumbers and greens in early spring.

It was not long before one of the members of our corps came round to each group of us, saying: "It's time to go to bed." Two men were expected to sleep in one bed, excepting an old man who was allowed to sleep alone in his own bed. I was expected to sleep with a boy one year younger than I. When the electric light was turned off, we all, probably having felt more or less relaxed, began to introduce ourselves, after mentioning what part of the Korean Peninsula we came from. My bed-mate's family name was Baek. As for the names of the other room-mates, I have totally forgotten. Thirty-four years have passed since then.....

● **What I have Remembered about the Land of my Ancestors: Goksan in Hwanghae-dō**

My bedfellow, whose family name was Paek, was so plump that he never appeared to be from a poor family. As for myself, I was very skinny. This led me to imagine the sort of circumstance he had been brought up so far, while looking up at the dark ceiling. Then I asked him:

"Have you ever been at school?"

"Yes. For six years," he said.

As for myself, it was only four years.

My family was living in the countryside about 20*ri* (ca. 8km) away from the nearest town. In those days, those living in the town attended school for six years, but those living in such countryside as I lived in, we were expected to leave school at the end of the fourth school year. The school I attended was 12*ri* (ca. 5km) away from my village. There was no age restriction in attending school. As for myself, I entered school at the age of eight, but I found some of my classmates had already appeared grown-up. In summer when we happened to take off our shirt, I found some had the hair at their armpits.

In the countryside we lived in, the school was rather small with less than two hundred pupils from the first year class to the fourth. The school personnel consisted of only five, including the principal. Each grade of class was attended by a teacher, and once a week the principal gave a class of Korean history, which sounded to me as if he were telling an old tale.

When I became a fourth grader, the principal was replaced by a Japanese one, who had just arrived to live in the neighborhood — with his house newly built there. We, in a group of about ten pupils, were taken there to see the house. We found the house was totally different in the make from what we had known so far. The pillars were square! In every house we lived in, the pillars were always round, because we used the trunks of the trees without turning them into any such artifacts. Around the entrance door, we saw a board fence with some open space in between the boards. This was something new to us. No house in our neighborhood had any such board fence as that. Ours were all built of mud mixed with yellowed straw cut in ten-centimeters long.

Here, I should like to recall how my own house looked like. The first thing I recall is a spacious yard ① — 50 *tsubo* at least. (1 *tsubo* = ca.3.3m squares) At the corner of the yard, there was an oblong pile of cut grass ② — about 10 *tsubo* wide — we had made during the summer season. From time to time, the pile of grass was watered so that it might not get dry. By the next spring, all the grass had get rotten to make natural fertilizer. Nowadays we all turn to the chemical fertilizer, though…..

In the corner of the other side of the yard, there was a deep well ③. We drew water from it with a sort of bucket with a rope. In

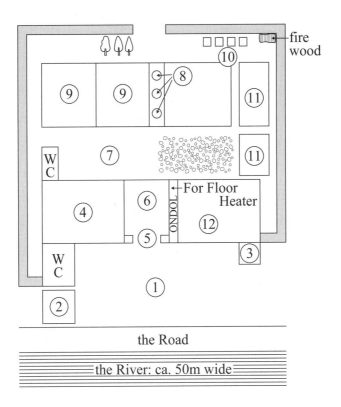

summer, the water was cool; in winter, it was steaming when seen early in the morning, The house stood with its long earthen walls facing the front garden. On the left side, there was a cowshed ④. The entrance to the house stood at the center ⑤. The gate was of a double-door, as is seen in a period film in Japan. Entering the gate, you would step on to the earthen floor ⑥. Then you would come to the courtyard ⑦. As the outside yard was, it was oblong, too. It was covered with rounded stones from the riverbed. Crossing the courtyard, you would come to the main house, which was oblong just like the outside house.

On the right, there was the kitchen with the three cooking stoves ⑧; at the depth of the right-hand side of it, there was a large pile of firewood; on the left-hand side, there were a couple of rooms each of which was eight *tatami*-mats wide ⑨. The earthen walls stood around the whole house. Along the back wall, there stood three or four huge tubs with home-made soy sauce or miso in them ⑩. There stood huge trees, too, which supplied us with peaches, apricots and Chinese dates, when their season came round.

There were also a couple of storehouses ⑪ and what was called an outhouse ⑫, too. All those buildings had round pillars. The courtyard, half of which was covered with rounded stones, was surrounded with the buildings. Sometimes in summer, we used to have supper on the mat spread there, while seeing the early-rising moon in the sky. Since I was born and brought up in such a house as this, the entrance to the new house built for the principal and his family seemed more or less strange to me. That was the first time when I saw a Japanese-style house.

● The First Day in Japan

We, who had slept in Japan for the first time — probably snoring — were suddenly made to jump out of our *futon* or Japanese-style bedding by the noisy sound of whipping that went along the narrow wooden corridor. That was the way the Japanese had adopted in making us jump out of our bed. They looked like us, Koreans in appearance, but the manner they had adopted in making us get up led me to feel they were somewhat different from ourselves. Until I chose to get away from here by over-riding that tall board fence, I used to be made to wake up in this way.

This was how our first day in Japan dawned. We all had carried our belongings in a *furoshiki* or a wrapping cloth with an arabesque design on it, which had later become a trade mark of "Tokyo Bonta," the hero of a T.V. drama we were to enjoy long after we arrived in Japan. Our parcel wrapped in a *furoshiki* had been taken away from us before we entered this room. When it was returned to each of us, we found the parcel had born a number ticket whose number was the same as that of our name tag. we had on our breast.

My parcel in the *furoshiki* was later to bring about a bitter experience to me. I had not undone that parcel since I received it from my father. This had left me ignorant of what sort of things was wrapped in it, even if I had felt it heavier than expected from

13

its size. This *furoshiki* was closely connected with my school days. In those days, we school children had not yet seen anything like a school rucksack or a school bag. All the textbooks and notebooks were carried in a *furoshiki,* while our pencil case was made for ourselves with some cardboard by turning it into a kind of envelope. That was probably why I felt keenly nostalgic on seeing "Tokyo Bonta" carrying his parcel in a *furoshiki.*

After having been roused from sleep that morning, we were led to the mess room. At the entrance to it, there was an office, and we were expected to call out the same number as we had on our chest in order to receive a wooden ticket. At the entrance to the mess room, we were expected to show that ticket before the meal was pushed out. That was what I did before receiving my breakfast. I had learned this procedure from one of those who had also been brought to Japan like ourselves, but he, somehow or other, seemed to be able to speak Japanese.

After the breakfast, we were ordered to line up in numbered order in the square before the mess room. A man, who stepped on a speaker's platform, began to speak. His appearance was far from a Korean, but he spoke an unmistakable Korean as we had learned at school — quite understandable even to the country boy like myself.

What he said first was the words of appreciation for the hardship we had to go through before we reached here. Then he went on; "We are now in Kyushu in Japan — more precisely, Tokusue in Saga Prefecture. You are now expected to work for two years at a coal mine — to dig out coal. There is a training period for a couple of weeks before you begin to work as coal miners. I hope you will be good trainees and good workers for the sake of the country, while taking care not to fall ill."

● Being Trained in a Military Fashion

What we were made to learn then was: how to receive a roll call by saying "one, two, three, four....," to follow the calls of "Right turn!" "Left turn!" "About face!" "Salute!" "Foreward!" "Quick march!".... After having mastered them, we were made to learn how to behave with a bamboo stick about 150cm long in our hands, according to such orders as "Go!" and "Stick!".... After having mastered them, we were made to learn how to behave according to "Go!" and "Charge!".... It took many days before we mastered all of them. Some had a poor carriage; others were bad at giving a word of command. We had a hard time mastering all of them. We were being trained even before we were able to speak any Japanese language. It being apparent that these actions were not indispensable in digging out coal, we could not help wondering what a strange training we were being made to go through.

Then we were ordered to run as long as three kilometers; some collapsed on the way. Most of them were elderly ones. As the days of training went on, food supply got scarce, while the taste was far from good. This did dishearten us. What had been served to us as "the boiled rice" was actually what was called "bean cake" or strained lees of beans. As for the side dishes, fish, which was served only occasionally as a treat, was no more than salted one. This had led me to wish to eat more whatever quality it might be.

At home, I had heard some who had been sent for commandeering starved to death. I thought I had been prepared to face such a fate, but it was not until I actually suffered hunger that I realized how hard it was to face hunger, even if I had not found the training itself so hard as the elderly had had to.

Hunger made me wake up even at night. Even before going to toilet to relieve myself, I went to drink water to relieve my hunger. I once asked a gray-haired old man what had made him come here as a drafted worker. His answer was: "My son, twenty years old, was to be drafted, but he had run away from home many months before. That was why I offered myself in place of my son." Hearing this, I felt as if I had done something good to my own father.

As the days went on, our training was becoming more and more militaristic in quality. We were trained to go ahead on our stomach, keeping only our elbows working. We learned how to make a salute while carrying a gun. Under the pretext of training, we were made to mow the grass in the open space behind the office building of the coal-mining company. Thus we were made to spend exactly a couple of weeks in such training as would never be of any help in the coal-mining we were expected to engage in before long.

On the final day of our training, *that* Japanese who spoke good Korean made his appearance and said to us: "Now your training was over. From tomorrow on, you are expected to work at the coal mine." Then, at night, we were invited to see a movie at a nearby school. Since the language used in the movie was not understandable at all to us, all we could understand from the scenes, the buildings and the gestures of the people appearing there was: a very sad story was going on. Neither the title of the movie nor the names of the actors and actresses had been given to us. Still I remember a song sung in that movie: "The glowing sky in the evening is gradually grading into gloom...." That was the first Japanese movie I had ever seen. In fact, everything that had occurred to me since I left home was what I had experienced for the first time in my life. This led me to say to myself: "I'll have a long series of "the first experiences in my life" before me, it seems."

The movie was over in a couple of hours or so. Then we were told to gather again to make it certain that we were all there. After the calls were given, it was found several of us had run away! Not only the staff of the dormitory but those who seemed to be school teachers also went around to find them out, but in vain. We, standing in rows, remained silent, while praying they — the first escapees of us — might not be found out.

It was not until we went to bed that we talked about the runaways in a low voice — how many of us and who they were, and the like — till late at night. It was unknown to us how many had run away, but it seemed four or five of us, when recalling the roll call we had

had before going out to see the movie. To us, drafted workers, this was something exciting as well as surprising.

● **Tunneling our Way through the Gallery**

According to the schedule we had been told about, we were sent into a coal mine. Talking of going to work, we are usually expected to arrive at a certain place in a work uniform, carrying a lunch with us. But here, at the coal mine, everything was totally different from what was expected. All we had on us as a uniform was a loincloth, 3 *shaku* long (ca.1m). That was all!

At the office at the entrance to the pithead, we were expected to show our number ticket to receive an instrument called cap with an electric lamp on it, and after having worn it around our waste, we put the lamp upon our cap. Then, we were carried in a tramcar (made of iron plate) as far as the vicinity of our work site. When I first took that tramcar, which went down the steep slope as if falling down, I felt simply so terrified that I felt as if the muscle of my hip had been shrunk!

What I was expected to do there was to put the coal sludge (brought about by blasting the rock) into the tram car. The work itself was not so difficult nor so hard to do, but the heat around there was simply annoying to us. Such a kind of work, as was done by the coal miners, was apparently hard to do. When they came out of the mine after the day's work, they were literally coal-black all over excepting their eyes which appeared goggling.

A couple of weeks had passed since we began to be engaged in such a work. Then, all the baggage we had carried from home, only to be taken away on the night when we reached that dormitory, was returned to us. As a matter of fact, I myself had not yet seen what had been packed into that baggage of mine. We were called to the office one by one, before our baggage was returned to us. But some of us — fifteen or sixteen of us, including myself — could not have our baggage returned.

On the day that followed, we were called to the office one by one, before our bag was returned. When my turn came and I entered the office of our dormitory, I found the contents of my *furoshiki* wrapper had been taken out and displayed on the floor. One of the staff members asked me if they were unmistakably mine, and when I answered yes, he thrust a white ring before my eyes and asked me if I could explain about it. I remained silent, simply because I could not tell anything about it. Then I was called down as "an unpatriotic fellow!" because "now in the time of war, such a thing as that ring must be offered to the Government instead of keeping it to oneself." After all, the ring was taken away, though the parcel was returned to me.

After returning to my room, I checked the contents of my own parcel: three pairs of underpants and a bag made of cotton — 15cm across and 30cm deep — which contained white rice powder, 10cm deep, in it. Most of the drafted workers in those days used to carry such white rice powder so that it might be taken after having been dissolved in water when they were unbearably hungry. The rest of the contents in the *furoshiki* were toiletries. As was found later, the ring they found at the office of the dormitory used to belong to my deceased mother, which my father had put in the rice powder I should carry with me in case it might be of any help for me to live on or to survive — by taking it after having dissolved it in water. The staff of the dormitory had examined even what had been placed in the rice powder, and that was why I was given such a sharp reprimand as "an unpatriotic fellow!" This hackneyed phrase — "You, an unpatriotic fellow" — used to be employed whenever anyone of any authority at the army, the police and any other national organizations reprimanded others. From then on, too, we were to be called "unpatriotic" again and again at various occasions until we "got calluses on our ears (got fed up with *it*)."

● A Scene of Beating up a Traitor

The time passed and all those things that had happened to us soon after our arrival here had already been rarely told about among ourselves. It was already summer. Every day, early in the morning, we were driven into the mine and returned late in the evening, and this way of life had prevented us from noticing even the changes of the seasons. As mentioned before, we were living in a long house with six rooms for about thirty men of us to sleep at night. Three pairs of bedding being provided in each room, we were expected to sleep — two in a single bedding. Immediately after supper, we went to bed. None could visit other rooms. Because at the entrance to the house, a member of the staff in the dormitory was keeping his eyes upon us till late at night.

One night, soon after we went to bed in the unusual heat we were suffering as if in a steam bath, we heard loud voices of crying and shouting from the office of our dormitory. Trembling with fear, I looked toward the entrance to the house and found no staff member, who ought to be watching over us, was seen. I was in the second room from the entrance. Looking toward the depth of the house, I saw everyone also looking with his neck turned toward the entrance. Then, though remaining silent, we all, as if having agreed to do so, went out of the room to look at what was happening in the office through its window panes — five or six of the staff members, standing in a circle, were crying and shouting.

One of them, I found, was a man who had come from Korea to Japan in the same group as I belonged to. His family name was Shiroyama, though I did not know his personal name. He was good at speaking Japanese; his manner of walking was what is now known as that of a *yakuza* gang (a crime syndicate in Japan). Why he was there with the staff members of the dormitory was because he had been appointed to be the chief of our corps since we were made to live in this dormitory. The chief was exempted from working at the coal mine. What seemed to me to be his work was to give us a number ticket at every meal we took, and a meal coupon for our packed lunch, besides giving bangs on the corridor with the handle of the pickaxe in order to wake us up in the morning and send us to bed at eight in the evening. That was why he was treated as a staff member of our dormitory.

Now, Captain Shiroyama, holding what looked like a black stick in his hand, was beating a man squatting before him with all his might. The face of the man being beaten was not seen. Every time the black stick was swung down upon him, he gave a groan of *"Ku! Ku! Ku!"* The black stick Captain Shiroyama was employing then was what we secretly called "the ox's penis." That was, like the ox's willie, it was neither hard nor soft, but it remained unbroken whatever hard object it might be hit upon. It was made of crude rubber. Being raved at as "an unpatriotic fellow" was much better than being blown by means of "the ox' willie." Though it was ceaselessly brought down, it gave only dull sounds of *"puchu! puchu!"* upon his shoulders, back, waist and buttocks, but always leaving bright red welts upon them.

It was only a few minutes since we began to peep at the scene, but we had already seen more than thirty slashes of whipping. The one suffering that violence, while crouching on the floor, was no longer able to give even a groan that had sounded *"ku-ku!"* Still Captain Shiroyama's whipping was going on. All we could do then was to exchange our glances and to start our way back to our own room in stealthy steps. Without any watchman at the entrance to our house, we were able to exchange words, and we all agreed that the one now being beaten was unmistakably one of the four or five of us who had run away on the night when the movie was entertained to us. The other fellows seemed to have successfully run away, but he alone was caught. We all agreed, saying: "What an unfortunate fellow he is!"

Then I felt as if I myself would run away someday. This also meant: I had already been prepared for it. But just as I remained silent about my resolution, none of us would reveal his intention to run away, It was hot even at night, while mosquitos were annoying us. What had become of the poor fellow who had been made to have a hard time at the office? I remained sleepless, having been made to wonder and worry about this and that.

THE DAYS OF OUR COMPULSORY LABOR

● **The Permission for me to Go out on the *Bon* Holiday was Suddenly Canceled**

Throughout the night, I remained sleepless. At dawn, I went to the mess room, as usual. I showed my number ticket to receive a meal ticket. I was feeling nervous, being afraid that I might receive any word of complaint, but in vain. At the dining room, I received my breakfast and packed lunch. At first, I ate breakfast, and then lunch, too, as I had been doing for a long time, because I could not feel satisfied with the breakfast alone. The breakfast we received consisted of an ordinary-sized bowl of boiled rice, which was far from what was known as boiled rice. What was served to us as "boiled rice" consisted of 50 percent of bean cake, 30 percent of crashed Indian corn, and 20 percent of rice.

This was the same with the packed lunch we were expected to carry to the coal mine. The *miso*-soup served at breakfast did smell of *miso,* but far from what was usually known as such. The rest of what we were served then was a couple of sliced *takuan* or pickled radish. This will explain how those meals served here were far from satisfying to a seventeen-year-old boy as I was then, even though I had had both breakfast and lunch at the same time, as I usually did. At every meal, I could not help feeling like eating more — at least as much as the eighty percent of what I had really wanted to eat — whatever quality it might be.

Three months had passed since my life here started. August had set in. We, the drafted workers, were permitted to go out according to how good we had been as the workers here. The one who had kept working for a full month was allowed to go out once in the next month. Even a single day's absence from work prevented one from obtaining the permission to go out. This rule had kept me from going out for the first three months I spent there. If my place of work had been on the farm instead of the coal mine, I should have been able to work even every day for a month or so. But the work in the coal mine had caused me to have a headache or other abnormalities in my health.

By and by, however, we began to have it by hearsay that: during the *Bon* Festival holidays (the Buddhist version of All Souls' Day), all of us would be allowed to go out. If this was true, I said to myself, I should be able to see what Japan was like. This prospect was simply pleasing to me, and I was looking forward to seeing what Japan was really like — its countryside with its farm and rice field and the farmhouses. On the morning two days before the *Bon* Festival holidays, I saw a notice on the wall of the office, which went as follows:

During the *Bon* Festival holidays (August 14th, 15th, 16th), those who have not missed even a single day at work will be allowed to go out every day during the holidays. As for the rest, a one-day outing will be permitted.

Anyway, I was looking forward to going out that day. First of all, I wanted to visit a Japanese restaurant to eat anything delicious to my heart's content. I also felt like walking on and on along a wide road or a street wherever it might take me. I also wondered what I should do in speaking to the Japanese I should meet here and there, and so on. This made me feel as if my working hours that day were passing much faster than any other days I had spent in that coal mine. This reminded me how eagerly I — in my childhood — used to be looking forward to the New Year holidays and the *Bon* Festival season.

Returning to the dormitory after the day's work, I took a bath and deliberately washed myself. At night, we were never tired of talking about what we should do the following day. None of my roommates had been at work every day. So we were to have only a single holiday. I think this was the same with those in the other rooms. The *Bon* Festival day dawned. The breakfast offered that day remained the same as the one we took every day. At nine, we were permitted to go out. All of my roommates, having agreed to go out together in a group, went to the office.

We found about thirty men had already been there, waiting to obtain their permission to leave this ground of our labor camp. We, one by one, showed our number ticket to receive the permission to leave the camp. Beside the reception counter, we saw the instructions given to us, which read:

1) You must return by four; otherwise you will be regarded as a runaway to be hunted for and arrested.
2) You must not steal.
3) Never employ any means of transport.

Among them, the final one was simply funny and laughable, because it was totally impossible for anyone of us to take any public transport, because we were still ignorant of where to take any such things and where they would take us. Even if we were ordered to take any such means of transport, we should have found it simply impossible to do so.

While waiting for my turn, I was wondering what I should do when I went out: First of all, I wanted to eat anything to my heart's content. Then I was to find out what sorts of public means of transportation were available, and where they started from and where their destinations were — along with their timetable. That was, I wanted to obtain any knowledge available in case I should run away some day in the future.

Now my turn came, and I presented my number ticket. It was Captain Shiroyama who was at the reception desk. I still remember how he (even though he was still as young as thirty-four or five years old) looked exactly like the man named Kodama, a key person who was to be known later throughout Japan by the Lockheed Scandal (1976), in which Lockheed Company in the U.S. had sent a huge sum of bribe to the Japanese Government.

Captain Shiroyama then, holding my number ticket, glared at me, and thrust it back to me, saying:

"This time, you are forbidden to go out, so you shall return to your room."

I, having been looking forward to that opportunity to go out, felt extremely mortified. When I asked him what had made him say *that*, he said:

"On your paper, you are branded as "unpatriotic.""

After the two weeks' training we had received here was over, it was discovered that a gold ring had been placed in the bag my father had prepared for me when I left home. I could not help saying to myself: "From now on, too, *this* would bring about a disadvantage to me." In other words, I was to be treated as "someone to be watched out for."

Now I could not help returning to our room. All but several invalids had gone out, and I was the only person left there. I felt sad and lonely. I think my father had put that ring in the bag as a farewell present to me and as something for me to remember my deceased mother by. But since it had been found in the bag containing rice-flour, it came to rub the staff the wrong way. I could not help thinking: it was far from fair. Because they had confiscated it, saying they would make obligatory sale of it to the Government, that matter ought to have been over at that point three months before. Still, they punished me in this way. How tenacious they were! I could not help feeling bitter against them.

● My Determination to Take off

Unable to enjoy even the *Bon* Festival holidays, I felt simply sorry for my misfortune. At that time, I was unable to tell what "unpatriotic" meant. This had led me to think the authorities concerned were overly tenacious. Nowadays, none call anyone "unpatriotic" nor any such word is employed in print. But in those days, "unpatriotic" meant "criminal." That was why "the unpatriotic" were forced to work but not allowed to go out to have a good time even on holidays.

Later on, I was to hear that: the Japanese who had made any

obligatory supply of anything precious — such as gold and silver and the like — to the Government used to receive a receipt to each of the items they had offered. As for my ring, however, I had *not* received anything like that, and it was *not* until no less than ten years after the War was over that I happened to hear of *the* receipt having been given to the Japanese who had "made obligatory supply of anything precious".... This was one of the many unpleasant things I had to experience in those days.

Thus my going out that day not having been permitted, I could not help returning to my room, which was quiet and hot. I felt lonely.... Then my eyes fell upon a few cigarettes left there. They were the rationed ones. I myself not being a smoker, I used to give mine away to anyone in the same room. Now, I took up one and lit it up and inhaled the first puff of it. At once I began to choke on it with my eyes filled with tears. At once, I put it out and went to gulp water at the tap at the entrance to our accommodation. Then I took a deep breath and wondered what I should do from then on. I didn't want to go back to my room, but it seemed to bring me another trouble if I left it. For a while, I wondered what I should do, but in the end I found myself going out of my room in fear and trembling.

Now let me explain what our accommodation looked like: its square ground was surrounded with the walls. The gate stood on the southern side. Entering it, one could see a vacant lot about ten meters wide and fifty meters long. On the eastern side of it, there stood three buildings; on the western side, too, the same number of buildings was seen. My accommodation on the eastern side stood nearest to the southern entrance.

When I left my accommodation, its entrance, facing west, was not yet in the morning sunshine. The entrance to the accommodation on the opposite side, facing east, was being bathed in the burning sunshine in summer. First of all, I looked at the office to make sure no one there was looking this way, to my relief. This led me to squat down with my back against the wall of our accommodation, which had remained in the shade. For a while, I remained there in that posture. By and by, having got my bottom too cool to remain so, I lifted my bottom though in the same posture. Without anyone to talk to or anything to be engaged in, I was simply watching over the office windows by certain implication. There was nobody watching over me, to my great relief.

It was around ten — on August 15, 1944.* I kept asking to myself about what my comrades were doing then. Walking or in any train or bus? Which would be their destinations? A variety of imaginations did make me wish to go out — to reach somewhere. By and by, however, my consciousness began to move northward!

*Exactly one year later, Japan was to have the Emperor's announcement of Japan's surrender, as is mentioned later.

It seems strange but interesting to me that: we, human beings, are quite likely to recall or think endearingly of our old home or childhood days, when we have fallen into some predicament or when we are happy with something pleasing to us. I myself then was neither happy nor annoyed by anything troublesome to me, but I think I was unconsciously feeling lonely, and this had led me to think of my own home as well as my fellow countrymen who had now gone out to enjoy their holiday, *Then* it came up to my mind that I should get away from here! First of all, I drew up my plan in order to put this determination of mine into practice. The walls around were as high as about three meters. As for the hour when I should put *it* into practice, the daytime as our working hours would be unavailable. If I were to take a day off, I must obtain a medical certificate given by the doctor. Then, this plan would not do.

How about running away at night? Darkness would be quite helpful to me!

But how could I get over that high wall? It was made of wood. If it were thin enough, it might be broken by a hammer or anything like that, but it did not seem to be broken so soon and so easily. How about employing a saw? But I simply could not tell how long it would take in making any opening for me to get through. It being quiet at night, my sawing would make a considerable noise to my disadvantage. While drawing the map of this dormitory on the ground with my finger, I kept trying to find out any successful means to get away from this dormitory or *Kōwa (Bringing Peace into Being) Dormitory*, whose plan was as follows:

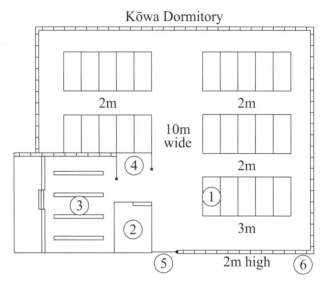

Kōwa Dormitory

① The room I was assigned to
② The Office
③ The Messroom
④ The Board to hung our number cards on
⑤ The Gateway
⑥ The wooden wall with barbed wire on top

Now I have mentioned the name of this dormitory for the first time. There were two more such dormitories as this, which also accommodated the Koreans who had also been taken here as drafted workers. Each dormitory having accommodated about 200 men, this company or Sumitomo Karatsu Coal-Mining Company alone had no less than 600 male Koreans, I think.

Let me return to what I was planning to do then. I, talking to myself: "I must get away from here by any means available," went on thinking about how to get away and stay away from here forever. In order to reach the coal mine, we used to walk about fifteen minutes. This had led me to wonder if I might run away from here forever — on my way to our workplace. But I soon found it far from practicable, because I was dressed in nothing but a loin cloth, as every one of my colleagues was.

I cannot tell what it is now, but at that time, we, not only Korean miners but also Japanese miners were all walking to our mine in nothing but a loin cloth. This, therefore, had never made me feel ashamed of it or discriminated against by it. Anyway, it was simply impossible for anyone of us to run away during the fifteen minutes we took on our way from our dormitory to the entrance to the coal mine. This led me to think of another plan: after breakfast, we received a lunch, which was expected to carry with us to our workplace. But we used to eat it immediately after the breakfast — even though at our own room, because we could not satisfy ourselves only with the breakfast. This was what all of us had been doing since we arrived here. Naturally, this was something we must not do. So, all of us were carrying our lunch box, even though it had already been made empty. Otherwise — or if what we were doing had been found out — we should have not only been reprimanded but also been made to do without supper! So we were all carrying the lunch box even though it was empty.

This led me to wonder if I were able to carry some of my clothing in that empty lunch box. But since our clothing in those days was all made of thick cotton, it was impossible to put even a single pair of trousers in it. As I mentioned before, all the clothing my father had packed up for me was made of thick homemade cotton. If it had been as thin and light as it is today, a single pair of pants would have been packed in it..... Then, all of a sudden, the bell began to ring. In those days, we used to hear the bell-ringing at various places on various occasions when many people were gathering. Since it was far-reaching, it was effective, indeed. But when rung close to our ears, it sounded so overly as to cause us some headache. Thus my planning of running away had suddenly been made to vanish, thanks to that bell-ringing!

● I had been Branded as a Traitor

It was already noon. Even though I was not permitted to go out, I was allowed to eat lunch here. It was not for the first time for me to have a lunch here since I arrived here three months and a half before, because we had lunch here on the holidays we were allowed to have three times a month. But now, I was alone. There ought to have been some others who had not been allowed to leave the dormitory. Probably each of us would have been made to eat at a different place so that we might not make any conspiracy among ourselves. Usually at meal time, we were simply crammed into this dining room, whichever tenement house or whichever room we were from. But now, I was alone. Eating alone made me feel even lonelier. My crunching of pickled radish seemed to give crisp echoes throughout that large dining room, which had usually seated as many as one hundred diners.

I took two or three mouthfuls of "boiled rice" but I did not feel like eating it any more. Most of what was seen in the bowl was grains of the Indian corn, which had been made sticky by the seedcake of soybeans. As for the rice, only occasional yellow grains were seen, as if it had given up being the leading part of the meal. Talking of the side dish, boiled radish cut into strips along with some fried fish-paste also cut into thin strips were all that were served, excepting the two pieces of pickled radish placed on a plate as tiny as the one used by children playing house.

I ate up the side dish and a piece of pickled radish, but I could not eat any more "boiled rice," because it made me feel as if I were chewing sand. So far I had never felt satisfied with any such "boiled rice" served here, having always wished to eat more — even a little more. What was it that had made me so lacking in appetite then? What was it….? Unable to find out any answer, I simply kept gazing at "the rice" left in the bowl.

None but I myself was seen in the dining hall, which was unusually hot and sultry. Then I happened to think of the other dormitories. I had heard there were three more dormitories like this one we were being accommodated in. Probably there, too, someone would be left alone like myself — being lost in deep thought, while being bathed in perspiration. I felt like talking to him, if possible. Unfortunately, however, we were both trapped in the enclosure as drafted workers — though not the birds in the cages…..

I was then seventeen years old, just having taken a step toward what was called adolescence. But having been born in what was called colony, I was about to be crashed down by my own fate, by the flow of my ill fate, by the strong power of militarism, by the forced labor after having been deprived of our liberty. These were what had been happening not only to myself but also to hundreds of thousands of drafted workers from our own country. We had been treated as if we were such lowly creatures as should be placed even below cats or dogs. This had made me wish to cry against this wrong we were suffering:

"What wrong have we done to you? What is it that makes us suffer so much? What are you going to do with my own youthful days? What you are doing is *not* for the benefit of the country *but* simply for keeping the war going on..... Right?"

I had clenched my fists so hard as I began to feel pain in them. The sweat had come falling from my brows to flow into my eyes together with my tears, which came falling down to my upper lip and then into my mouth. It was warm and salty. I pulled one of my short sleeves and wiped around my mouth. I knew: however much I might cry over this situation I had been driven into, I should never be able to change this situation of mine.

Now, I was about to stand up, intending to leave the dining hall. Then I heard a sharp voice coming from behind: "Hey you! What makes you stay here so long? You, an unpatriotic fellow!" I saw Captain Shiroyama there. "Pardon me, please!" I said, lowering my head meekly, and left the dining hall, quickly slipping away from him. If I had returned any word of resistance, it ought to have led directly to my disadvantages. At that time, there was no need for me to bring about anything that would add to my disadvantage. By that time, I had already made up my mind to run away….. Not yet had I found the way how to do *it,* but I had already made up my mind to run away, and that, without fail! I had already been labelled as "an unpatriotic fellow." Then, even if I were to be caught as a runaway, my identity would remain unchanged. What had made me mind then was that: I should have to receive much slapping, if I were caught.

I left the dining room, and when I walked as far as the middle of the central passage, I looked back to the office building. No one seemed to be watching over me. "I'm always ready to change my plan, according to the situation," said I to myself, walking to where I had been seated until before lunch, and sat down there as if crumbling down, my back against the wall, my knees drawn up. It seems that we, human beings, if equipped with any purpose to achieve, are likely to let it reveal itself through our body or mouth or hands. Even before I knew it, I had drawn a cross on the ground and repeated writing the Chinese character "北 (north)" on the right edge of it. This would have revealed my hidden intention to run somewhere toward the direction of my own home in Korea, even if I might not reach there. My intention to run away remained unchanged whatever I might be called or even if I might be executed. To my mind, my running away was something natural and justified.

What had made me wish to run away from here even to such a desperate extent was my helpless hunger. To myself, it seemed simply satisfying if only I were allowed to fill my stomach with anything eatable, whether it was bitter or salty. My greatest incentive for running away was to fill my stomach, it seems. If only I had been allowed to eat to my full even at this coal-mining company, I would not have been so much obsessed with an idea of running away from here, I think.

As would usually be the case with all the living things on earth, human beings especially — if left hungry — come to get angry first and then get cruel. For example, when eating together with my roommates face to face at that dining room, I myself entertained a moment's wish that *he* might get a stomachache the moment *he* took up his chopsticks. Even if such a thing had happened, I knew it would be impossible for anyone to eat the food that had belonged to *him,* and still I could not help imagining such a situation. This does reveal how hunger could make us vulgar and immoral. Later on, I felt angry at myself who had become so lowly and immoral. I said to myself: if I were to get along with such a lowly way, I might come to lose my own self; while I was still remaining myself, I must have caught up with my own self; otherwise I might have to give up remaining a human being.

I was saying to myself: "Run away from here! Otherwise, I shall have my mind discard myself!" Every time this notion occurred to me, I felt my back get so hot, while the top of my head got unusually hot as if it had caught fire! On the other hand, the mere sight of the dormitory office never failed to make me say to myself:

"Those who are over there are all ogres. I myself am a human being. Ogres are dreadful. It is only natural for us human beings to get away from such dreadful things as ogres. We were born as human beings of all creatures on earth. Why is it that we human beings have been sent to the ogres — only to be ordered to work under them — all naked but for our loincloth, while being kept hungry and forbidden to talk freely? What on earth had sent us to such a miserable situation? …. Now I'll run away…. get away from this hell! What if I were caught? I shall simply choose to die. *That* would be much better than keeping alive here with such a dirty mind within myself."

While being kept trapped into such a notion as getting away from here, it naturally led me to the thought of my own home. It was only three months since I left home, but to myself it seemed as if three years or even four years had already passed. My father had remained silent, when we parted at the bus stop on the national highway. My younger sister had just begun to go to school; my younger brother, four years old, who had been bereaved of his mother even before his first birthday, was being brought up by his father without receiving any help from any woman. How was he growing into a little boy? Wouldn't he fall into the river running before our house?

Talking of the river, the old familiar Yeongbong did help me to grow into a man! It was as broad as 200m across, and the water always remained ample. It was 4m or even 5m deep at the deepest. But at the shoals, it was only 1m or so even at the middle of the river. At the edges of it, it was only 30cm deep. So until I became a schoolboy, I used to spend most of the daytime in summer there — in and around the River.

In those days, all the little boys were naked. After having enjoyed swimming for a while, we hunted the little fishes at the shallows of the river. Then we enjoyed *sumo* wrestling on the turf of the riverbank. We never minded whether we won or lost. When we got hungry, we used to eat anything we were able to find — tomatoes, cucumbers, or egg apples — in the fields, whomever they might belong to. We never minded washing whatever we were about to eat; just rubbing it on our own belly was all we did before eating anything — and that to our heart's content. Occasionally, we were discovered by the owners of the fields, but they never scolded us. All they said to us was: "Don't eat too much, or you'll get stomachache." When we contented ourselves, we returned to the river to keep enjoying ourselves again until it got dark.

Occasionally, we enjoyed peeping somewhere very deep. There was also a depth for us little children to peep into. It was where a rock had protruded from the foot of the hill at the back of our village. Its top was about one meter above the water surface.

Looking down from there, we could see a large fish looking like a black porgy resting at the depth — while moving its gills like a bird on the wings. There were some other slender fishes swimming by, with their flanks glittering. Such sights of them did make me wish to catch them someday, and this wish of mine had been realized to a certain extent before I was sent to Japan. The fish looking like a black porgy was easily caught by making an earthworm the bait, but this was *not* the case with that slender one, which had simply swum away with its flanks glittering. In fact, that was the only sort of fish I had never succeeded in catching there. Even today all those things in my memory never fail to excite my nostalgic sentiment.

● Living in the Double Discrimination against the Koreans

The colonization, the war-making, the militarism and the commandeering were what we Koreans at that time were suffering. The last mentioned — the commandeering — was the term employed when the Japanese Government forced us Korean males to come to Japan to work at coal mines, munitions factories, airports, and so on. In other words, it meant "forced labor" or "*chōyō*" in Japanese. Nowadays this word is not found in the dictionary of everyday Japanese. But in those days, hundreds of thousands of male Koreans were forced to come to Japan to offer their labor under the pretext of "*choyo*" or "commandeering" — only to dismiss *the* word itself from everyday Japanese dictionary when the war was over. How extremely cruel and thoughtless they could be, including the modern scholars and experts in learning!? During the wartime, who on earth had worked to keep Japan as she was? Politicians? Servicemen? Scholars and doctors? Or women and children? As a matter of fact, everyone was of any use or any help, I think.

But would Japan have been able to be engaged in the war if it had not been for us, hundreds of thousands of drafted workers from the aged to the high-teens, who had been dragged to Japan proper from all over the Korean Peninsula? Would the Japanese women and children alone have been able to produce all the food and the munitions to be consumed by millions of soldiers being engaged in the war? It was not only for the soldiers but also for those tens of millions of civilians, including the women and children, the aged and the disabled, that we Koreans were made to work to keep them alive. The mere thought of it does make me tremble all over. Why? Why had such things happened? I could not help demanding the Japanese to ask themselves sincerely who on earth had kept them alive during the wartime.

But when the war was over and the confusion after the war was beginning to subside and Japan began to regain its social order little by little, we Koreans in Japan began to notice that: the Japanese Government's discrimination against us have begun to reveal itself. Firstly, they did not admit us to have a nationality as Koreans. The reason given for that was: Japan had no diplomatic relations with the Democratic People's Republic of Korea. This situation still remains as it was then — even if thirty-five years have passed since the end of World War II. (Note: the author wrote this chapter in 1980) That was, seen from the standpoint of the Japanese Government, we Koreans remain stateless. Then would we be allowed to become Japanese citizens? No, we would not be allowed to, even though we were taken out of the Korean Peninsula as Japanese citizens to be commandeered. This was an obvious fact, and still we have been treated in such an unreasonable manner, to our dumbfounded astonishment! I may not be so strict as to require them *not* to forget the evils they have once inflicted upon us, but considering what has actually been happening to us, the way they have adopted to employ even at present is unusually cruel. I should say this is none other than the discrimination against us.

I cannot tell when this system of commandeering started, but whenever the Japanese army occupied anywhere in China or in any other countries in Southeast Asia, we, the Koreans, used to be made to celebrate it by holding a lantern parade. Korea and the Korean people at that time used to be treated as Japan and the Japanese nationals and this had led to the conception of commandeering of us, the Koreans, under the pretext of "doing something for the sake of our land (Japan)." Thus we were to be driven into the coal mine, left hungry, deprived of freedom and tyrannized over. But we, the commandeered, simply kept working, as we were told to, even without being conscious of our having been discriminated against. Our having been suffering those discriminations at that time might be accepted as those from a colony of Japan, but the discriminations we are suffering even at present is something impermissible to me. Looking back, I am able to give a large number of examples of discriminatory treatments we have kept suffering even to this day. But if I were to begin to write about them, I simply cannot tell how and when I shall be able to put the final period to it. So let me return to that first holiday I had badly missed.

● Those who had been out Returned

The sun around the *Bon* holidays burnt down relentlessly. The sun itself had already started to decline, but it remained still hot. I had simply been planning to run away. Excepting the lunch time, I remained seated at the same place. When I felt unbearably thirsty, I went to have a gulp of lukewarm water at the tap. Then I incidentally sat down on what was called *agari-gamachi* (the timber frame at that part of the house through which we stepped into the house proper). It was all quiet. This reminded me of those who had gone out, saying to myself: "Where are they walking now? What are they seeing? What did they eat? What are they thinking about?" "They will have many things to talk about when they return," until I finally said: "Well, isn't it already the time they'll come back?"

Usually working at the coal mine, we had never guessed the time by seeing where the sun was poising itself on its way to the sunset. But that was the only day in Japan when I felt the daytime was really long. This led me to have an illusion in which all my fellow workers had run away never to return! At that moment, I found my body stiffened. Yes, that was the way I myself might take! If things went well, I might succeed in running away from here! There was an ample hope of success in it! Since we were permitted to go out to enjoy the *Bon* Buddhist Festival Season even though only for a single day, they would surely give us the New Year Holiday! It was still far away, but this meant I should have much time to make an ample preparation for it, including the money that would help me put that plan into practice successfully. Once I decided to run away, I must do it successfully! Otherwise, I should be half killed! This prospect made me thoughtful and patient. So far my patient wish to run away from here had prevented me from finding the right way for me to take. One must remain cool and calm in finding out an unfailing manner of doing anything. I then realized how childish I had been so far.

Now I decided to be successful in achieving that plan of mine. Otherwise, I should have to fail in making myself a respectable member of the society. It would depend on myself whether or not I should be able to achieve that aim of mine. It would be impossible to tell what would become of it without carrying out that plan. "All right," said I to myself. "From tomorrow on, I shall be facing my purpose of achieving my aim — planning for it and preparing for it, while taking sound steps toward it. In whatever manner I might have been bound, it would be natural that what was bound should be unbound sooner or later." Then I found myself feeling as happy as if I had already succeeded in running away!

Then, all of a sudden, I heard some noises coming from outside. This led me to jump out of the room; as I had expected, my comrades were coming back! What a long day it had been to me! I might have been missing them so much that I had rushed out of my room! What had become of my wish that they might run away, making use of this opportunity? I then realized: I had been wishing they all would come back to get together with me again. One group after another entered the house by the hinged door. None of them looked either tired or happy. When I jumped out of the room to meet them, I was expecting them to be appearing very happy, after "having had a good time in town." As it happened, however, they simply appeared as usual, to my great disappointment.

"What happened?" said I to myself. "Have they *not* enjoyed their outing so much?"

I myself, left alone, had been feeling miserable all day long…. But the life outside they ought to have enjoyed was not so pleasing nor so exciting as expected. If so, I had no need to have expected so much…. Still, I had kept my eyes on the hinged door at the entrance gate to the dormitory. Face after face I saw coming in. But they were *not* of those living in the same room in the same tenement house as mine. What was it that had made them so late in coming back? Already dozens of other groups living in other tenement houses had come back…..

Why! They are there — five in all! Now one group after another had come back! And, after having shown their own number ticket while giving their number orally, they were coming this way, and went into their own room. Seen from behind, they appeared lonely, their shoulders having dropped, their waist appearing loose. Was it because of their fatigue or because of the prospect of their daily life from the following day on? Then, I caught sight of my own roommates — nine of them, after having returned their number card and reciting their own number, came walking this way. Those in the other rooms in the same house walked away with a bitter smile on their face. I said to them: "Well done!" This was what we usually said to each other after having returned from our daily work. It sounded more or less unsuitable to those who had returned from their outing, but I simply could not find any other proper words to give them.

Now, my roommates were coming this way. They stopped walking before me, appearing rather embarrassed. I said: "Well done!" as I usually said to those who had returned from work, even though I felt it was not a proper greeting to those who had returned from their outing. The eldest man among them said: "Sorry, but we have nothing to bring back to you." The others had kept their head dropped. I knew they were feeling sorry for their having returned with empty hands. I asked the old man:

"Was there anything pleasing to you?"

What I had really wanted to say was: "Did you have a good time?" But, seeing them all having cast their eyes down, I simply could not ask such a question. The old man gave a few nods, took my arm, and urged the others to follow us. Thus we soon found ourselves seated in a circle in our own room.

The old man took a single cigarette out of the crashed case of *Kinshi.* "*Kinshi*" was the brand name of the cigarettes in those days. We received several cigarettes a day as rationed goods. One of my roommates was also a non-smoker, as I was. This had led us to distribute ours equally to the three smokers in the same room. Now the old man, puffing the smoke around his mouth, said: "As I was walking all day long, I've got tired." The three others, still looking down, remained silent, as if they found themselves in an awkward position. This led me to think I must make them feel relaxed.

Now, I asked the boy whose family name was Paek: "Have you eaten anything good?" Then he turned to me, and said: "Yes, I'll tell you something funny. When we entered an eating place and ordered *udon,* I heard a woman at the kitchen say: "*Udon* naai!" This led us to leave there (because we took "naai" as "nonexistent") and entered another, and ordered *udon* only to receive the same answer: "*Udon* naai!" This led us to take the seat at the table and began to consult what we should eat instead of *udon.* Then the waitress came and asked: "Four of you?" We answered: "Yes." This led her to leave us and entered the kitchen. Upon the walls, we saw the menu they served there. This led us to discuss in whispers what we should eat. But excepting *"udon"* and *"soba,"* we simply could not tell what sorts of food they were able to offer there. Then, the steaming bowls of *udon* were brought to us, to our joy and relief! Thus we found: "naai!" means "all right!" in this area.

While this episode was being given to me, we began to feel relaxed, and this led us to exchange pieces of information and discoveries they had gained that day, saying: "Wherever we may go, all we saw were women and children; *not* a single male person was seen," or "The persimmons were green and inedible," or "The buses were running along the main street," or "The terminal station for the trains is about 2km east of this coal mine."

Whatever they might have seen or found, they seemed to have been walking around all day long. Hearing them talk, I had begun to feel as if I myself had been accompanying them.

Among us, there was a man who remained silent, though he was always smiling. His name was Kim; he was six years older than I. This meant he was twenty-three. I had once heard that: his family at home had a hardware store, but since he was neither so sociable nor so talkative as was expected from a merchant, he remained dissatisfying to his father. He had not attended school, but when he talked, he was trying to make himself understood by everyone. This had led me to think: if he were to make himself a teacher, he would surely be a good teacher. In other words, I had seen a dependable person in him. This had made me decide that: if I were to have any opportunity to get away from here, I should reveal it to none but this person or Mr. Kim.

Ring-rung, ring-rung.... The bell was telling us: "It's time for supper!" By this time, the awkward air we had been feeling when they returned to the room had gone, and now we were all smiling as if we had all agreed to do something interesting. I had got extremely hungry, and this had made me wish to run out of the room before anyone else, but I did not do so. Because I was afraid that the friendly air we had regained among ourselves might have been lost again. Then, Mr. Kim said, rising to his feet: "Now, everyone, let's go to supper, shall we?" and walked out of the room, passing those sitting near the entrance. I took this opportunity, and said: "Yes. Let's," while urging the old man sitting in front of me, and followed Mr. Kim, saying to myself: "Mr. Kim has grasped our heart and mind best of all among us." Usually he remained far from talkative, but his speech and behavior seemed to me persuasive as well as dependable. At the reception to the mess hall, I gave my number, as usual, in order to receive my number card before entering it.

● We had Two More Watchmen at the Mess Hall

At the entrance to the mess hall, I noticed something strange. So far we had had one watchman beside the entrance — Captain

Shiroyama, who was in charge of those from North Korea —
and the other watchman beside the kitchen counter — another
Captain from Chungcheong Dō, who was in charge of those from
South Korea. But now, we saw one more watchman added at each
of those two points — four watchmen in all. Their expression
appeared unusually rigid. So far they used to be smoking in a
casual manner….. It seemed strange. Something undesirable must
have happened. Had anyone who had gone out run away? If so, *that*
would be kept secret from us. That was the way they had adopted
so far. I felt excited. But, trying to make myself appear as calm as I
could, I put my number card into the ticket window, following Mr.
Kim. Thus I had a rice bowl and a side dish pushed out. Holding
them in my hands, I looked around, wondering where I should seat
myself. As for Mr. Kim, he had already settled himself just in front
of the watchman or at the last seat anyone — including myself —
would take. But, on that occasion, I seated myself *there* just beside
Mr. Kim, who had steadily been taking his meal in total silence —
under the nose of the watchman. This kept me saying to myself:
"Calm down! Calm down! I haven't done anything wrong."

Just before my eyes, I saw a large, shabby kettle placed,
appearing as if asserting its own importance of being placed there.
Beside it, the small, blue tea cups were casually piled up in an
oval bamboo basket. The edges of those cups had been badly tea-
stained. Beside them, the rice bowls appeared less dirty, and this
had led me to make it a rule to drink tea not by the cup but by the

rice bowl I had emptied. Now my supper was over, while I had my attention carried away by that kettle and the tea cups.

This had given me a lesson: when I need to calm myself down, I should concentrate my attention *not* on something main that has occupied my mind *but* on something trivial or irrelevant that has happened to come up to my mind.

Honestly speaking, however, it is something fairly hard *not* to reveal my inner disturbance. But what had saved me then, I now realize, was my confidence in innocence on my side.

This made me learn something important. Still I knew it was something fairly hard to achieve not to reveal my own uneasiness or presentiment. But what had saved me then might have been my own clean consciousness that: I had not done anything wrong that might make me feel guilty. Certainly I had not done anything to make me feel guilty, but I had kept in my mind a certain cause for me to feel agitated. That was, if anyone had run away, I knew he would have adopted the same method as I had kept in my mind. This meant that: I had been anticipated, and the ratio of my successful escape would be halved. The success or failure in flight did not matter to me then. What mattered most to myself was the motive itself. I had aimed at the opportunity of the New Year holiday, when we should be allowed to go out. Because of the gold ring they found in my rice bag and confiscated under the pretext of obligatory supply of goods to the Government, I had still been suffering a penalty even when three months had passed. Now we had four full months before the New Year holiday. By then, the situation would be changed. My excellent workmanship as a coal-miner might give them a favorable impression. If so, there would still be some hope for me to be allowed to go out on the New Year holiday! But what if anyone of us had run away by making use of this *Bon* holiday? My plan of running away would have been badly — more than fifty percent — damaged. When I had thought of running away by making use of that occasion, I did feel some other persons also might have had the same idea as I had. But I never thought then that: *that* had occurred that very day! Having two more watchmen over us did cause me to feel uneasy. After the meal, I filled the rice bowl with the tea till it overflowed, and drained it to the last drop. This helped me to feel less stifling before I left the mess hall.

● The Three of us had Run Away

Leaving the mess hall, I saw our tenement house across the wide central road. About the center of the open ground at the central road, I took deep breathing several times. Then I wondered who had run away and which of the tenement houses they had lived in. Then I felt as if they might be those living in the farthest section of this tenement house. They had never talked to us, even though we exchanged greetings when we met in the morning or in the evening. They remained simply unsociable and apart from us. So we simply could not tell what they were or what they had in their mind. Then I remembered I had not seen them come back nor had I seen them at the mess hall. This led me to decide to go and see if they were there.

I went to the entrance to our tenement house, and looked back to make sure that I was not being watched by anyone in the office, I, passing the entrance to our room, went farther on. In the second room where the paper door was kept open, all the roommates were seated, talking something among themselves. The same scene was seen in the third room, too. All were present in the fourth room, talking something among themselves. Probably because of my footsteps they heard, they had stopped talking. The fifth room at the end of the tenement house had its sliding paper doors all closed. There were two pairs of rubber thongs left kicked off. I called to them: "Hello! Is anyone here?" There was no answer. This led me to slide the paper door quietly to make it half open, and I saw a couple of men seated there, looking forwards, their back on the wall below the back windows, with one knee drawn up, their hands kept around it. In this heat, both of them appeared as if enduring the coldness they were feeling. Having been embarrassed to see them there, I said:

"Why, you are here! Having had no answer, I thought no one is here. Have you finished supper?"

Both shook their head. One of them said: "We are not allowed to eat it, because our roommates have run away." I felt sorry for having mentioned the supper forbidden to them. The other urged me to leave there, saying:

"You, too, will be found in the wrong room. So leave us now."

"All right. See you later," said I, while closing the paper door, and returned to my own room. It was only a few words that we had exchanged, but since we were able to understand each other, I felt as if we had had a good talk.

Returning to my room, I found Kim and Paek there after having finished their supper. Paek asked me:

"You have been to the room beyond, haven't you? Have you seen them all?"

"Two alone. They said the three of them had run away."

This led Paek, who had been lying on his stomach, to turn himself over to say:

"Only three? Why? What happened to the other two?"

Then, there came back the old man and one more. Then Kim said:

"As I had expected...."

The old man and one more who had just come in and heard Kim saying so, stood there, as if being puzzled at what they had heard. This led me to urge them to seat themselves there by shaking my hand, while sending them an eye-signal to obey me.

Then I told them what I had just seen in the room at the end of the house, and then added that: this had made Kim say: "As I had expected...."

"Ah, yes. I see," the old man said. "That was why I felt

something strange in the dining room."

For a while, all of us had sunken into silence. I had been aware that Paek had fallen into silence after saying: "Only three? Why?...." It seemed to me that his unspoken question was: "Why were the two alone left behind?" or "Why had the three alone run away?" What Paek wanted to say must have been that: "As long as they were room-mates, they should have naturally run away all together. Don't you think so?"

That brief comment given by Paek pierced through my heart. So far I had kept saying to myself: "I shall be alone when I run away." What had made me decide *that* was: because the running away in a group would be easily found, and when caught, it would turn out a mass tragedy. If alone, even if caught, it would remain a personal misfortune; the others would be left safe. But Paek's remark had moved me, because of his sincerity toward his comrades. This made me realize that I was wrong. But I knew it was not the right time for me to reveal anything like that. "Let me wait till I am ready to run away," said I to myself. "When *the* time comes, I shall talk with the others to decide on "who would run away with me and who would remain." That would be what we should do as human beings and as comrades. Running away by oneself and for oneself cannot be regarded as fair and humane.

I felt as if I had been taught what we, human beings, should be by Paek, my junior: we should help each other, while talking each other among ourselves. Otherwise, we shall cease to be human beings. It seemed to me why I had regarded those in the office as demons was because they had never treated us drafted workers as human beings; those would-be human beings treated us, drafted workers, as if we were even below cats and dogs. Seen from above, they might have made themselves inferior even to the animals. Under the pretext of the obligatory supply of goods to the Government, they never minded appropriating anything belonging to others; as for food, they dined on gourmet by making a special request; during the daytime, they simply spent their time in gossiping or taking a siesta. For all that, they made it a rule to shout to us: "You shall go and work hard for the sake of our land!"

What was it that had made them say such an impertinent thing as that? The first thing they should do for the sake of their land would be "to make themselves like human beings" by "behaving like human beings," and by "keeping their mind humane." This is something needed as human beings and most indispensable to any human beings. Thus I had made up my mind to live a life worthy of the name of a human being, however lowly I might be brought down socially or financially.

It was a long day for me — August 15, 1944. It would not be long before we heard the bell ring to send us to bed. Captain Shiroyama, carrying the handle of a pickax, would come round, while knocking the wooden corridor that led to each of the entrance to our rooms. The Old Man took his bedding out of the closet and prepared for going to bed. Everyone remained silent, but each seemed to be thinking about something different from each other. The old man had already been in bed. As usual, Kim was the last to go to bed. I also lay down beside Paek. The one to turn off the light was the Old Man, but he still remained in bed for some reason or other. The bell rang. This led me to pull up the top layer of my bedding to cover my head in order *not* to hear Captain Shiroyama's order — "Go to bed! Go to bed!" — which went to the end of the corridor and returned. I put my head out of the bedding to find the light had gone out. It was hot. Mosquitoes were noisy around my ears. Someone was heard to hit himself, trying to hit on the mosquitos. The old man, as if in his sleep, said: "I do wish they would succeed in their attempt to run away…." No one gave any response to him. I myself remained sleepless, while thinking this or that aimlessly and endlessly…..

● What Happened at the Mess Hall

Pattan, pattan..... I heard Captain Shiroyama walking heavily along the corridor toward the end of it and coming back, calling to us: "Get up….Get up…." The summer night seemed to me unbelievably short. I was still feeling very sleepy. While yawning, I said "Good morning" to my roommates. Everyone of us hurried out of the tenement house. I seated myself on the timber frame at the part of the house through which we walked into or out of the house, while waiting for *the* two in the room at the farthest end. By and by, they presented themselves and soon they were passing me. This led me to say: "Good morning!" Both of them gave me a nod and walked away toward the mess hall. Having seen them enter there, I went to wash my face before I began my daily routine — reciting my number at the window of the office to receive the number card before entering the mess hall. That morning, I saw Captain Shiroyama standing alone at the entrance. At the side of the window through which we received our meal, too, I saw another captain — from Chungcheong Dō — standing alone. Since I was late in coming, I found the service counter was not so busy. While putting the card into the slot, I just peeped into the kitchen. Then a round-faced young woman lowered her hips and said, gazing at me; "You are working with Ura-*san,* the hewer, aren't you?" Having been spoken to so abruptly, I could not understand what she was talking about, but since "Ura-*san*" was my boss at my working place, I simply gave her one nod or two. In the meantime, a bowl of rice and another bowl of *miso*-soup had been pushed out. I was about to have the rice bowl in one hand and the bowl of *miso*-soup in the other hand. Then, I saw something round wrapped in a yellowish pulp paper being pushed out by the round-faced woman. She gave me a signal of "hide *it* quick" with her eyes and chin. I, though unable to understand what she meant, hid *it* with my hand. I looked to the left. I turned my head toward the entrance. None of the watchmen had noticed what I had done. So I quickly put *it* around my naval, and while pressing it by my left elbow, I held the bowls of rice and *miso*-soup with my hands. I felt my heart beating wildly.

In a moment, I was able to reach the nearest table. While eating the breakfast, I had kept that gift between my crotch, which made me unusually hot. In August, it was already hot even in the morning. Still I persevered, keeping my knees closed, heels wide open. This made me sweat all over. All I had worn then were a large-sized half-sleeved cotton shirt, whose color was khaki mixed with light blue — and a single loin cloth, through which I was being made warmer and warmer, because of what I had hidden there.

While eating, I guessed that the extra food I had received was a rice ball. Now, having finished the breakfast, I must go to receive my packed lunch. I gripped that gift in my right hand and put it into the left-hand underarm in my shirt. I gave it more or less pressure upon it. It got indented like a rubber ball. Then I put the lunch I had just received also under it. Thus I was able to leave the dining hall safe and sound. But it was not until I came to the central road that I had finally felt relieved. Indeed, that was one of the most strained experiences I had ever had!

It seems to me that: man is so made as *not* to be able do anything wrong. Even receiving what was offered to me secretly by deceiving some authority did make me unusually nervous. Still, when I found myself having got over that nervousness, I had already been planning to escape from here, giving a thin smile on my lips, saying: "Serve you right!"

Now, I briskly walked into our room, only to see my roommates vigorously eating their packed lunch, keeping their back toward the entrance, as usual. I entered the room, trying to appear as calm as possible, and sat down below the back window, facing my roommates. I pulled out my packed lunch from under my left arm and placed it before myself. Then I put my right hand into my shirt and took out the round package I had received some time before.

Everyone was watching what I was doing: I took out a round package and took off the wrapping, only to find that it was *not* an ordinary rice ball *but* a rounded scorched portion of boiled rice! Paek was the first to give a cry:

"Why! It's scorched rice!"

This led Kim to warn us to keep silent by putting his third finger on his lips. Everyone there was gazing at that single rice ball made of slightly-burnt rice usually left at the bottom of the rice-cooker. The old man, glancing at me, asked in a whisper: "How have you got *that?*" I had already been feeling proud of having received it, but since I had not expected to have any such question, I simply remained unable to think of any proper answer to give him. Thus all I could mumble then was:

"Haa, well…. I have received it from somebody."

Then he said: "I know, you have received it from somebody. I am asking what has made you get *it?*"

I shook my head and said:

"Well, I cannot tell. Since a woman in the kitchen asked me if I know of Ura-*san* as "*sakiyama* (a leading miner)," I said "Yes." Then she gave *this* to me. That's all I can tell."

The old man — simply saying: "Well, well, is that so?" — returned his gaze upon the ball of slightly-burnt rice. This led me to push it before the old man, saying: "Anyway, please share it with everyone here."

This led him to say: "All right. We must hurry to work, or we shall be scolded," and after having divided that rice ball — as large as a baseball — into five, he handed one to me, while others were taking one for themselves.

This reminded me of my childhood days. Until I began to go to school, I often ate *o-koge* or burnt rice left at the bottom of the rice cooker. Nowadays, we cannot see what was called *o-koge,* and no children can tell what it is like. Nowadays we use gas or electricity in cooking rice, but in my childhood, boiled rice was cooked upon what was called a cooking stove. That was, washed rice in a proper amount of water put in an iron rice-cooker was placed upon a kitchen stove. When the water began to boil, the wooden lid, thick and heavy, began to be lifted by the bubbles rising from the rice being boiled. This was the time to abate the flames. By and by, you might choose the suitable time to lift the lid to see the doneness. When you see many potholes on the cooked rice, it is done. Then you will put out the fire. Still the iron rice cooker remains quite heated. This produces some slightly-burnt rice at the bottom of the rice cooker. Since it takes considerably long time before it is properly burnt, it tastes fairly attractive in its own way. That was why we, children, used to eat it every day as a sort of snack.

Now everyone was thankful to me for that unexpected gift of the scorched rice ball I had brought back, saying: "I haven't eaten it for a long time. It has tasted good! Thank you!" Then, after having eaten it, they all hurried to work, carrying their empty lunchbox. As for myself, I had no time to eat up my lunch. Or I should say I did not feel like eating it at least that morning, because I was not only happy to have received "that scorched rice ball" but also sensible enough to think: I should fail in obligation to that round-faced woman at the kitchen if I had not carried my lunch just as it is at least today."

It was fifteen minutes' walk from our dormitory to the entrance to the coal mine. On my way there, I thought of showing Mr. Ura, my boss, my having carried the packed lunch *that* day (just as we were expected to). Be that as it might, what was it that had led the woman to give me *that o-koge* that day? I had never met her nor talked to her. Judging from her appearance, she seemed to be four or five years older than I. It was simply puzzling to me. She seemed to be well-acquainted with Mr. Ura. That was all I could tell about her. Then, I thought of asking Mr. Ura about her when I saw him that day in the pit — so that I might find something about her — what sort of person she was or what her name was. Then I found myself having already arrived at the front of the office at the entrance to the coal mine.

● Working in the Coal Mine

The office there was several times larger than the office of our dormitory. Its appearance was that of the schoolhouse in those days. It was all built of wood. Not only the pillars, walls, window-frames and floors but also the desks, bookstands and doors were all made of wood. The eastern side of it was the office with more than ten desks in it; at the center, there was a space — wider than ten *tatami* mats — for us, drafted workers, to wait or to equip ourselves. Seen from the front, there was a small window to let the light in, and on both sides of the walls, our number tickets — 5cm long and 3cm wide — were seen to be hanging closely. The entrance to that space had no walls so that all of its interior could be seen from outside.

The western side, which was called "cap," was where "the lights," indispensable in the mine, were kept in custody. At the depth of it, there was a charging station. What we did here every morning was to show our own number ticket, as we did at the dormitory, to receive an electric torch and a battery. The former was as large as what we have on our bicycle today; the latter was 5cm thick, 15cm wide and 20cm high — about the size of the notebook used by the school children at present. At the top of the battery, there was a plug with a thick rubber band fixed in the middle. The light had an electric wire about one meter long fixed at its back. At its head, it had a plug for a battery. The battery was expected to hang at our side, but it did prevent us from moving around. This led us to put it just above our buttocks. The light was put above the visor of our cap.

The electric light employed at the coal mine was expected to be placed above the visor of our cap. Our cap had been made of thick cloth, while the directors and coal hewers, who were all Japanese, covered their head with a steel helmet. Today the lamp on the bicycle is fairly light in weight, but the light employed at the coal mine at that time was so heavy that the cloth cap we had worn easily came down when we moved around, preventing us from seeing ahead, to our immense annoyance.

Now, when we were ready, having been equipped with the light, the battery and the cap, we were to go behind the western side of that building. The entrance to the coal mine or the pithead was seen there. A long train of iron trucks was waiting for us there. One iron truck was able to carry more than ten of us if crammed into as was seen in the subways in Japan now. If the maximum capacity regulation was observed, one iron truck — with the three benches to accommodate three men — would be able to carry nine men. The trolley train was composed of twenty to thirty trolleys. In the morning, hundreds of men must be sent into the mine within a limited time. Thus every morning and every evening, nearly two hundred of us were to be carried into or out of the coal mine.

Now I got on a trolley train in the rear, which remained empty, as my roommates did. Before long, we heard the whistle blown to notice our starting. Our trolley train began to move. I was on my feet, while seeing the rail leading downward, with the iron wall behind under my arms. Along the midst of the rails, a wire rope as thick as 5cm in diameter was seen to go down, increasing its speed. This led the trolley train to rush down to the bottom like an arrow. The unshaded electric lamps along the rails appear to be going up, giving a shrill twittering sound of *pyu! pyu!* It took only five minutes or so to reach our destination, but even my daily riding on it had not yet made me believe it was such a short time. In the mine, do we have a different sense of time? After leaving the trolley train, we hurried to our own place of work, while exchanging our parting word of "May you be safe!" Here in the mine, that was the only greeting everyone of us exchanged.

My place of work was at the farthest end of the pit. As "a tunnel-man," I was expected mainly to find out the vein of coal. In case of petroleum, we were to find it by boring downward, but as for the coal, we had to find out a new coal bed by boring our way in every direction — upward, downward and sideways. When anything promising was found, we were to dig our way toward that direction. Digging through the rock formation was something unspeakably hard to do.

I was expected to work under the leadership of Mr. Ura or Ura-*san,* as we called him. He was then fifty-two, if I remember right. He was a quiet person with a strong sense of responsibility. Whatever might happen, he remained cool, calm and collected, as if he had kept a strong faith in his mind, always taking pity on us, who had come from overseas as drafted workers. In my own case, since I was a new-comer in his group, he was kind enough to tell me how to "do it properly" by deliberately showing his own example. He also said: "Come and tell me first, if you come across anything annoying or unable to understand." This made me adore him and I felt happy to have had such a kind person as Mr. Ura as my own boss. Even today, I occasionally think of him, endearingly recalling him for the kindnesses he had offered me.

Now I saw Mr. Ura having already arrived there, thus waiting for us, drafted workers. Then, after it was checked that everyone was there, we set to work. Mr. Ura had six men and one woman under him. As for the work, the man of responsibility or Ura-*san*, his wife and an apprentice, who was one of us, drafted workers, were to engage in boring. Then we — in pairs — dug a hole, employing a jackhammer, toward the coal bed. The tip of the jackhammer, equipped with a six-angular iron chisel, 3cm across, was so made as to go on boring a hole by shaking it by air. The central part of the coal bed was to be dug about 1.5m deep. It got shallower, as it approached the both ends. That was, how we were to dig a tunnel.

When the hole was brought into being, we charged it with dynamite equipped with a fuse to be lighted on it. The coal-waste brought into being then was expected to be loaded up into the tramcar by the rest of us or myself and one of my fellow workers. While putting the coal-waste into the tram before our break time, I was thinking about "the slightly burnt rice" I had received that morning. I wish you would not laugh at me, who had been so conscious about such a trivial thing as that. We, the drafted workers, had been made to live on such a humble meal as "a single bowl of boiled rice" — mainly consisting of unpolished rice largely mixed with barley and bean cake. This had left us always hungry. So, to us, the drafted workers, even that burnt rice left at the bottom of the rice cooker was something unusually precious.

That was why I could not help minding it. What if what we were doing had been found out *then* and *there?* Not only I but also that woman would not have been overlooked. When I thought of her courage or boldness she had shown for me then, I could not help being moved by her kindness. On the other hand, I shall never forget that thrill I was feeling on my way to the dormitory. I still feel as if I could feel the flush on my face and the warmth of the burnt rice I was carrying on my crotch. On the other hand, I could not help feeling unbearably miserable and ashamed of what I was doing then, trying *not* to be observed or found out by the watchmen around the entrance to the dining hall. What a lowly and miserable period of time I had to spend in my youth! Thirty-five years had passed since then. If I were asked by someone what the springtime in my life was like, my immediate answer would be: "It was a period of hunger." I say this *not* as a metaphor *but* as a physical reality. Our youthful days at that period of time was simply inseparable from our physical hunger.

At home in Korea, I had often heard the people say: "When young, you are in the bloom of life." But looking back at that miserable life in my youth then, I still remain simply unable to understand what that message dedicated to our youth really meant. "What's the bloom of life? Stop joking! Just look at us! Haven't we been simply made the fertilizer for the soil of the other nation?" said I to myself, feeling resentment against my miserable situation.

The noise of the jackhammer stopped. The scene around, which had remained vague because of the powdered rock, gradually began to be seen clearly. To myself, the lunchtime that day seemed to have come sooner than usual, probably because I had been made to keep my mind unusually busy with what had been happening not only to myself but also to those around us since the day before.

● Who was it that had Brought me the Package of the Burnt Rice Ball?

I took off the lid of my lunch box for the first time in the long time. My colleagues or the other drafted workers had gone behind the tramcars a little away from us. Our boss, Mr. Ura, and his wife had been looking at me and at my lunchbox by turns, before he talked to me:

"Why, you have brought your lunch, haven't you?"

"Yes," said I. "What makes you say *that?* I myself am able to bring my lunch, even if only once in a while."

Then I got to my feet and went to sit down beside Mr. Ura, carrying my lunch box in my hands, because I had wanted to ask him about *the* woman who had given me that scorched rice ball.

Mr. Ura then, having picked up something in his lunch-box with his chopsticks, casually put it on my yellowish rice, while giving a sidelong glance at my lunch-box. This led me to say to him, while gazing at what had just been placed on my boiled rice:

"Well, this morning, I received some scorched rice...."

This led Mr. Ura to stop chewing the rice in his mouth, and after having asked me "From whom?" he swallowed it up. Then he resumed eating, as if he had heard nothing particular. This led me to explain him about how I had received that ball of *o-koge* or burnt rice that morning, and closed my speech with: "I had never seen her nor talked to her before, so it's simply puzzling to me why she had given *that* to me." Then, Mr. Ura, having noticed that I had not yet even begun to eat my lunch, urged me to eat it by jerking his chin up. This led me to eat it quick. I had expected him to say something to me while eating, but he remained silent until I finished eating and received a cup of tea from Mrs. Ura.

When I finished drinking my cup of tea, Mrs. Ura asked me: "What did you do with that scorched rice you'd received?" I told her how I had hidden it between my thighs while eating breakfast and how I carried it under my arm as far as my dormitory — before I ate it with my roommates, and that: *that* was what had enabled me to bring my lunch with me that day, adding that: *that* had still made me feel warm at the crotch. This led Mrs. Ura to give a big laugh of *"Ohhoho! Ohhoho!"* Then she said: "Well…, that was our daughter. Yes, she had given *it* to you!" before she resumed her laughter of *"Ohhoho! Ohhoho!"*

The first laughter she gave had not affected me at all, but the second one she gave led me to laugh with her, but soon I began to feel rather ashamed of myself. That had led me to feel miserable.

On the other hand, Mr. Ura himself was nodding, looking serious, as if he had been impressed by something. Mrs. Ura said, as if to herself: "Well, she…," then went on, looking at Mr. Ura: "The other day, we were talking of the dormitory. Have you told her about *him?"* She said, pointing to me with her chin. "Surely *not!…. She*…."

Mr. Ura, remaining silent, had kept his eyes on the rock wall just in front of him. As for myself, having found that: the round-faced woman at the kitchen — the woman who had given me *o-koge* or that burnt-rice ball — was their daughter, I felt my heart filled with even greater emotion for the kindnesses Mr. Ura and his family had given me. This left me speechless, but I was saying to myself: "I'll do my best here, working for the benefit of Mr. Ura. If I were to find any opportunity to run away from here, I shall not be able to let *it* go, but if I could not find any opportunity to do so, I should have to resign myself. Then, I should like to work under him even to the end of my life!"

We were then hearing the boring machines working while giving a faint sound of *shhu-shhu-shhu* of the rolling belt. The belt had kept working from morning till evening when the work was over. Mr. Ura, turning his eyes toward the boring machine, stood up, saying to himself or to anyone there: "That's *the* way, I see....." and walked to the machine to supply oil on the toothed wheels to turn the belts or on the shafts before he wiped around the motors clean with the oiled cloth.

Mrs. Ura was wrapping each of the emptied lunch boxes in its white wrapping cloth or *furoshiki*. Probably having been so made, each cloth fitted each of the lunch boxes of different sizes.

Mr. Ura, the captain, called to my fellow drafted workers who had been sitting behind the trolley train: "Let's begin, shall we?" This did make us resume our own work. I myself began to fill the trolley train with coal. The rock-powder blown out of the rock drills having grown thicker and thicker around us, it did make us feel as if we were in the thick fog.

The day before seemed to me immensely long, but that day I found was unexpectedly shorter. After the work was over and the tools were placed in order, Mr. Ura and the two men remained there to embed the dynamite in the holes that had been dug with the rock drill. After the two left, Mr. Ura alone remained there to light the fuse before he quickly left there. This was how our work of the day was over. Then we all hurried to the trolley train waiting for us. When it moved thirty or forty meters onward, we were to hear the burst of the dynamite that had just been embedded. Hearing that vigorous sound behind, we were to come back to the outer world. The sun in August still remained high as if hesitating to fall in the west.

● The Pieces of False Information Given by the Imperial Headquarters

The moment I put myself into a hot bath after having washed off all the coal dust I had got that day, I used to say to myself: "Why! I have made a safe return from that underground hell once again!" In the bathroom for the exclusive use of us, drafted workers, we had neither watcher nor supervisor. In fact, that was the only place for us to be able to relax ourselves. So we all talked about what had happened that day and consoled ourselves. What was more, that was a perfect place for obtaining any knowledge or information indispensable if one wished to get away from here. This was also the only place for us to talk about anything secret or to talk to someone living in the other dormitory. But since our daily schedule having been grasped by the dormitory authorities, we had to be careful in the passage of time…. Still thirty or forty minutes being available, we were able to consult with anyone there about anything we would like to.

I usually did not spend much time in bathing. But now that I had come to feel it necessary to obtain any information available, I made it a rule to prick up my ears for any whispering obtainable there. Neither watchman nor guard was seen around, but when we came to talk of the war, everyone lowered his voice, because of the wariness we could not help keeping. According to the whisperings that came into my ears, "it was a downright lie told by the Government that Japan was steadily on its way to the victory; as it was, it had kept being defeated, and it would not be long before the Americans marched into Japan proper, even though it was kept secret to the people in general; it's simply deplorable and pitiable for them; anyway, what would become of us if the Americans made their appearance here? I'm afraid we might be regarded as the Japanese and be taken prisoners." Then the other voice said: "As for that, there is no need to worry. We shall find it much better to be taken prisoner of war by America. I'm sure it will be much better for us than to be made to work in such a coal mine as this. I wish it would come sooner! Say, even tomorrow! The sooner, the better!" I myself had found this opinion quite reasonable.

In those days, all the information given to us had come from the Imperial Headquarters. They simply informed us of "our victory" being achieved one after another. Not a single word was given to refer to their losing battle or lost battle. In other words, all pieces of information being given in those days were of complete fabrication. All the women and children, all the old men and old women, and even the disabled persons had been pressed into labor, until at last even we, Koreans, were drafted to be driven into hard labor. What was worse, even kitchen utensils as well as articles made of gold and silver were forced to give up under the name of the obligatory supply to the Government. There followed the volunteer labor of housewives and young women. The old men and women were made to work on the farm, while taking care of the babies and children, until the lower part of their back was badly bent — while being made to believe in the false pieces of information given by the Imperial Headquarters, even though they were soon to be found out nothing but a web of lies!

As it happened, what we had been whispering in the bathroom was to turn out to be a reality exactly one year later — on August 15, 1945 — when Japan accepted the unconditional surrender, which had remained unheard of so far. Be that as it might, I thought I had got an important piece of information. It was easily imaginable that: if Japan suffered the defeat, we, Koreans, would naturally be made prisoners of war. Then, we might be better fed. But what I had wanted more than anything else was: the physical freedom or the freedom of action and the freedom of language. Should I be able to get them all? I was not sure. This led me to decide to run away, as I had expected to! I was saying to myself:

"Even for a brief period of time, I'd like to live like a human being. I'd like to seek freedom. No more coal-mining! No more being a prisoner of war! No more war, the worst of the evils! All the evils had come from the war! If it had not been for the war, I ought to have been enjoying my youthful days in the mountains and forests in my own dear old homeland! The way I'm living now does not seem to me the way the man should live.... especially in his youth...."

Feeling unusually miserable about my own way of life then, I was hurrying to my dormitory.

● **My Thoughts on My Homeland**

That night I was lost in deep thought, while being made to hear my roommates snoring — after the bell rang to make us go to bed and Captain Shiroyama's knocking along the corridor was over. In the darkness, my eyes had been wandering feebly around the ceiling. Because of the war now going on, for the sake of the land called Japan, and in order to keep ourselves alive, we had been making immeasurably great sacrifices. Not only we, the drafted workers, but also the whole land of Korea had been made to sacrifice itself. We could not help obeying the executors of Japan's militarism. We, the Koreans, having been born in the colony of Japan, must witness the gap between the conquerors and the conquered. I want no war! No coal-mining! No death! No colonialism! Then, where shall I turn to? Where is my own place? Nowhere on earth can I find any place for myself?

To myself, what I had heard in the bathroom — America would soon be here to occupy Japan — was the matter of great importance! Since we were serving here as Japanese nationals — even though only ostensibly — it was quite probable that we were made prisoners of war. As for myself at that time, I had not minded so much whether Japan would be defeated or America would come over or we were made prisoners of war, as what would become of our land of Korea. Would Korea as a colony of Japan be transferred to America? America, too, had once enslaved the black people, hadn't it? It would only be the developed and powerful nations that would be able to invade into another country to conquer and colonize it. America was powerful enough to do such a thing. Then it would not be impossible. Even if the U.S., after having won the war against Japan, should have made Korea its colony, I wondered if any other nation on earth would complain about it. All I could do then was to pray to the god — if the god is in this world — that: my ancestral land might not be made into the colony again; it would simply be too cruel of him if he were to force us to bear even greater sacrifice we had been suffering so far.

This reminded me of what I had always been told by my father since my childhood: "Do not turn to others; you must not rely on gods, either; the one who turns to others is an idler; the one who turns to gods is a criminal." It seems that I had been much influenced by my father, and I had never turned to others for any help, not to mention gods. But now, I did pray to god, if anything like that exists, saying: "If any god is, please see to it that we shall be kept independent!" I myself, far from being a criminal, had always remained good or even too good. Still, I was then suffering such cruel treatment as might be given to slaves. What was worse, our homeland might be made a colony once again! We might be made slaves there. "Still, my dear father," said I, "must I not pray to any god? They say: we are so made as to catch at a straw when about to be drowned. Right?" At this point, I could not help giving a wry smile to myself, facing the dark ceiling.

Rumor had it that: the Japanese on these islands had had no arms to fight with, even though they were in the midst of the war. I heard that: each of the people had been equipped with a bamboo spear, usually placing it at the entrance of their house. This reminded me of that saying: "A drowning man will catch at a straw." Still, everyone in Japan at that time seemed to have believed in their victory. What was it that had made them so crazy? Ignorance? "Overdoing anything is by no means recommendable" is among our popular sayings. Placing too much trust upon the current government is by no means recommendable. I cannot tell what the Japanese people at that time were saying to themselves, but as long as seen from outside, they remained too blind to see through the true nature of things. If one puts a blind trust upon anything — whatever it may be — one is quite likely to fail to see the true nature of things. This still remains a lesson to myself; Even though I am living a lonely life now, making myself blind is the last thing I shall choose.

According to the announcement from the Imperial Headquarters, they were still giving a declaration that: they would exterminate "the brutal U.S. and U.K." But it seemed quite probable to me that the U.S. would soon make their entry into Japan. What would happen to us then? It was tolerable for me to be made a prisoner of war. But never should I be able to tolerate my homeland Korea to be colonized again! Until recently I had believed that: if this war was prolonged, I should be forced to make myself a soldier even if I were to run away from this coal mine. But the information I had just obtained at the bathroom that day seemed to have ordered me to "think *it* all over again." Muttering that order to myself, I fell into a deep sleep.

● The Packed Lunch

On august 17, 1944, I woke up to be dazzled by the sunshine falling upon my face, as usual. But the sunshine that morning seemed to me unusually dazzling. Probably because of the want of sleep, I found my legs unusually heavy on my way to the dining room, even though I had poured the tap water all over my head as soon as I got up. But I must go on, because I had to receive my packed lunch, and also had to offer my thanks to her for the scorched rice ball I had received on the morning the day before. While pushing my number card into the slot, I looked in. I saw a woman's hand come stretching to take my card. In no time, I had a bowl of rice and a bowl of *miso* soup placed before my eyes. Then I saw a round paper parcel pushed on toward me — as it was the day before. While covering it with my hand, I looked at the woman who had sent it to me. That was unmistakably the same woman I had seen the day before. Though I remained silent, I sent my "thanks" to her only with my eyes. She also, though in silence, gave me her facial expression of "It's O.K.."

I was able to leave the dining hall without any trouble, exactly as I had been the day before. When I returned to our room, I placed the package of the burnt rice before my roommates, as I had done the day before. Everyone turned his eyes upon it, when the Old Man grasped it and placed it softly before me, as if it were something very precious, and said: "This is yours. Yesterday, we received it as your kindness, but today, this is *not* for anyone of us, *but* yours."

Mr. Kim, whom I had mentioned before, also said to me:

"He is right. This is none other than her kindness offered to you. So we shouldn't have accepted it, as we did yesterday. We have all agreed: what you have received shall be yours."

Then Paek also said to me:

"Yes. We have all agreed. So you need not hesitate to take it."

These words of them choked me, leaving me silent. Everyone, as usual, began to eat their lunch in the box, This led me, to follow them in silence.

"Do you eat it now?" asked Paek. "Yes," I said, while eating on and on. Then, I packed the empty box with the scorched rice, which had been wrapped in the paper. Then we all went to our place of work in the mine.

At lunchtime, the Uras and we, drafted workers, used to eat at different places: the latter in the shade of the trolley train. That day I went to join my fellow workers without giving any notice to Mr. Ura.

After lunch, we all were to take a brief nap with our back on the smooth part of the rock surface. I took out the lunchbox and divided the rice there into five equal parts and brought them to each of my mates. They asked me what had made me do that. This led me to explain what had been happening to me since the day before. But as for the information I had got at the bathroom, I kept it to myself. What if it were to spread by word of mouth till it was known to the office of our dormitory? It would be quite probable that I might be called "a traitor" again, to my fear.....

Anyway, we were able to have such a pleasant lunchtime then as we had never had for a long time. After having eaten a scorched portion of boiled rice, one of us requested me to bring us such an extra portion of rice again if I were lucky enough to receive anything like that the next day, too. This led me to take him as someone comparable to a little devil, but I was quite ready to promise him to do so. After having a chat for a while, and when we were about to set out for the work, we received a cup of tea from Mrs.Ura, who had always prepared the tea for us, too. This had led us to have tea *only* at the lunch time, so we might not take too much advantage of her kindness. After having sipped the tea, we all returned to our work.

● The Hard Labor in the Coal Mine

In the mine, it was properly cool when we were not at work, but once we began to work, we were kept bathed in perspiration. Still, I had been working in the situation less hard to bear. Roughly speaking, there were three types of work in the mine. As for the tunneler, I had already mentioned. The pitman is the one who actually engages in digging the coal out. This is the most dangerous and the most exhaustive work to do. The coal-mining is done along the vein of coal; if that vein was 50m wide, the miners would work in a line — about 2m apart from each other. The problem then was how high that vein was.

The highest part of the vein here was 3*shaku* (ca.1m); the lowest was 2*shaku* (ca. 60cm). We were to work side by side, holding the pickaxe in our hands. The one short in stature worked on his knees; the tall one must employ his pickax while lying on his side. This way of working made them look like black ogres — clad only in a single loin-cloth; their body, drenched in sweat and covered with coal-powder, gave a black luster even in the dusk inside; their lips and skin around their eyes alone had managed to reveal something like human skin. The sight of them did remind us of what is called "a hell in this world." The eighty percent of the drafted workers in the mine were made to work as coal miners, I presume, because all the miners here, excepting the bosses, were drafted workers.

Beside the work mentioned above, there is the work performed by those called *shikuri*-men, who were to go planting logs (from

50cm to less than 10cm across) — 2m apart — so that they may prevent the ceiling of the newly-made cave from falling down. Then the further effort is made in this line — by planting *torii**-like archways along the tunnel we have already drilled. This work is comparatively less dangerous to do, while they are said to draw the highest salary among the laborers here. The *shikuri*-men worked in a group of four or five, but drafted workers were rarely included in it. Even if included, those who were tall and strong were not employed but one.

*an archway to a *Shintō* shrine in Japan: 冂

I had been made to work as a *"kusshin*-man" (a man to dig on and on)." It was rather fortunate of me. If anyone was made *shikuri*-man, he was regarded as having been promoted. There were many other kinds of work for us to do — pushing on the trolley train, the sewage disposal in the mine and so on. But even today, I cannot forget what those pitmen at work used to look like. Whenever I recall *the* scenes, they lead me to get goose pimples. Thinking that: that was the way the Japanese were making the war — by driving us, drafted workers — it simply makes me stand aghast and speechless. Who would compensate us for that lost time and that abused energy of ours? And how?

During the War, we were helplessly driven to work "for the sake of *our* land (Japan)." But when the War was over, everything had vanished in the air.

● The First Salary I had Received

Now — 1987 — I am free to write anything like this, and *that* has made me write this memoir. Looking back, I had once been blessed with a chance to run away, to my great good luck. My having been forbidden to go out on the *O-Bon* Holiday (the Buddhist version of All Soul's Day, which occurs in mid-August) led me to work hard so that I might return the kindnesses I was receiving from the Uras. I was to receive *o-koge* (the burnt-rice ball) from their daughter every other week. This was because of her schedule: in one week, she was expected to arrive at her workplace at 4 a.m.; in the other week, at 11 a.m.. In the former, I received a mass of *o-koge;* in the latter, I did not. Whether I received *o-koge* or not, I kept working regularly even when I had a little headache or stomachache or a cold, excepting the 5th, 15th and 25th of the month as our regular holidays.

When August was over and September arrived, I received what was called salary. Four months had passed since we arrived here. I never asked what had made them pay us the salary then. I had never expected to receive anything like that. What if I might ask them any such question? I was afraid I might receive another shout of "you, an unpatriatic person!" and this had led me to decide to work without saying anything provocative. By the time I reached our room, I had read the details printed on the back of the yellowish envelope. I still remember how it was like, since that was the first wages I had ever received: 120 *yen*. The details went as follows:

The board and lodging charge: _____ Tobacco: ¥15 Alcohol: _____
Payment in Advance: _____ Clothing: _____ Daily Necessaries: _____
Remittance: ¥70 Recoupment: ¥85 The Remainder: ¥35

I opened the envelope and shook it upside down to find there an unmistakable sum of money of ¥35. I cannot tell how much the tobacco called *KINSHI* cost then, but all I thought about that proviso was: How much I had spent on the tobacco! As for the Remittance or the money to be sent home, I thought it would be told us sooner or later. All that I did then was to hold the cash tight in my palm, saying to myself: "This is mine."

When I returned to our room, I saw everyone seated there, staring at his money with his wage packet before him. Mr. Kim alone had already been writing a letter to his father at home. This led me to follow him. I borrowed the two sheets of letter paper from Mr. Kim and began to write to my father. At the beginning, I apologized him for not having written to him sooner, and wrote that: I had been in good health, even though I had found the meals offered here were not sufficient for me, and that: since I was working at the coal mine for the first time, it would take several more days before I got accustomed to the work there. Then I asked if my brothers and sisters at home were living in good health. I also wrote that I had received the salary for the first time, and that I had got the money — ￥70 — sent home, too. At the end of the letter, I wrote: there is nothing for him to worry about me, so I hope he would feel easy.

On the day that followed — before I went to work — I left it at the office without putting any postage stamp on it. When I saw Mr. Ura at our work place and told him I had received the salary for the first time, he told me that: the drafted workers could not receive the salary for the first three months because they still remained mere trainees, but from the fourth month on, they were to be treated as the full-fledged to receive their salary. I had remained unconvinced at heart, but I simply said: "Was that so?" as if I had understood him. Be that as it might, that salary seemed to be a divine assistance to myself, because I had been planning to run away from here. The more money I had kept with me, the more helpful it would turn out, I was saying to myself. The money my father had equipped me with when I left home — ￥70 — still remained exactly as it was in my bundle. So the money I had kept with me had now become ￥105!

By the New Year, I should receive the monthly salary three times. Then I was to be equipped with more than ￥200. That would surely be helpful to me. In those days, it used to cost less than ￥100 to take the ferryboat from Busan in Korea to Shimonoseki in Japan. I say this, because I found the following year (1945) at the port at Hakata, it cost ￥100, as I shall recount toward the end of this book.

Anyway, ¥200 at that time was a large sum of money. This did help me to feel free from being worried about money. On the other hand, I was feeling as excited as if I had taken my first step toward running away from here! This led me to feel the need of making even greater efforts by adopting a suitably respectable attitude not only for the Ura family but also for myself. What had made me say this was: from mid-July to the *Bon* Festival* holidays in mid-August, I was among those who had been carrying out a slowdown or what was called *noson*. That was, we behaved as we were expected from leaving our dormitory to entering the mine pit, but instead of working there, we hid ourselves in the abandoned mine or the dead pits, until the time came for everyone to leave the coalmine. Then after taking a bath to join our fellow workers, we returned to the dormitory with an unconcerned look.

Strangely enough, this slowdown of ours was rarely brought to light. We, drafted workers, even though we had a headache or stomachache, could not take a day off unless we got a certificate from the doctor. This led to our invention of *noson*. In other words, the perfunctoriness of the office side had caused *it* or helped *it* to be brought into being. If we had been paid by the day, it would have been known to them whether we worked that day or not. But we were paid by the month, without any proof of our having worked every day of the month. It seemed that those in the office had good-naturedly believed in our perfect innocence to follow the orders they had given us. That had kept our *noson* from being known to the office. *Noson* was usually practiced when one was sick or not feeling well but was not able to get from the doctor any certificate for one's complaint about one's physical condition.

*the Buddhist All Soul's Day

II

AS FAR AS WHERE THE STRAIT WAS SEEN

● A Letter from Home

My *noson* had been practiced *not* for any such reason, *but* for the purpose of expressing my resistance to their cruel treatment to us, Korean laborers. But after the *Bon* Festival holidays or the Buddhist *all Souls' Days* were over, my state of mind had been changed by 180 degrees. I no longer needed to turn to anything like *noson,* or the situation itself had led us not to do anything like that. Excepting the regular holidays of the 5th, 15th and 25th, I kept working without indulging myself in *noson.* Even the heat of summer seemed to be easily bearable when September set in, probably because it was only at night when we were staying at the outside world.

At home, the harvest season or the busiest season for the farmers would have already set in, when even the children were expected to lend their hands; Father used to cut the soybeans in the field — from which I had unexpectedly been drawn to this forced labor — and to place them in a small pile along the ridge in the field, which I collected to bring to the roadside so that we might carry them home by oxcart in the evening, when the bright red sun was about to hide itself behind the western mountains….. Where was the sun going? Anyway, we seemed to have another fine day tomorrow, too.

Saying so to myself, I ought to have been going home.... As it was, I had been made a coal miner with my dear old home far away beyond many mountains and fields and the sea..... My father, having been suddenly deprived of his son — like a man who had unexpectedly had a black kite take his *abura-age* away from him*— ought to have been left in grief and resentment, even unable to give any protest against this absurdity. As for myself, I had seen for the first time what the autumn scenery looked like in another country. On our way to work, I saw the mountains beyond the huge heaps of coal adding to their autumnal tints day after day. This did remind me of those dear old mountains I used to see at home, making me feel nostalgic for my dear old home.

*a turn of phrase employed to describe someone who has unexpectedly been deprived of something special to one. *Abura-age* is a thin slice of deep-fried *tōfu* (soy-bean curd)

Early in October, I received a letter from my father at home. That went as follows:

Our harvesting is over for the most part. At present, we are busy preparing for the winter. Thanks to the money you sent us, your younger sister, Hana, is dancing with joy at her belated tuition having been paid and a suit of Western clothes having been bought for her. Your younger brother Funryur, who is taken to his aunt every morning to be left with her all day long, is making himself a good boy — eating, playing and sleeping as properly as he should, to our great relief. I hope you will also be in good health, taking good care of yourself. We shall be able to get along with anything as long as we are in good health. And one more thing I must say to you is: you may come to need your own money at any moment. So do keep your money to yourself instead of sending us any money.

From your Father

This letter written on a single letter paper was to be the first and the last letter I had received from my father. By then, all the bonds between us had already been severed. When I read this letter, I felt he had already seen through what I had held in my mind. What made him write — "you may come to need your own money at any moment" — was understandable to me to a piercing extent. And this led me to believe: Father would surely allow me to run away from here. But I did not send in any application to stop sending money to my father, partly because I had simply wished to do something for my father, and partly because I had felt confident of my own ability to earn my getaway money even if I might keep sending him some money.

● Preparing for Running Away

One of the pieces of information I had obtained at the bathroom was how to make a perfect runaway from the coal mine. That was to run into any military factory or anything in that line. The reason was because it was so made as *not* to receive any approach from any coal mine. This was something new and valuable to me.

One of these days, I asked Mr. Ura if he could lend me a map of Japan. This led me to obtain a map of Saga Prefecture, though not the map of the whole Japan, because he had not possessed anything like that. When he handed it to me in the mine, he kindly gave me a piece of information: to the farther north of this town of Tokusue-cho, there is a naval port in the town called Karatsu*; to the south, there is another port town named Imari*. He also added: if I had any opportunity to go out to enjoy myself, I should make a visit to either Karatsu or Imari, for it offers a pleasure-place for men only. In my heart of hearts, I was moved almost to tears by the kindness Mr. Ura had shown me then.

*Both Karatsu and Imari have been known for the chinaware or Karatsuware and Imariware they produced. (This is closely related with what is known as *Bunroku-Keicho no eki* — Hideyoshi's expeditions to Korea in 1592 and 1597.) Hideyoshi had destroyed the Hōjō clan and united the country. He then planned to subjugate Ming China and expected Korea to be instrumental in asking tribute from China. Korea, however, fearing the powerful Ming dynasty, refused to mediate. Hideyoshi then decided to conquer Korea and in 1592 (the first year of the *Bunroku* era) sent an amphibious force of 150,000 men to Korea. They reached Pyongyang, where they ran into Ming forces. Hideyoshi had to conclude peace and to withdraw his troops. This expedition is referred to as *Bunroku no eki.*

As the peace treaty of Ming China had used abusive language, Hideyoshi decided to send a second expedition to Korea in 1597 (second year of the Keichō era) But he died before the expedition could fulfill its mission, and, following his last injunctions, the expeditionary forces were withdrawn. This expedition is known as *Keichō no eki.*

The two expeditions ended with a great loss of men and materials. However, one result was good — the Japanese had brought home thousands of Korean artisans and scholars, and the arts of printing, dyeing, weaving, and ceramics were studied in a new light.

—— *A DICTIONARY OF JAPANESE HISTORY*
By Joseph M. Goedertire, C.I.C.M.

When I asked him to lend me a map, Mr. Ura might have read my thoughts, and that had led him to give me a hint in a casual manner. At a later date, I was to make a successful runaway by making use of this hint Mr. Ura had given me then. But all I could say then was: "Thank you for your kindness." I folded the map and put it in the wrapping of my lunch box so that it might not give any noise even if swung back and forth.

While I was at work, I was wondering how I should carry *it* as far as my own room. I had to return the lunch box at the mess hall. All I had on my body then were the loincloth and the rubber-soled socks! No! I had a half-sleeved shirt! Since October set in, we had been permitted to wear a half-sleeved shirt. Now it was left beside the lunch box so that we might wear it on our way back. It might be helpful for me to bring *it* back.

In the evening, after the day's work was over, we left the mine. After taking a bath on my way to the dormitory, I took out the map out of the lunch box, and pressing it hard under my arm in my half-sleeved shirt, I walked past the office building to reach the mess hall to return the lunch box. Since the map under my arm seemed to be about to drop, I pressed it hard, inevitably causing *the* shoulder alone to appear unnaturally stiff. Far from good! But now I was walking past the office building, gripping the strap of my loin cloth in my hand. Then, unfortunately, I saw Captain Shiroyama staring at me in my unusual posture.

"Hey!" he called to me. "What's happening to you walking in such a strange manner?'

I, pretending to be as casual as I could, gave him an answer:

"The cord of my loin cloth has failed me…."

Thus I made a successful run to our own room, even though I had to find the cover of the map had been softened with my sweat.

Now I spread the map before me. Kim and Paek and one more came to join me in studying it. The old man alone remained unconcerned, while smoking. First of all, I looked for where Tokusue-chō or where we lived was; then I let my fingertip return to Karatsu, and then go to Imari. They moved their eyes along my fingertip, as if being dragged by it.

My fingertip returned to Karatsu and encircled *it*. Kim alone answered: "Yes." The other two seemed to have failed to understand what I had meant by encircling the name of Karatsu. I swallowed my saliva and looked at those around me and told them of my own plan of running away from here, *if* I were allowed to go out on the New Year holiday. Everyone remained silent. Kim, while moving his knees a little said: "I'll join you." The old man followed him, saying: "I'll remain here." The other said: "I'll be giving a thought about *it* till then." Paek was the last to express his intention: "I'll remain here together with the old man." After all, those who had decided to run away were Kim and myself; those who had intended to keep staying were the old man and Paek. The other had remained indecisive.

By and by, the bell rang to send us to bed, followed by Captain Shiroyama's hitting along the corridor, before the light went out. Everyone was lying in bed in silence. Then the old man muttered, as if to himself: "You must give *it* a good thought, so you may not lose both principal and interest."

As for myself, I had thought I should reveal my intention to run away just before my putting *it* into practice, but now that I had spread the map before them, I could not help revealing my intention. Now I think I had done something good by revealing my intention to them, because it did give them the opportunity to think about *it* themselves. So everything went all right. All I should do from then on was to wait for the opportunity for me to put *it* into practice. Saying so to myself, I let myself go to sleep so that I might be able to keep working the following day, too.....

From this day on, I made it a rule to hurry to the bathroom as soon as I finished the day's work, so that I might obtain any information available. October had set in, and it was growing noticeably cooler in the morning and in the evening. The mountains beyond the huge coal-waste heap, which had been displaying the autumnal tint, were gradually turning less and less bright. The winter season seemed to be approaching even to this southernmost main island of Japan. Looking back upon that heat and humidity during the summer season, I could hardly imagine the winter season here would bring us anything like snow! Still the autumn season we had seen here for the first time had gone and the winter season was about to set in. When we entered the mine in the trolley train, we felt chilly, and even at work, we were less sweaty. On the other hand, at the bathroom, we were able to have the most blessed time.

One day, also at the bathroom, I had a piece of particularly interesting information: there was a remarkable difference between the Army and the Navy even in the supply of food and commodities. The latter was said to have been amply supplied either in food or in commodities. I could not tell why, but I had felt any information obtained at that bathroom was fairly trustworthy and reliable. In fact, according to my own experience I was to have after having run away from here, all the information we used to obtain *here* proved to be literally authentic.

One day toward the end of November, when I returned to my dormitory after taking a bath, as usual, I found Captain Shiroyama there. When he saw me, he gave me an unusual grin and said:

"Hay, you, just make a visit to the office."

This set me to hold my breath. Because it occurred to me that: what I had talked to my roommates of my having planned to run away from here had become known to the office. If so, it would be all up with me. I should never be allowed to return here without receiving any such violence as might give me any physical defects. This led me to turn defiant, saying to myself:

"Well, if I must receive *it,* I will make myself a dignified receiver of *it!"*

● I had My Salary Raised from November on

While shutting the entrance door behind, I shouted, as usual: "No. 320!" The man, about sixty years old, who had been seated at the long desk beside the front wall — with his hair split seventy-thirty, wearing the dark orange glasses — placed his tall tea cup with a click on his desk. Moving his eyes and nose, he made his glasses slip down to the tip of his nose, and cast a quick glance at me through upturned eyes from above the frame, and said:

"I know you are No. 320. But don't give me such an angry look. Just feel easy, since I have no intention to bite you."

Captain Shiroyama, standing beside me, said to me:

"He is the Superintendent of the Dormitory. Just behave yourself meekly."

I simply kept staring hard at him without changing my countenance as well as my posture.

Now the Superintendent of the Dormitory said to me, looking at a piece of paper held in his far-stretched hand:

"Well, No.320, I have received a written report from the site supervisor of your place of work, saying that: You are a very good worker, steady and dependable, and that: you are worthy of having your salary raised. So, after quitting all scores so far, you will get a raise in salary — ¥10 — from November on. We hope you will continue to be a good worker. If everyone makes himself such a good worker as you are, we shall surely win the war. Do you understand me?"

When I came to stand before him, I had assumed a defiant attitude, keeping myself stiff, intending to let him attack me as much as he liked. But when his speech was over like this, I found myself having collapsed on the earthen floor — as if I had had all the wind taken out of my sail.

Seeing what had happened to me then, the superintendent of the dormitory swung his palm from side to side, saying: "All right. All right." He, probably having mistaken what had happened to me then had come from the respect and gratitude I was feeling toward him, had narrowed his eyes. I rose to my feet, employing both of my hands, and after bobbing my head in salute, I left the office, while hearing a boisterous laughter behind me.

As soon as I returned to my room, I laid myself. The old man asked me:

"You are late in coming back. Do you have a stomachache?"

"No. I've got tired," said I.

"Have you? That's quite probable."

The old man seemed to have relieved to hear that. This led me wonder if I should tell him about what had happened to me at the office. By and by, I came to a conclusion that: I had better *not* tell anything about it. In fact, I had kept silent about it — even after I had run away and after the war was over — until today.

Probably because I was born and brought up in the severe climate, I had always remained perseverant and persistent in keeping *something* in secret — say, even to my comrade in flight! I myself like this perseverance of mine, but I cannot help disliking that persistency or obstinacy in hiding something from others. Now, by writing out all of these defects of mine, I hope I shall make myself light-hearted in the true sense of the word.

Even after all my roommates went to sleep, I kept thinking

about what had happened to me at the office. I felt sorry for the superintendent of the dormitory who had kindly raised my salary, but to myself, it was much more important and relieving that my plan had hit the mark! I said to myself: "I must say thank you to Mr. Ura when I meet him tomorrow, and at night, I will write to my father, saying that: he need not send his answer any longer, and that: even if I might not write to him so often, he need not worry about it, keeping himself at ease, while believing that I am always remaining safe and sound."

In November, my wages for the previous month were raised, while my remittance to home remained unchanged; all the other recoupments remained also unchanged, thus causing only my share, having been raised by ten *yen,* to have risen to 45 *yen.* This meant: all the money I had kept then became 220 *yen.* If I were to receive my salary for December before the New Year's Day, it would make as much as 265 *yen.* But I thought: now that I had got the money enough to meet my purpose, I would not need any more money. This led me to think: I must make another advance arrangement with my roommates before long. So far it was decided that: I and Kim would run away, while the old man and Paek would remain. Only one of us in the same room still remained indecisive. In a week — on December 15 — we should have a day off. This decided us to have a good talk about *it* by making use of that opportunity.

I remained a regular visitor to the bathroom to listen to any more information available there. By that time, we had come to get many such rumors as: the U.S. planes came flying to the Kantō Region (where Tokyo is) to drop the bombs there, or the Japanese people were now making bamboo spears in order to fight against the U.S. soldiers who might come landing in Japan proper, or the Americans were fond of women and this would lead them to kill all the menfolk, while leaving the womenfolk for themselues, or all the Japanese would kill themselves before they saw any such miseries, and so on, and so on, until we could no longer tell the mere rumors from the rigid facts. The only thing that seemed probable was: Japan would be defeated, and the U.S. soldiers would come to land in these islands of Japan.

This led me to say to myself: "I must get away from here before the Americans come to land here. If they come on, we Koreans, too, would either be taken prisoners or be kept strictly confined in this mine as coal miners. Either prospect seemed quite probable. Even if we asserted ourselves to be Koreans — *not* Japanese — it would *never* be understood by them. All I could do then would be to pray that: the Americans might *not* come on until the New Year season came round. Somehow or other, I had become confident that I would surely be able to run away from here when the New Year season came round!

Thus on the day off or on the 15th of December, I had a talk with those who had not yet made up their mind. After all, it turned out that it was only Kim and myself who had been ready to run away.

● Our Plan to Run Away

Within that very same day, I talked with Kim about how we should carry out our plan. All that we had come to agree with each other were: all we should prepare for *it* would be that pair of suit in which we had arrived here; each of us should carry only 30*yen* for the moment; the rest of our money should be hidden under the piece of cloth we had patched upon our loin cloth; excepting *this*, we should be carrying nothing with ourselves; even if one of us might be caught, the other should keep running away; if anything unexpected might separate us to leave each of us alone, we should *not* leave our contact to any other *but* do it ourselves." Then Kim added: "If I were to be caught, I'll give them an *opposite* direction, so you must keep running toward the direction we have decided at first. Don't forget *this,* I'll warn you!"

This made me answer him: "All right. If I were caught, I also would do as you have told me." The direction we decided to take was northward or to the town named "Karatsu." (P.91) The reason why we had chosen Karatsu was: firstly because it was closer to our own homeland; in fact we had wished to bring ourselves closer to it even by a single step: secondly because it had a naval port there, and thirdly because the name of Karatsu or 唐津 — which literally meant "Chinese Port" — had made us feel rather familiar to ourselves. (P.92・93)

When that plan of ours had been made up, Kim gave me another theme for us to consult about, saying: "I think we had better have told about this plan of ours at least to our roommates. What do you think?" This led us to talk again about our plan, but it was not long before I said: "Please do *it* as you like or as you yourself think *it* better. I agree with you on any decision you'll make. But, come to think of it, I've come to feel rather depressed now that only two of us have come to run away, leaving the three behind....."

This led Kim to tell me what he had had in his mind:

"It cannot be helped. Everyone has his own contrivances. What is more, there is something one *must* do — regardless of the number of one's comrades. Even if one might be sent to death, one must do what one must do."

"As you know," he went on. "Long ago or about thirty years ago, when our land of Korea was about to be colonized by the Japanese, many Korean patriots came out, filling the streets, while crying out for keeping our land remaining independent. This caused a large number of men and women to be killed or to be sent to prison, as is recorded in history as "the 3.1 Incident." — This also led to the assassination of Ito Hirobumi (1841-1909), at Harbin.... (P.247)

All this while, the Korean patriots had kept raising their outcries against Japan's colonization of their Korean Peninsula. Probably, even today, our compatriots might keep crying for our independence against Japan's lawlessness somewhere unknown to us without being known to us. Both you and I, though unable to join them, must at least help ourselves obtain our own freedom."

"Talking about our own running away from here," he went on, "if seen from the standpoint of the general public in Japan, it will be taken as nothing but a mere escape of the drafted workers from the coal mine, but seen from our own standpoint, it is not a mere escape from work, but a part of our resistance movement against their colonization of our land."

"If seen from the standpoint of the Japanese officialdom," he went on, "our running away would certainly be regarded as something unpatriotic and unpardonable. But just think who on earth will come to unchain us to make us free from such cruel treatments as "the transportation for forced labor," "the detention by legal force" and "the forced labor." No one will come to cut those chains around us. Then we ourselves must cut the chains for ourselves."

"Everyone of us, human beings, wishes to live a life worth living. That wish comes from the real nature of us human beings, But now, we are not placed in such a situation as will enable us to wish to lead any such worthy life. So at any rate, we must take even a single step forward by setting ourselves free from the chain that has been wound around us. Even a single step will do. We must step forward to follow the path to freedom."

"I know what has made you plan to escape is *not* just to satisfy your wish to fill your stomach. So I can understand your guilty feelings, when we two alone — among five of us — are planning to escape, but to my mind, we ought to keep such personal sentiment only to ourselves for a while. Once we run away, we shall never be allowed to fail. What if we were to fail? It's quite apparent that those remaining here will surely be thrown into grief and sorrow. So we cannot die in vain. Don't you think so, Mr. Ri....?"

This was how Mr. Kim had made sure of my preparedness for our planning. I, having been deeply impressed by his admonition, made up my mind again to make our running away a successful one. I now realize that: what has enabled me to speak and write in Japanese as I do now — though in my own way — was the envy I had been feeling toward Mr. Kim, whose thoughtfulness and ample knowledge had always remained stimulating to me. In fact, I never got tired of making efforts to catch up with him. This was how I made myself confident in myself and learned how to survive not a few trials I had to face in my life.

Ten days had passed since we decided to run away. Now we had only three days left before this year — 1944 — was over. It goes without saying that those seven months I had spent here since I was taken to this coal mine were to bring me one new experience after another. What had impressed me most naturally included the forced transportation, the forced detention and forced labor, and that they had all occurred, to my surprise, in Japan proper, where we caught glimpses of differences of the nations in the yellow pickled radish and the tea prepared from the leaves of the tea plant; after having been hazed in the name of the training for the armed forces for as long as a couple of weeks, we were sent to the coal mine only to make us stand aghast. Could all that be a comic, in which none could laugh? Every morning and evening, we were to get up and go to bed by the signal of hitting along the corridor with the handle of a pickaxe. The runaway, if caught, would receive his baptism of being hit with a whip of crude rubber. What a miserable youth, in which I had to hide a package of the slightly-burnt rice ball in the crotch of my trousers! The miseries I suffered there would be endless, if written down. Indeed, those two hundred days I had spent there simply deprived me not only of human dignity but also of even a brief time to rest my mind.

On the night of the last day of my seventeenth year* — 1944 — I was in bed, feeling the growing coldness. This bed, which had never been adored by me, would never see me again. I prayed that I might not return here as long as I had kept my soul within myself. Having been humiliated was unbearable. But all those kindnesses I had received here were unforgettable. This led me to send my tears of thankfulness to the coal hewer, Mr. Ura, and his family, who had always been kind and fair to me, a mere drafted worker who was having a hard time.

*One's age used to be counted as one year old at birth with one year added at every New Year's Day.

Regardless of my thoughts in confusion with sorrows and bitter feelings, mixed with expectations and uneasiness, I heard *the* devil in this world coming round to wake us up even on the morning of the New Year's Day — by madly whipping along the corridor. Still remaining half asleep, I was wondering how such a lowly fellow as Captain Shiroyama would get along when the war was over. Some people in the shade had been making use of such a lowly fellow as he — as the leader or the boss of a certain group of people.... The leader, who was to lead the nation either to its rise or to its downfall, ought to have been chosen with the utmost care..... Then I could see the primary factor that would lead Japan to her downfall. None of us in this dormitory had ever regarded this person, Captain Shiroyama, as a human being. Not a few of us had fled from here, because of their total disgust they could not help feeling against him. I myself used to intensify my wish to run away from here every time he came into my sight.

I gave repeated yawns, and feeling like telling my fortune *that* day, I looked around to see my roommates. Everyone of them gave me a nod as if sending his agreement with me in my plan. Kim also nodded to me. I lowered my head to him, inwardly saying: "Thank you for everything." Kim himself, who had been allowed to go out on the *Bon* holiday, too, was free from any worry. But I myself had still remained in uneasiness itself. Six months had passed since I was branded as an unpatriotic person, and it was only recently that I had been set free from the distrust with which I had been looked down upon. Should I really be allowed to go out? I kept asking to myself. Kim had placed a bet on me who had placed a bet on the possibility of my winning a permission to go out that day. It was to such a companion of mine that I could not help lowering my head.

● The Last Meal I had Taken *There*

Even on the New Year's Day, we were expected to finish our breakfast by 7, as usual. Urged by the Old Man, we all went to the dining hall. Not a single tip of cloud was seen in the blue sky. Indeed, it seemed quite a suitable day to celebrate the arrival of the New Year. The window glass in the office had been steamed up. Only the reception window had been cleared off by someone obviously with the palm of his or her hand. I recited my number, and after having received the wooden tag with my number 320 written on it in black ink, I entered the dining room to find that the five tables for as many as thirty diners had already been occupied. To our disappointment, however, the meal we were served then simply remained of the same type as the one we had usually been given, excepting the five or six pieces of diced *tofu* we found in the *miso* soup. In my life so far, this was the first and the last New Year's Day when I had to do without any piece of *mochi* or rice cake.

After the meal was over, we were expected to receive "a leave permit" in exchange for our number plate. While chewing the boiled rice without haste, thus savoring the taste of it, I spoke inwardly to that number plate of mine I had placed in between the dishes:

"You are a mere wooden plate with No. 320 written on it. And yet, you have deprived me of my own name, preventing me from obtaining any meal without you. Yes, you have had control over me for as long as seven months. Now, I'll implore you to release me, if you have any such mercy as is possessed by any human being. Before long, I'll make a trial of you: if you are kind to me, I'll keep you in my mind throughout my life; *if not*, I'll spit on you!"

After the meal was over, I brought myself to the window through which we had received our meal, wishing to say something to express my heartfelt thanks to the daughter of Mr. and Mrs. Ura, who had kept supplying me with *o-koge* or burnt-rice ball. From inside the kitchen, a woman strange to me asked: "Can I help you?" I asked her in whisper:

"Is Miss Ura in?"

She nodded, saying: "Ah," and called out to her, saying: "Toki-*chan!*" At once, I saw her coming into my sight, tilting her head a little.

"Can I help you?..."

She gazed at me. I had not prepared anything to say to her for that moment. And all I could say then was:

"Well, …. Thank you. Yes,… that's all…"

I simply turned back and walked away.

● I Got the Permission to Go out

Saying to myself that I had done something I should do, I walked on toward the office building, keeping my number plate in between my palms. That might have made me appear as if I were praying for something. At the reception counter, I held it out as it was in between my palms, and chanted my number: "320." What answer should I get? I felt my heart beating high. From the reception window, I peeped into what was happening over there: Captain Shiroyama I had often mentioned stood up and walked to me. He had held a piece of paper as large as a name card between his fingertips. Then he saw me through upturned eyes, and said:

"You have done it! You've kept working for four months on end. The dormitory chief has been satisfied with your diligence. I hope — from now on, too — you'll remain as good as you have been. This is something for you — as a bonus. So, here you are!"

He put a piece of paper he had kept behind him upon the counter board with a click.

There I saw the five Chinese characters — 外出許可証 (A Permission to Go Out) — clearly stamped in blue! Overjoyed, I stuttered out:

"Th-th-thank you very much!"

In spite of myself, I felt moved to tears — while receiving a written permission as large as a name card with both of my hands. This new card reminded me of that old number plate I had just returned or parted with. It was a piece of wood, upon which my number — 320 — written in Indian ink, could hardly be seen because of the dirt from my hands.

On leaving the office, I started to run and jumped into our room breathlessly, thus attracting all the gazes from my mates upon me. In silence, I just thrust *the* leave ticket, looking like a magician showing his card to his audience. On seeing that, they all gave groans of "Oh!" or "Uhoo!" as if in surprise. Then, I said to Mr. Kim:

"I have now made myself your mate at long last! I hope you'll kindly guide me along."

Then I bobbed my head to him, who said:

"Well, well, that's good news to us all, too! I myself can stop worrying now. All of us, too, have been worrying about you, haven't we?"

The Old Man responded, saying:

"That's right! Well, well, I'll be able to feel relieved for the time being. Before you came back, we had been worrying about you, hadn't we?" He went on: "But now, you are making the very best departure. Well, Paek, just bring us some water in the lunch box, so we may have a drink, wishing them their best of luck on their way, according to the traditional ceremony for the farewell cup."

Then, the Old Man ordered Paek to prepare for it, employing his hand gesture.

Paek, probably having been in haste, soon came back, carrying the lidless lunch box filled with water, trying not to spill it with his hands. Then the Old Man urged everyone to take out his lunch box. When everyone did as they were told, the Old Man gave another order:

"Paek, pour that water into each of their lunch boxes."

Paek, beginning with Kim, did as he was told. When each had some water in his lunch box, the old man said:

"Well, I don't think it quite right for us to drink water (instead of *sake*) from a lunch box (instead of a *sake* cup) on New Year's Day (of all days), because it does remind us of our custom of "drinking *water* together from a *sake* cup at what may become our final parting." But let's drink success to Mr. Kim and Mr. Ri,, praying for their good health and safety!"

Thus they drank success to us!

Even after that ceremonial drinking was over, the old man, probably feeling worried about us, said to us: "The first thing you should do when you are out in the town is to obtain some salt — about a handful. Even if you had nothing to eat, salt water will keep you alive for three days or so. And keep your match box carefully — not to get it wet with rain. If you had loose bowels, burn the dried wood to get some charcoal; the powdered charcoal will stop *it*. If you cannot take a bath day after day, you should rub yourself down with a dry towel before going to sleep. This will keep you from catching a cold and from becoming lousy, though I hope you may not have any such sufferings. Anyway I do hope you will not come back, once you have left here. So this is our final parting. We wish you good luck!"

The old man seemed to be feeling as if he were about to send his own sons into the depths of the forest in the mountain. This moved me almost to tears, but I tried hard not to reveal my being tearful.

Thus we began to prepare for our outing, keeping our parting deep in our bosom. It was not long before we heard the bell ring to permit us to leave here. The old man seated himself — on the timber frame through which we stepped into or out of the house proper — had been studying what was happening around the office. We were all waiting for the direction he would give us. About twenty minutes later, he gave us an order, saying:

"All right. This is the time. Let's go!"

We all jumped out of our room. In front of the office, we saw a line of twenty to thirty people. The five of us joined it — the old man, Paek, myself, one more and Kim, according to the direction given by the old man. As I mentioned before, this old man had made himself a drafted worker instead of his own son he had let run away before *the* authorities came round. My father also must have had the same idea as this old man, but the then circumstances had failed him to put it into practice….. When I thought about it, I could not help feeling pity for and familiar with this old man, as if he were my own father; the trust I had placed upon him was also profound.

According to the order of our arrival there, we had to pass the censorship of our permission to leave, before we finally stepped out of the ground of our dormitory.

● **The Decisive Action we Took**

Since we stepped on the land of Japan to work in the coal mine there, seven months had passed, and all this while, we had always been deprived of our freedom, whether we were working in the daytime or sleeping in the dormitory at night — always remaining fearful of the watchful eyes upon us. And now, I was finally able to walk around, to eat what I wanted to eat, and to say anything I liked. I was feeling as if I were breathing the air totally different from the air I had been breathing so far. Unlike my companions, who had already been acquainted with the outside world, I was more eager to see things that came into my sight rather than talk to my companions. By and by, we found ourselves at the station named Tokusue — where we had got off the train for the first time in Japan. On that occasion, we got off the train as if driven away from it, and I had no time to keep in memory what that station looked like, and that, it was at night.

But now, when I saw it all over again, I was rather surprised to find what a small, timeworn station it was! There was a single window to sell tickets, and the other window beside it was to handle packages. In the waiting room about six *tatamis* wide, a wooden bench was seen beside the wall; on the opposite wall, a faded timetable was hung. Not a single decoration was seen around. But on entering the waiting room, we had our eyes caught by a group of young women in their New Year *kimono*. Even in the midst of the wartime, young women in their beautiful *kimono*

114

made us feel happy and restful. In fact, they made me forget all those miseries of the wartime and commandeering. When we were appreciating those feasts for the eyes, we had a startling figure come to pass in front of us. The figure in a military uniform was walking around with folded arms to our disgust.

Kim, my companion, whispered to me: "It's not the right place for us." This made me respond in a suppressed voice: "Let's go somewhere else," and we walked out on to the station square.

The square was far from spacious; even the bus could not turn its direction, The bus stop was seen by the roadside over there. I saw the timetable there to find that: the bus usually started ten minutes after the train's arrival there. The bus started six times a day, and the final one was 5:30 P.M. It was about once a couple of hours that both the train and the bus arrived or started. This meant: if we missed the train or the bus, we must wait for about a couple of hours. This led us to talk and decide that: we two should part *here* with the Old Man, Paek and one more. We shook our hands, praying for each other's good health and good luck. The three, who were to stay on at the coal mine, were looking back again and again until they had turned the corner that led to Imari* in the south.

Soon we found ourselves walking unconsciously toward the direction where our companions had vanished. Soon we found ourselves to have come as far as 1*cho* (ca.109m) southward from the bus stop, but we, instead of going back to the bus stop or to the train station, decided to kill time, walking back and forth around there. On the other hand, our appearance being none other than that of the drafted workers, we could not help being nervous about it. As for myself, I was in a white cotton suit my father had given me when I left home, and in black sports shoes made of artificial silk at that time. As for Mr. Kim, he was in a dark green suit made of something like jute bags, which had been offered by the coal-mining company to anyone who wished to have it. His shoes were of the same kind as mine. Anyone would easily be able to tell what we were — the drafted workers from the coal mine.

Even while walking up and down the street, we were feeling restless. What if we were to come across a military-police officer? If he saw what we were doing, he would not let us go in silence. Then, it would be all over with us. Still we had nowhere to go and hide ourselves. If we were to go to the countryside, the local farmers would surely inform the police of us as the questionable ones. Then all we could do would be to remain as we were until the time the next bus came to take us somewhere else. We simply kept walking back and forth, while wishing the bus would come sooner. In time, we saw one person after another walk into the station, probably because the train would arrive before long. This did encourage us, though a little. If the train arrived and left the station, the bus ought to arrive here — the bus we had been waiting for — for as long as two hours, while worrying about what the people would think of us.

What had made us choose to take the bus instead of the train was what we had learned from the precedents: Almost all of those who had taken the train after having run away from the coal mine were caught only to be taken back. According to the hearsay, the plain-clothes-men in the train were always keeping their watchful eyes on the drafted workers on the run. So the precedents and the information had led us to choose the bus.

At long last, we heard the whistle blow from the other side of the station, and it was not long before those who had got off the train left the station to make themselves scatter toward their villages. Seeing those scenes around, we made a slow approach to the bus stop to find no one waiting for the bus. But when we were cautiously walking toward the bus stop, still half a *chō* (ca. 109m) or so away, intending to run and jump into the bus as soon as it arrived there, a couple of middle-aged men in their civilian uniform presented themselves as if from nowhere and stood at the bus stop.

As for "the civilian uniform," it had been brought into being for men in place of their business suit. The newly-introduced uniform with a stand-up-collar had four or five buttons in the opening in front. I could not tell what sort of standard had led it to be made into what was called "the civilian uniform" for men. But since I had taken "the civilian uniform" as the full dress for men, I could not tell those who had made such an abrupt appearance before us were whether on their official business or merely for their New Year's outing. Anyway, they were eagerly talking about something. If they were local villagers, we should not mind them. But if they were in public office, they ought to have known that the drafted workers must not take either the bus or the train. If we were found to be runaways, they would be able to catch us! This sent us to a predicament. I tried to find out what my companion, Kim, had in his mind. Kim, also unable to decide what to do, said: "Let's let it go." This led us to take the next bus that would come round a couple of hours later. It was before noon. So the following bus would be here around 1 p.m..

Then, we decided to fortify ourselves with a meal, and began to walk toward Imari in the south — which was the direction opposite to Karatsu as our destination. From that bus stop at Tokusue, we walked as far as the third bus stop before we finally found an eating place. Entering it, we found it was six or seven *tatami* wide, with three small tables — each of which was about one meter long — arranged to form an oblong table, with as many as five chairs on one side. Because we had kept moving since morning, I felt somewhat relieved when we sat in the chair. It was not long before we had a steaming bowl of *udon* and soup served before our nose. The fragrance of the chopped spring onion seemed to reach to the bottom of my stomach. A couple of pieces of sliced *kamaboko* (white fish meat made into a seasoned paste, steamed and typically formed into a semi-cylindrical shape) placed on top of *udon* in the soup did stimulate my appetite. That was the first time for me either to see *it* or to eat *it*. When I ate up the *udon* itself, I took up the bowl in my hands and slurped the soup to the last drop. That also tasted good! This led us to order one more bowl, and again we ate and drank everything in it. This made us warm and full, and much more collected than before.

Then Kim took out a cigarette and said to the woman in the kitchen:

"Madam, may I have a light, please?"

Then she brought a new match box and handed it to him, saying:

"Here you are. You may take it with you."

Kim, while saying "Thank you very much," gave a meaningful grin at me, and lighted a cigarette and breathed in the smoke with a relish. To me, it seemed that he had wanted to say: "Now, I've got the matches!"

Now we decided not to return as far as the bus stop at Tokusue, but to take any bus at the nearest bus stop from this *udon* shop. The bus stop at Tokusue was the third stop from here. Now we decided whether we should get off at Tokusue or we should go on as far as Karatsu, according to the situation we would find at Tokusue. Seeing the timetable for the bus, we found we still had twenty minutes before the bus arrived.

Waiting outside would not only make us feel very cold but also raise suspicion. What should we do then? After having found it difficult to decide what we should do, I gave a loud question toward the kitchen:

"Madam, may I ask when the next bus will come?"

Then the woman said, her head popping out of the slit of the short curtain hung outside the kitchen:

"There is about twenty minutes, whichever way you may go. Anyway, you can wait here, because it is very cold outside."

"Thank you, Madam!'

I gave a prompt answer to her. Thus we were saved from waiting in the danger and the coldness outside! This made me happy. Kim looked at me, giving me a silent comment of "You did it!" This made me say:

"You've got the matches for us. So it's my turn to do something for us."

● In the Bus of our Destiny

Thus we waited for the bus, and we were able to get on the bus without any trouble. We passed the first bus stop and the second one, too, without anything troublesome. When we came in sight of the third stop of Tokusue near the train station, the conductor gave an announcement, saying:

"The next stop is Tokusue…Tokusue. If you get off there, please let us know in advance."

We remained silent. When I saw the bus stop from behind the driver's seat, I said to myself: "Oh, no!" Because I saw there a couple of men neatly dressed in the same kind of suit we had seen that morning! I looked at Kim. He shook his head. We left the bus, saying: "I'll stop over," after having handed the ticket to Karatsu to the conductor, only to return to that roadside at Tokusue.

According to the pledge we had made at the beginning, we were never allowed to fail in performing this running away. Whatever sort of men those in the civilian (wartime) uniform might be, we still had half a day before us. There was no need for us to be in haste or to run a risk. We had known that: waiting for the opportunity being our first prerequisite in running away, we should wait without haste until the final bus came to take us.

Now all we could do was to wait and wait. The bus would come three more times — at 3:00, at 5:00 and at 7.00, though the last one was too late for us. Thus we decided to place a bet on the bus to arrive here at 3:00 or at 5:00. If unable to take the bus by 5:00, we thought we could not help returning to the coal mine. If we failed in our attempt that day, our hope of running away would be reduced to zero, but if we returned to the coal mine, we should be able to expect another opportunity to run away. Talking about such prospect of ours, we kept waiting for the next bus to come round, while enduring the coldness. We had kept ourselves about 100m away from the bus stop — while coming this way and that — pretending as if we were simply hanging around.

That turned out a hard job. In that cold weather, I had had no underwear; all that I wore under the jacket was a green half-sleeved cotton shirt; as for the lower half, a loincloth and a pair of trousers were all I wore. This made me feel cold to the marrow of my bones. It was indeed at long last when we finally saw that long-awaited bus come into our sight without giving any sound from the recess of the mountain!

This led us to hurry back to the bus stop. Looking back, the bus, appearing larger and larger, came rushing toward us. This made us run. Then I saw two soldiers coming out of the station. They were in a tight-collared overcoat of yellowish green. On their arm, they wore a white armband with a couple of Chinese characters that read 憲兵 (MP = Military Policeman) written in red. From the hem of their overcoat, a brown sheath of the sward was seen to have stuck out beside one of their leather boots. We, breathing out white breath, reached the bus stop a little earlier than the bus, and this led the MPs to watch us by turns, as if seeing something uncanny. We found ourselves having gone too far to retreat, while we could not get on the bus, which had just come sliding before us, giving the loud sound of the engine. The two MPs got on the bus, letting their footsteps sound noisily, while looking askance at us. All we could do then was standing there, hiding our sheer resentment in our bosom.

The woman conductor kindly asked me, while putting her hand on the folding door: "Won't you get on?" We both at once raised our hand and waved it off. This led her to close the folding door, with her head tilting a little. We saw the bus going off, leaving a tremendous amount of smoke behind. "Ah, we have only one more chance left to take the bus!" I sent a voiceless cry toward the western sky, which was giving the fading light but no warmth was left in it. Only the coldness came infiltrating into the marrow of my bones. But we kept ourselves moving all over, expecting to catch one more chance to get away from there. We shook our shoulders, or rubbed ourselves from the knees to the tips of our feet, trying to regain any warmth in our body. We tried squat-hopping, too. In fact, that was one and only opportunity for me to have gone so far in my attempt to keep myself warm.

At home or in my birthplace in Korea, the temperature in the New Year season drops as low as 15 degrees below zero, and snow falls to a depth of 50cm, too. On the other hand, here in Japan we have no snowfall. The temperature does not drop below zero, either. Still, what was it that had made us feel so cold then? Could it be that our inner selves were being affected by the coldness outside? All day long, we had been trembling in the coldness of midwinter, while being made to fail in achieving our aim again and again, and now in the evening, we were gazing at the smoke rising from the chimneys of the local houses on the farm. There came the signs of the dark night crawling down the surface of the mountains in the west. By and by, it began to wrap us up into the dusk. This led my blood go faster, making me feel less cold.

Then, far in the south, I saw the spots of pale light. This time, we slowly walked toward the bus stop. When we came to the point where the signboard of the bus stop was clearly seen, we saw no one there. Looking back, I saw a large figure of the bus with yellow lights approaching. Just at the moment we reached the bus stop, the folding door opened for the three or four passengers to get off. The bus was nearly full, excepting near the doorway. Many were standing. We quickly got on the bus. Unable to go farther, we stood at the doorway and gripped one of the iron bars of the baggage rack. My heart kept throbbing so loudly as might be heard by the one standing beside me. The woman conductor produced the tickets from the bag hung on the belt around her waist, and while looking up at me from a step below, she said to me:

"Have a ticket, please. What's your destination?"

"Karatsu," said I.

That was how and when we finally stepped out of the life as coal miners — after having survived the hard life over there and after having wandered around on that cold day.

● What I Thought in the Bus

I was pretending to be innocently looking at the scenes outside — the rice fields in the winter season or the landscape at the foot of the mountains clearly seen in the distance. I had made myself an actor — as had occurred only once in my lifetime — in my desperate effort *not* to be found what I was. This led me to have greasy sweat on my forehead, which made me feel as if I had something heavy around my forehead. In fact, I had been convinced that: if I were to fail in playing this part of mine, I should have to see my own life come to an end. This was by no means my exaggeration. I could not help feeling as if someone had kept watching over me from behind. But I could not look back, because I was feeling that: if I were to look back, everything would be over. I had kept my nerves on my back. What if anyone should touch me on the shoulder with his hand? My heart was throbbing violently, while the sweat on my back came falling down to my hips.

To myself as a runaway, the interior of the bus seemed to be as good as the cage to keep an animal in it. In case of emergency, there was no exit for me to get away. I felt all the more keenly just how inappropriate the bus was to the runaway! Before I knew it, the sun had set and it was growing dark outside. We passed two or three villages; all that attracted my attention then was the roofs and walls which appeared deep black, while neither street lamps nor domestic lights were seen. Why? That was also a backwash of the war. Toward the end of the 19th year of Showa (1944), the enemy planes began to attack the urban areas and harbors in Japan proper. This led the Japanese Government to issue a variety of orders: white roofs and white walls should be painted black; all the outdoor lamps should be left unlighted even at night; all the domestic lamps should have lampshades covered with black cloth; all the window curtains should be black in color.

These counter measures had not been brought about voluntarily by the general public, but by the Government's order under the newly-invented rule of the black-out. This had led the whole of Japan to remain pitch-dark at night. Even in the running bus, it was kept vague as if lighted by a midget lamp we have today. Ironically, however, this vague light in the bus did help me keep my nerve less strained.

The bus kept running, while stopping at many bus stops, but after dark, it no longer had any new passenger to get on, though some got off, to my great relief. When I got on the bus at Tokusue, I saw nearly ten passengers standing. But since some got off and others took the empty seats, it was only four or five still standing. Fortunately I had a man about forty in the thick overcoat keep standing beside me. In fact, I could not help giving thanks to him, though inwardly.

Since it was dark outside, we had our faces reflected on the window pane. I, pretending to be as cool as possible, kept my eyes toward the darkness outside. By the time the bus had passed five or six stops, I had come to feel less nervous, and began to feel my shoulders relaxed. Even in the dim light in the bus, our figures reflected on the window glass were fairly clear.

My face I saw there had become far from what I had known so far, to my immense wretchedness. My hair closely cropped, my face appeared pale and haggard…. My eyes appeared larger than before. With my middle finger, I rubbed around my eyes to make sure that they were mine. Unmistakably, these were my own eyes in my own face. I muttered to myself: "How utterly changed I have been!" While I was working as a coal miner, I had never looked at myself in the mirror. We having been brought to Japan as drafted workers, none could afford to think of bringing any mirror with us.

In the coal mining company, we had no mirror even in the

bathroom, to say nothing of our dormitory. Once in a week, a barber came to the dormitory to give a haircut to those who had needed it. Even on that occasion, all the barber had brought with him was a single chair and a single washbasin filled with water placed in front of the office building. When he finished close-cropping our head with his hand-operated hair-clippers, he shaved our face little by little while splashing the water upon it. What had mattered most then was *not* how well the haircut was done, *but* whether it was done or not. That was why no mirror was seen around.

Seven months had passed since I was brought to Japan to engage in the forced labor. In the meantime, I had never had any opportunity to see even my own face, because we were expected to work only for the sake of the country. And now, even though I was in the midst of running away, I was able to see my own face on the windowpane for the first time in a long time! But what on earth had happened? I could not see *there* anything like my own face! Still, *that* could not have been any other person's face. Indeed, that was something tragic and far from laughable! I felt as if my face were being made distorted. What on earth was it that my life in Japan for only seven months had completely changed my facial appearance — including the color of my skin and my physiognomy! Indeed, that was an astonishing experience to me. This made me feel: a man is naturally made according to the cause brought about by men.

I was born to be a farmer, and by the time I was brought to the coal mine, I had got such a good tan all over as might be comparable with anyone from the South Sea Islands, and I myself used to be proud of it. And now, I found myself completely changed! I felt simply sorry for myself I saw on the window pane, and this made me almost forget where I stood — as a runaway from my work place.

Probably another bus stop was approaching, and this had led a man standing beside me to take down his bundle from the baggage rack. This made me say to myself: "If he gets off the bus, I'll have too much space around me. That'll make me less safe." For a moment, I felt myself being endangered. I had been made too nervous to imagine his situation and his way of life. The bus stopped, and he got off the bus, while turning up the collar of his overcoat. Seeing him going off, I said to myself: "He has his own home to go back; judging from his age, he must be the father of several children. Can that bundle he is carrying in the *furoshiki* wrapper contain his New Year gifts to his children? How fortunate he is to have his own home to return to! How enviable!"

After seeing him off until he had gone out of my sight, I could not help saying to myself: "Now we are heading for Karatsu, but even if we arrive there, we haven't had any prospect of being able to have even a bowl of rice and even a night's lodging. All of these passengers in the bus — unlike ourselves — would have their own home and their own family to return to and none of them would be worried about their meal to eat and the bed to sleep in. Come to think of it, what wrong have we done to have been deprived of all these things? What on earth makes us suffer such cruel punishments?"

We have had our own land conquered. And now, we have reduced ourselves to escapees with the heavy burdens named "drafted workers" — always nervous not only about what was happening around us as if we were criminals but also even about the motions of the other people's eyes and behaviors. Still, we were deprived of any inn to stay at at night, of any food to relieve of our hunger, and even of words to exchange with others. Where do such absurdities come from? What wrong have we, Koreans, done? Doesn't *any good god* exist anywhere? I did wish to give all these heartfelt questions to *him!*

The war they were making then was lacking in justice from the beginning. The imperialists in Japan, when they first succeeded in invading Korea to conquer it, went on to the northeastern part of present-day China and established what they called the Manchurian Empire (1932–1945), and succeeded in placing the whole land of China under their control. The battle front gradually went farther and farther southward until it covered all over Southeast Asia. Still, they kept going on until at last they attacked Pearl Harbor (1941). That was a surprise attack upon it!. Since they invaded into Korea first of all, they kept invading on and on without any justice to hold up high. How much exasperated the Americans were, when such a surprise attack was finally made upon them! This led America to form the Allies with the United Kingdom, France, Poland, the U.S.S.R., India and China in order to fight against Japan. And this finally led to the atomic bombings upon Hiroshima and Nagasaki in Japan, and to her unconditional surrender to the Allied Nations (1945).

The peoples of the invaded countries had been driven into that aggressive war which was injustice itself. Among all those unfortunate nations, we Koreans had most readily been made into their slaves, to the greatest convenience of the Japanese. It goes without saying that: it was not only we Koreans but also the Japanese people themselves who had been forced to make unmeasurable sacrifices. Tens of millions of young men were made victims of the war by being killed or being made disabled in battle. Their parents, siblings and relatives — even unable to weep over them or to utter their sorrows or harsh realities in life — did hold back their tears of lamentation.

In those days, it was considered virtuous and the expression of their loyalty *not* to reveal their sorrow even on the deaths of their sons or brothers,

Now that the war is over, I cannot help feeling chagrined at the thought that: if such courage and virtue had been directed toward peace-making, instead of having been devoted to the war-making, we should have done without suffering anything so miserable as has been regarded as the worst miseries in the world history. The war, whenever and wherever it might be made, cannot do without any human sacrifices. War-making is the worst and the most sinful actions on earth. Whether justice exists or not, I shall never make myself cooperate with anything called war. If I were forced to lend my hand to war once again, I shall never hesitate to escape death! I shall subordinate my principle to my own life.

Now, I had made up my mind to live in freedom in the true sense of the word — if only I succeeded in this running away. While pondering over this decision of mine in the bus, I came to notice the winter rain was striking the window panes only to pour down. "What an awful rain this is, when everything seems to be going well with me!" I could not help grumbling to myself.

The rain was now coming down in real earnest, and after dashing against the window panes, it cracked open before falling down, looking like so many waves. How long does it take before reaching our destination, Karatsu? Will this rain be over before we reach there? What if it was still raining? Considering our real identity, I felt like praying intently for our success in overcoming this unexpected water accident.

Now I reflected on what I had clad myself in, and rubbed down the breast of the white cotton suit in which I had arrived in Japan in May the year before. But, however hard I might rub it down, it never worked like magic. Outside the windows, it simply remained dark, cold and rainy.

The bus kept running through the rain in the dark, as if it

had never minded carrying anyone like myself — a young man trembling in fear and coldness. Even though I could not tell whether or not there was any bus stop on our way, the bus seemed to have kept running for a considerably long time. Then the sound of the engine seemed to get lower and I found myself on my feet much less swinging. It seemed the bus was sliding quietly into somewhere. Suddenly we saw our way being lighted, and the bus crawled toward it, as if being swallowed into it, and stopped as if diving into the lighted space under the roof. The woman conductor called out in a thin and piercing voice:

"Karatsu. Karatsu. This is the terminal of this bus. Please take care not to leave anything behind when you leave the bus."

This led me to move quickly from near the entrance — where I had kept standing — to the space right behind the driver's seat. What made me do *that* was my guilty conscience I had kept as a runaway — or I simply could not get off the bus *before* anyone else of my fellow passengers. Holding on to the straps in my hands, I was following those who were leaving the bus with my eyes. The woman conductor — with a black large pouch hanging a little below her waist — was putting into it the tickets she had received from the passengers. Kim, my companion, had already been seen walking off without even looking back at me, after having handed his ticket to the conductor. It was on the night of the New Year's Day in 1945.

III

EMBRACING THE UNSEEN LAND
OF MY ANCESTORS

THE ESCAPEE FROM THE COAL MINE

● **In the Town of Karatsu**

Could the winter weather be so changeable? By the time we arrived at the naval port town of Karatsu, the heavy rain had eased off, while the sky, which had been pitch-dark, began to clear up. Still my cotton suits with no lining having sucked up the cold rain, it did make me tremble all over. What if I had not kept my tension unusually raised in that strange town? In fact, even though that might have been regarded as our departure to the heyday of our youthful days, it simply remained chilly and joyless. Be that as it might, the map I had received from Mr. Ura, the coal hewer, turned out to be really helpful to us then, since it had informed us about which direction we should take.

In our life at that dormitory we had left behind, going out at night was the last thing we could think of, and this had kept us from seeing any night life in Japan. As I had been noticing in the bus, too, this town of Karatsu had also been left in total darkness, to my greater disappointment and sorrow. We could not tell what the citizens themselves were feeling about this, but Kim, walking beside me, probably unable to keep it to himself, mumbled to me, as if he had forgotten his own situation:

"I feel sorry for the town being kept in such darkness as this. It's piteous, isn't it? I simply cannot believe: this is the way the people live in Japan or the nation that has driven us Koreans into such miseries as this..... Darkness.... It's darkness itself, isn't it?"

This remark of his, however, sounded to me as if he had felt some sympathy or pity for the Japanese people whose ambition had driven themselves into such darkness as this. This led me to retort to him, saying:

"This is nothing but the case of "As one sows, so one shall leap!""

But wasn't it the Japanese people themselves who were being made victims by being led to dream of their victory — by their cruel leaders? How cruel and wicked the monster named WAR can be! If we had had our due, we, too, should not have been running away in such a misery as this, while being made to feel unreasonably guilty! The Japanese people would not have been forced to lead such a miserable life as having been deprived of any lighting even at night, either. These thoughts on certain extremely ambitious politicians, certain aberrant elements and the most pitiable general public being operated by the tyrannical government placed under the evil stratagem — led me to the pity on the general public in Japan. Indeed, this runaway trip made me feel that: this world we lived in was darkness itself and the future in which we might live in would also be deprived of any light to guide us along.

The bus had brought us farther and farther northwards, and now we were heading farther northwestward. My gym shoes — made of rubber soles and cloth — had sucked as much water as they could, and this led me to feel like kicking them off and walking in bare feet. But unable to overcome our habit of wearing any shoes, I kept walking in them, even though my steps could not help being very heavy.

Since Mr. Ura, the coal-hewer, had told me of Karatsu as a port town full of life and energy, I had been looking forward to seeing it. As it happened, however, we could not see even a single outdoor lamp lighted nor even a single person walking along the street. It was also apparent that they were extremely careful *not* to have their lights seen from outside even to a nervous extent. How could we expect any active life in such a town? All the impression I had received then and there was: "There is something abnormal here."

We kept walking for nearly an hour, while dragging our sports shoes badly soaked with rainwater. When we came to the end of the road that parted right and left, we wondered which way we should take. Kim decided to take the left one. Not a soul could be seen around, even if we wanted to ask where these roads would take us. So we decided to take the left one. According to Kim, the right one ran simply straight northward, while the left one "moderately" turned toward northwest.

● We Found Ourselves at the Guard House

Thanks to his decision to choose anything "moderate," we were fortunate enough to come across someone helpful to us within our ten minutes' walk. No sooner had we heard the voice of "Stop!" than we were caught by the floodlight. To our astonishment, we had had our breast pointed by a gun!

Of all places on earth, we had come blundering into a guardhouse for defending the naval port! At once, we had a body search carried out to what seemed to me to an extreme extent — from head to heel. Then we were subjected to put through a severe cross-examination, willy-nilly — not only our names and from where to where we were going but also what was the purpose of our journey — thus subjecting us to searching inquiries. All this while, we had had their bayonets kept pointed to our chest. Indeed, they were boorish and ruthless. Even after those examinations were over and it became apparent that we were by no means dangerous characters, they still kept holding their bayonets. I felt as if I had witnessed the weaknesses of the Japanese military that never allowed any outsiders to approach them, remaining obstinate and fanatically devoted only to their own side.

However systematical and rigorous the armed forces might be, we were all human beings and the members of the Japanese society in the final analysis as long as we were within the boundary of this country. Within their own sphere of influence, and that, in their own defense position, they had carried out a body search, and even after they had confirmed that we were not dangerous, they still kept trying us, while thrusting a bayonet at us. Indeed, I could not help calling them abnormal rather than having gone too far.

It seemed to me that: the Japanese military at that time having been so frightened at the enemy's oncoming that they had been made too eager to observe their military discipline and they could no longer afford to make sure whether it was right or not. And still, they seemed to have properly developed a sense of discerning what would benefit them. After giving us inquiries for a while, they seemed to have been convinced in their own way, and one of the guards wrote something on a piece of paper and handed it to me. The guard, who had been thrusting his bayonet at us, said to us, while handing that paper:

"Bring yourselves *here*, and you will find your work and you'll also be kept safe."

We received that paper with proper thankfulness, but having been finally released from them was more relieving to us than anything else.

Seemingly we then ought to have been revealing the foolishness of us human beings. Simply having had no nerve to read that note on the spot, we made our way back according to the direction given to us: "About face!" Because of the floodlight which had been focused upon us, I was feeling dizzy, while realizing what it meant when they say: "The future is a closed book to us." To us then, however, this was not a laughing matter. We kept walking for five minutes or so, feeling our way back in darkness, until we came back to that three-forked road we had seen before we strayed into that guardhouse.

This led us to feel like reading the paper we had just received. We struck a match to read the memo:

"Ōshima, Yasuyama Group: Cross the bridge and turn to the left."

The one who wrote this might be able to tell what this message meant, but to us it was simply puzzling. Still we had no nerve to throw away this memo kindly offered to us for the sake of our safety.

All we could do then was to walk on and on according to that direction — in order to approach our homeland, even by a single step!

It was apparent that: even if we were able to return to our ancestral land, Japan's administration upon us would not vanish nor bring any change in our life, then all we — the helpless and powerless — could do was: simply keeping doing something useless.

I feel it was then and there that I learned a lesson: once we were born in this world, we must live on, keeping ourselves alive. It seems to me that it was then and there that I came to notice that: there is nothing useless in life: even what once seemed to be useless in life is quite likely to turn out to be useful, or far from useless, thus to make us feel confident in ourselves. What was more, I came to learn: any experience we may have in our life is quite likely to bring momentum to our life.

Now we, remaining silent, followed the road according to the direction given by that memorandum. To me the situation then seemed to be comparable to a large *furoshiki* wrapping me up all over. That was, I could not help feeling that: this running away would not come to an end. On the other hand, I had been impressed by the way the guard had thrust out his bayonet upon me. Its point, though having been made so close as to touch the breast of my jacket, the cloth *there* remained unbroken, to my horror! If anything wrong had affected him, I might have been stabbed to death on the spot! This thought did send me a chill going up and down my spine!

As for my having run away, I had retained my own spirit of self-respect, and in carrying out this plan of mine, I was feeling a pride in my own intention to get back at Japan's rigarous militarism. But, to my dismay, I simply could not help feeling hungry all the time. I had not minded either the hard labor at the coal mine or the lack of freedom in the life there. So I could not have been so foolish as to run away from there only for such reasons at the risk of my own life.

Even if I was an immature boy as I was, since I was determined to risk my own life, I had naturally evaluated it and hope for the proper reward for it. When driven into a corner, it is easy for one to kill oneself, but it is by no means easy to keep oneself alive safe. In my own case, I had spent as long as half a year before I finally carried out my plan of running away. Meanwhile, I had carefully been working out a plan for the process of running away.

On the other hand, even if we had succeeded in running away from the coal mine, we could not help remaining in Japan, unless we crossed the sea. This meant: we could not help running and running around this country endlessly. The militarist government of the Japanese Empire had set up a network all over the country. While all the Japanese — young and old, even schoolchildren — had unanimously been turned into militarists. As a matter of fact, I myself, a green youth from Korea, who still remained unable to speak Japanese properly, had to find it very hard even to make up my mind to perform a runaway trip that seemed endless to me. So it took me as long as half a year before I finally made up my mind to carry out that plan of mine or what seemed to me an endless runaway journey. In the meantime, I had carefully worked out the plan for the process of our flight.

But even if we had succeeded in fleeing from the coal mine, if we remained in the territory of this country without making a voyage to somewhere else, we should be remaining in the territory of Japan all the same, wherever we might go. On the other hand, Japan's militarist government had set up a dragnet in every corner of this country. Both young and old — even the elementary school children — had been turned into militarists. This had naturally led me — still young and inexperienced and even unable to speak Japanese language properly — to pluck up my courage before making up my mind to make an escape journey which seemed endless to me.

My greatest concern then was: how to make myself survive — instead of abandoning my life. To my mind, making light of one's life would lead to making light of anything one might engage in, and it would be the last thing one should do. So it was not until I made up my mind *not* to abandon my life to the very end that I started to carry out *this* plan of my flight.

On the other hand, for the militarists in Japan at that time, human life was considered something beneath their notice. This reminds me of my own experience at what was called a young men's school — which was brought into being a little later to give the young men military training. The teachers there used to say to us: "One horse is better than ten of you!" or "The horses are much more serviceable to our country than you!" Believe it or not, these comments used to be given to us in a loud voice without even the slightest compunction. This does explain how badly our human lives were being made light of or exploited at that time. To my mind, *that* was why Japan was defeated. The human lives being irreplaceably precious, how to save them ought to have been our greatest concern, I think.

It was still bearable to us that: Japan had taken us Koreans out of our land on the Korean Peninsula in order to make us work here as coal miners. But how could we bear the sight of that devilish scene in which a Korean who was groaning with high fever was being made a target of a bucketful of water thrown at him, and that together with the bucket itself ?! Sending the sick or the invalid to the hospital was out of the question! If one's desertion in the mine was discovered, one was deprived of one's three meals a day and bedding even in mid-winter. Whether we died or not, it did not matter to them; only punishments mattered to them. Indeed, we had to suffer numberless humiliations and hardships to bear!

Still those who were naive like myself did not take it as discrimination but scolded ourselves for our weakness or ignorance, while keeping ourselves stoically patient throughout our youthful days. According to the official stance, we — the drafted workers — were expected to work under a two-year contract. As it happened, or as I found it later, some were made to keep working even *after* three years or even five years had passed since they were brought to Japan as drafted workers. That might be no problem on paper, and it had been so made that they could not run away from the coal mine as long as Japan kept making the war.

I myself, being innocent and incompetent, not having thought of any other means but to remain perseverant, made up my mind *then* to keep running around as long as the war was going on. Looking back, I now realize that: what had really led me to make up my mind to run away from the coal mine was my attachment to life itself, as all living things on earth have, even though my constant hunger and relentless oppression we were suffering then also helped me to make that decision.

Since then, I have been living in order to keep myself alive. To my mind, it is impossible to find any such person as may sacrifice himself for the sake of his own country or for the sake of any specific person. To my mind, a man is so made as to sacrifice himself only for the benefit of himself or in order to satisfy himself.

What had brought about such a shameless action called war appeared to me nothing but a collective action to satisfy themselves. That was why even a green youth like myself — only seventeen years old — could be so desperate and brave as to risk his own life. Seemingly, I had come to realize *then* how precious our human lives could be, even before I knew it. I cannot help thinking that: none other than the then administration of the Imperialist Japan, which had made light of human lives as if they were cattle or horses, had kept in it the very cause of its downfall. To my mind, it was the Imperialist Japan's invasion into Korea that had finally led to the ruin of Japan. And at a corner of that process to that crushing defeat, we, a large number of Korean people and the drafted workers from Korea had to be badly dragged along. I myself had spent half a year as a drafted worker at the coal mine, and it was no more than fifteen months and several days from my running away from the coal mine to the end of the war. But, even to this day, I cannot get over my personal feeling as if I had been struggling much longer — for as long as ten years or even twenty years.

● **Guided by the Note Handed by the Guard**

Kim and I kept walking in silence. Still keeping that fear we had felt at that guardhouse, we spent all the energy left to us in dragging our frozen bodies. I kept wondering what we should do if we came to find a hangout for the military police officers at the end of that road. Should I bite off my tongue? Or should I leave myself at the mercy of them?

At that three-forked road, after having read the memo we received at that guardhouse, Kim said, looking up at the dark sky:

"I don't believe in such a memo, but since it is in the north (as we have been heading for so far), I'll follow this road to the north, as is directed here. What will you do?"

This led me to give a prompt answer: "I'll go with you."

This made us resume our way. But the farther we went on, the more uneasy I felt about our destination. We were hurrying our way in agony; I kept looking downward, even though my eyes had been kept turned up at the corners.

It was only fifteen or twenty minutes since we were released from that guardhouse, but in the meanwhile, I had exhausted all my energy I might have spent for three years — both physically and neurally. I still believe: if I had been left in such a nervous tension as that for as long as an hour, I still believe, my life would have been shortened by ten years. I simply could not guess what Kim, who had kept walking before me, had had in his mind. But recalling how silent he had remained all that while, I guess he was also full of tension and apprehension, just as I was.

A few days later, I happened to talk to him about what I had been feeling *then,* and this led him to disclose his own feeling then, saying: "I was also being frightened. Anyone, if brought into such a situation, would be turned into a picture of tension and apprehension. No one would be able to remain calm." This led me to learn that: we, human beings, when forced to face a certain ultimate, will be folded into only *that* pressing matter before our eyes both mentally and physically, regardless of our ages or qualities.

Forty years had passed since then, and on the New Year's Day in the 60th year of Showa (1985), I was saying to myself, looking back upon *that* memorable day with careful deliberation: "During the past forty years, I've been driven into several difficulties. But I had already learned through that experience of mine: straining every nerve and thought upon something that had driven us into *the* difficulty may accompany a danger of exceeding one's abilities to deal with it."

Seemingly, this knowledge of mine has helped me to survive to this day. Speaking more simply, this had added to my desire to keep living. In fact, on that occasion, too, I had been overwhelmed by the tension and uneasiness so much so that I remained unable to give any proper thinking to anything — excepting the final desire to avoid death or being killed or being arrested.

I kept walking, dragging my feet in the frozen shoes, through the darkness of horror, while glaring at the concrete road which was gleaming black. If caught and thrown back to the coalmine, my life would come to an end at that point, I thought. Then, I saw Kim come to an abrupt stop. This led me to bend my legs to look ahead. The uneasiness I had kept feeling so far had led me to assume such a defensive posture. We saw, beyond the darkness, a pair of something whitish standing on both side of the road. I fixed my eyes upon them and listened to catch anything like human voices. The uneasiness I had kept feeling so far seemed to have hit the mark! Saying so to myself, I crawled on the ground, while keeping my attention to them.

Certainly, they stood on both side of the road, but seen from a distance at night, it remained vague in the darkness. But they appeared simply far from human beings. If they were human beings, their upper half would easily be able to tell from their lower half. As it happened, they had nothing like any such halves. Could they be flat boards or pillars? What was more, I came to notice some human voices, though faint, approaching to attract my attention.

I, still remaining on my knees and hands, said to Kim:

"They remain still, do they? They are not human beings, it seems."

"Right," said Kim. "But here come human voices. We had better take care. Let's make sure from both sides."

This led me to begin to cross the road, leaving Kim behind.

We had kept our eyes fixed on those objects, which remained simply still. The human voices, which had remained feeble, were now growing more and more audible until we could tell they were three or four in number. We both remained cautious enough to keep silent. When *the* time came, I would run and run and run, whether I could get away or not! Such an active thinking of mine had led me to go on and on at a brisk pace, leaving my companion far behind.

When I finally came to face one of those mysterious things, I simply sent to my companion such a loud cry as I had never given for a long time:

"Why! It's a bridge! They were railings of the bridge!"

Then I saw him — looking like a black lump — coming briskly like a visible wind and said in a tone of angry voice:

"You speak too loud. Have you forgotten what we are?"

This did remind me of our situation then.

"Sorry," said I.

"Never forget we are always at the risk of our lives," said Kim.

Then he brought himself to the side of the railing he had come from, and squatted down to light a cigarette. Leaning myself on the railing, I was seeing what he was doing. This did make me feel like warning to him, saying: "Doesn't *that* attract *their* attention?" But all I could do then was to be gazing at the light of his cigarette keep going on and on, to my irritation, till it went off for a while.

Then there came — from beyond the bridge — the human voices which sounded fairly clear. This led Kim to trample down his lighted cigarette under his shoe.

Those voices were so mixed together that I could not tell how many people were coming along but their voices sounded simply free from any reserve or affectation. What was more surprising, their language was Korean! I doubted my ears, and breathlessly pricked up my ears to listen to them. Unmistakably they were Korean, and they sounded as if they were having fun among themselves! Peeping through the parapet, I saw several people approaching, mixed in confusion! I turned to Kim to see what he was looking like, and found he did not seem to do anything with them. This led me to make a clear-cut decision as to what I should do. Should we let them go past? No sooner had I asked myself than I found myself having left the parapet I had stood by to bring myself at the center of the road on the bridge!

Dressed in white, I cut a conspicuous figure in the darkness of the night. Those people in that lively group seemed to have noticed me at once, and they drew near to us in a black mass of people! Inwardly I was saying: "May anything come out!" On the other hand, I had reached my definite decision that: even if I were caught, Kim might make his getaway.

Just before we came to this side of the bridge, I had got beset with doubts and fears, but when we approached it to have a good look at it, we found it was nothing but a prop of the parapet of the bridge, to my great relief. This had led me to give a cry of joy to find that: the direction we had received at the guardhouse was *not* false and that: this might lead to the success in our flight; and now I saw "that big brother" of mine, who had warned me against my being too easy-going, was smoking in the dark, revealing the spot of a smoker in the darkness! This led me to say to myself: "Are you doing *that* — at the risk of our lives?" My having run to the center of the bridge had also been prompted by the similar sort of desperation

● Our Encounter on the Bridge

It seems to me that a man sometimes behaves in a manner he has never expected before. In my own case then, I was to meet that black mass of people, while keeping myself standing bolt upright. As their figures were becoming clearer, I could see, to my surprise, as many as six men approaching us. This decided me that it was wrong of me to have thought of letting them go while hiding ourselves behind the props of the parapet. I also realized that: my decision to run away in case would be of no use if we were to have so many pursuers behind us; it would not be long before we found ourselves "the mice in a trap." Then what should we do?

Before I found any answer to it, I found myself running toward them and speaking to them in Korean:

"Help us! Save us!"

I went on to say also in Korean:

"You, my countrymen. Right? I've just run away from the coal mine!"

Then a man, much taller than others in the group, came up to me to grasp my arm, while saying in a low voice: "Why, you did it! I see, I see." Then he took off his workman's livery coat or what was called *hanten* he had worn, and simply hung *it* on me, saying:

"Now put it on, so you may not stand out so much in the theater."

The others were also saying something, but to me it remained unable to understand, each saying something different at the same time. Anyway, the warm kindness I had received then along with the *hanten* did fill my heart with warm thankfulness.

I now realize: this encounter on that bridge had occurred when I was in the most miserable situation in my life, but soon it turned out it had also provided me with the supreme pleasure in my life. But even before I might be appreciating such a grateful sentiment, I — together with Kim — was to be taken into a theater along with those Koreans. When I repeated my wish to help us and told them of our having run away from the coal mine, they had already made up their mind to take us with them. When the man had quickly put his livery coat on my shoulders, their action had started. The man who gave me his livery coat said to those behind him: "Let's go on anyway," and resumed his walk at the head of his party, who went on — surrounding me — along the road we had just come down. That was the last thing I had ever expected to happen.

Be that as it might, I was simply upset, even unable to tell the whereabouts of my companion, Kim. Was he, a cautious fellow, still hiding behind the prop of the parapet of the bridge? Or had he run away anywhere, while I was coming to know of this group of Koreans?

To my embarrassment, I simply could not tell where he was. But how could I leave him behind and vanish with these new companions of mine? This led me to say, as if to myself or to anyone else around me:

"Well, I have a mate to go with me...."

The man who had put the livery coat on me — now walking ahead of us — stopped short and asked me:

"Where is he?"

"Over there," said I, pointing to the prop of the parapet Kim had hidden himself behind.

This led him to send a calm voice of invitation to Kim:

"We are your countrymen, so just come out to see us, will you?"

I was not quite sure whether or not Kim was still remaining there, but after a while, we saw a black figure rise to its feet abruptly! This moved me to tears for the reason unknown even to myself. Had I been dependent on him so much? Had he chosen to remain there instead of leaving me alone? Had our reunion made me feel so reassuring?

Now we — a group of eight Koreans — walked on, crossing the junction of the three roads — from which we had wandered into that guardhouse — until before long we reached a theater situated below the inner road on the right-hand side.

In front of the theater, there was an open ground, about 20 *tsubo* wide. (1 *tsubo* = 3.3*m* wide) A single electric lamp with its shade was seen at the entrance. On the right side, there was a hut for the ticket counter. I could neither tell who had paid for our tickets nor how much they cost him. We two, surrounded by the six men of our group, were pushed into the theater, which had already been overcrowded. No empty seat could be seen, even each aisle being packed. This naturally led us to get mixed among those in the standing room in the center, even though no one had directed us to. When I looked around with diffidence, I found again we were being surrounded by *the* six men as if we were being escorted.

The performance seemed to have started long since. The first stage we saw was probably a skit, in which two men were talking or singing to each other, at one time pushing on, at other time retreating, while inviting constant laughter from the audience. Being surrounded by the people and being dressed in the livery coat, I never felt cold as long as my upper body was concerned, but there being no heating system there, and my shoes having sucked ample rain water, I was beaten by the coldness coming up from the soles of my shoes even toward my abdominal region. Kim — standing next to me, with no livery coat on him, as I did — ought to have been feeling very cold, but I did not feel like offering that livery coat to him, partly because I must put obligation to the person who had offered it to me, and partly because I was still feeling disagreeable to his speech and behavior when we came across what had turned out to be a bridge.

As for the stage, the curtain had fallen and from behind it, there came ample rattling and clattering even as far as the audience in the standing room. It was only after what we felt fairly long when the curtain rose again.

While the stage was being prepared, the auditorium was kept dusky. Soon this intermission turned out to be our drinking time. What was called *doburoku* (homebrewed *sake*) had been brought in — not in the bottle but in what was called "water pillow" at that time. It was made of Indian rubber and large enough to carry about one-*sho* (1.8 liter) of *doburoku*. Filling it in a cup, they passed it around to drink in turn. Naturally, it came round to me, and I, receiving a cup of it, drained the cup at one gulp. My stomach being empty, my body wet with rain, I poured it into myself in one gulp — feeling it going down through my throat into my stomach! Even after the cup went around all of us, the *sake* seemed to have still remained. This led us to have another round of drinking — but half a cup this time. That was my first experience of drinking *doburoku* in a manner of "drinking an equal amount of it."

I drink alcohol, but not so much as to get drunk. Seeing that this was the same with my father, this might be the case of "Like father, like son." Anyway, I have never seen any member of my family have got so drunk as to be unsteady on his feet. On that occasion, too, Kim had left half a cup for me, but I returned to him as it was. I simply could not drink it in case I, a homeless person, should get drunk *then* and *there*. Until then, I had kept myself less cold by keeping my toes moving, but now that I had a cup of unrefined *sake,* I had begun to feel warm all over.

Since we met on the bridge, they never asked me anything. Looking at what was happening on the stage in quick succession, they were eagerly talking about it. But I myself — having been taken here before I knew what was happening to me — had simply been driven by doubt about those compatriots of mine, and this had prevented me from enjoying what was happening on the stage.

The time went on and on, and it was steadily approaching midnight. All this while, I was simply anxious about what on earth they were going to do with us. This had prevented me from remembering how many stages were there and what was the story about. Though only once, the man who had offered his livery coat to me whispered into my ear:

"Have you found *doburoku* (unrefined *sake*) good enough? That is made from genuine rice. If you've found it good enough, you may drink it as much as you like. Leave everything to me, and now just enjoy yourself with the show!"

But I could not make myself so relaxed as the other members of his party. The time I had to spend in an uneasy feeling seemed unusually long, and when I was finally released from that Japanese play, I could not help feeling really relieved in the true sense of the word..

● The White Rice and the Korean-Style Pickles

When we left the theater, we found ourselves in the pitch-dark, and the cold air kept us trembling all over. This led everyone to give cries of "*Hyaa!* How cold!" I went to the man who had lent me his livery coat and said, holding out the coat I had just taken off: "Let me return this," but he refused to take it, saying: "No, you shall be in it. As a matter of fact, it's too bad for you to appear so conspicuous."

This led me to see myself all over. Certainly he was right, since I had been dressed in all white. This decided me to accept his kindness to keep myself warm as well as safe. It was not long before we — while making ourselves gradually share their feelings — headed for the bridge on which we had met them. Judging from their way of talking, they seemed optimistic, free and open-minded.

By and by, we came to the point where we had been saved. But they simply passed it on without showing any response or concern about it. When seen on the bridge, it seemed that the end of the bridge led to an island independent of the land we had just left behind. Looking at that bridge all over again, its width was fairly large, while its surface was smooth. In a word, it was a fine bridge at that time. It seemed considerably long, too, and the opposite bank was seen reflecting itself in deep black on the water. From about the middle of the bridge, the land over there began to come into our sight. Not even a single light was seen in the houses on the shore, while water surface alone was giving a scale-like glimmering, thus adding to the desolate feeling in the scene.

As for myself, I had been kept more and more uneasy, simply unable to tell who on earth they were, and what they were going to do with us — even though they were talking among themselves all the way. This led me once again to assume a defiant attitude in desperation, saying to myself: "I don't care whatever may happen to me!" I had been wondering if I should talk of the memo I had received at the guardhouse, but even if I were to do so, I needed to have had a talk with Kim about it, but being unable to do so while walking along surrounded by others, I could not help leaving everything to take its own course.

As was expected, the bridge was considerably long — about three hundred meters. Probably because it had already been very late at night, we safely finished crossing the bridge without meeting any other passengers. By and by, we arrived at their home or a house that stood by the roadside — after having followed several lanes. Opening one of the sliding doors, they stepped into the house in rapid succession, along with someone sending a greeting: "Haai! We are here!" This led us, new comers, too, to enter the house, as if being pushed on from behind.

There was an earthen floor there, about eight to ten *tatamis* wide, or what might be called a dining kitchen. The first thing I saw there was a table — long and wide. On the other table near the entrance, there were three bamboo-baskets filled with three kinds of chinaware — bowls, plates and cups. On the dining table was seen a massive rice tub put in the basket knitted up with thin straw ropes.

Unable to tell what to do, I had just planted myself with the entrance door behind, simply looking at what they were doing or at the make of the house. On the left side of the entrance, I saw a staircase leading to the second floor. On the right side where I had planted myself was a wall painted white with a time-worn clock hanging about in the middle. It was just 11:30. In the dusk of the back room, something like kitchen stove was seen.

Those who had entered the house in a bustling pack began to eat or devour, while serving themselves freely! To myself, who had just run away from the coal mining company that morning what I was seeing there was simply amazing and unbelievable! What was it that had made so much difference? Things were going wrong? Or could this be a different world? What they had piled up in the bowl by serving themselves was undoubtedly white rice! What was even more amazing, there was Korean-style pickles of Chinese cabbage and white radish! This led me to almost drivel. The man, who had offered me his livery coat, talked — while piling a bowl of rice to himself — to someone behind the sliding paper door before him:

"Hey, Boss! We have picked up two of us — young and fresh this time. I'm sure they'll soon make "fine horses" if trained properly. Please see them before you decide."

Then he seated himself on the wooden bench beside the table, while carrying a porcelain bowl of piled-up boiled rice in his hand. Then he said to us, too:

"Hey, you also must be hungry. Come and eat plenty."

This was followed by many other voices to invite us to the table:

"You need not hold back! Holding back will lead you to a loss, you know?"

Even though I had been overwhelmed by the new situation we were facing, I simply could not suppress my appetite, and this led me to look at Kim, who also seemed to be amazed at the vigorous appetite shown by those menfolk.

Then, there opened the sliding door on the left side, and we saw a man around fifty — with a square-cropped head, in a black livery coat, revealing his under shirt — was sitting cross-legged, while smoking. He, looking out upon us, was observing us with his chin turned up. When our eyes met, I gave a bow for some reason or other. He did not give any response to it, but before closing the paper door, he said to the man I had mentioned before:

"Hey, Yama! Why don't you feed them properly, instead of helping yourself so liberally?"

I myself, though not a fluent speaker of Japanese, had already been able to understand Japanese to a certain extent. This led me to give a voice to address to him: "Ah—ah—" though unable to speak Japanese fluently. The sliding paper door, which was about to be closed, stopped, and I saw him nod to the man he had called Yama. This led me to ask Kim beside me to give me *the* memo we had received at the guardhouse, and on receiving it, I handed it to the person who had been called "Yama."

Yama, having received it in silence, handed it to the man with a square-cropped head, who, while seeing the memo, said:

"Yama, they seem to be on their way to the Yasuyama Group. So give them a good guidance to the way there."

Then, the man in his livery coat said to us in Korean:

"Why! You are on your way to the Yasuyama Group! I see. That's why you cannot have a meal here. Now I'll give you a proper direction to reach the Yasuyama Group you are heading for."

Then he spoke in Korean, instead of Japanese he had adopted so far:

"Well, I'll tell you how you'll get to the Yasuyama Group you are heading for. Just open the door and go out to see the sky, and make a tour around this vacant lot, and when you find the door exactly like the one you have seen here, just open it, saying "Hello!" That's your destination — the Yasuyama Group. By now, those who had visited the theater must be back to have a late-night meal. So, to my mind, you will arrive there at the best hour imaginable."

While listening to him, we realized that: "the Yasuyama Group" was nowhere but *here!* This led Kim, who was standing beside me, to apologize to him in a calm voice: "I'm sorry we had not known *that.*" I myself was also feeling rather embarrassed at our ignorance. So far, none had mentioned "the Yasuyama Group" since we met on the bridge, and *that* had prevented us from knowing they were of the very group we were about to visit to turn to. This led us to give a bitter smile on our face, and no sooner had Yama-*san* finished his speech than there rose a burst of laughter from those who were there!

● We Entered our Accommodation

Thus our runaway trip turned out to be a really lucky one. The boss with a square-cropped head closed the paper door, gazing fondly at us, while narrowing his eyes. Now, we, too, were able to have a late-night meal that was also our supper. I was chewing the boiled white rice and Korean-style pickles, feeling as if in a dream. Then I suddenly found myself being moved to tears. Not only the boiled white rice and pickles but also my dear old delicious Korean-style side dishes were being offered — each in their own pans, from which we were expected to serve ourselves with anything as much as we liked.

What had made me tearful was the boild white rice I was eating then. As I had mentioned before, since my childhood, I had never eaten the boiled white rice excepting those three annual occasions — the *Bon* Festival Holidays, the New Year Holidays and my own birthday. The first reason for this was: we were too poor to live always on rice. The second reason was: our farmland was more for vegetables than for rice, and the facilities for rice-growing were far from enough. The third reason was the war Japan was being engaged in, and this had forced us to make obligatory supply of rice. Even if we were poor and short of facilities, if it had not been firstly for the war Japan was engaged in and secondly for its system of obligatory supply of rice to the Japanese Government — in other words, if we had not been invaded to be colonized by Japan — we ought to have been able to retain our self-sufficient lifestyle, as we had been so far throughout our history.

As it happened, even though we were rice-growing farmers, we remained unable to live on rice. Rice boiled with barley still remained better. We, children, had to be raised mainly on foxtail millet, Indian corn, potato and the like. That was, the boiled polished rice was served only three times in a year. What a miserable life we were being forced to lead during our growth period! We often say: "Nothing is fiercer than the resentment concerning food." But this never conveys what I mean. What had engulfed my heart then was the sadness of the weak oppressed by the strong and powerful.

The supper I was offered then and there naturally led me to imagine what would be happening to my roommates in the coal mine. They would be praying for us, even if they, having got a by-blow in our flight, ought to be suffering from the pain of the hunger inflicted upon them as punishment.

This thought moved me to infinite tears from the bottom of my heart which had remained hard and dry for a long time. Now upon the grains of white rice in the bowl in my hands, the endless tears came falling to soak through them, while those grains of white rice still staying in my throat were being brought back because of the sobbing I was giving.

No longer could I make my chopsticks reach the rice in my

bowl. Kim, who had seated himself beside me, noticed what was happening to me, and asked me in a low voice:

"What's the matter with you, Ri?"

Kim warned me against *it* in a low voice. This, having made me even more sorrowful, led me to sob, while burying my face into the china bowl I was holding.

That was the first night of the New Year, and they had just returned from the theater to enjoy their New Year banquet there in great good humor. Now, having been astonished at the least expected sight I was giving them then, they came over to see me, saying:

"Hey, what's the matter? What has happened to you?"

I, suppressing the sadness welling up in my heart, said to them.

"It's nothing. The food here, after the food I had at the coal mine, is simply too good..... too good-tasting to me, and it has filled my heart.... but I'm all right, now. Thank you."

Then I pushed all the boiled rice left in my bowl into my mouth.

Those who had crowded around me returned to their seat, looking as if they were saying to themselves: "Well, that's nothing so serious."

Then, there occurred nothing in particular; everyone left his seat soon after his meal was over and disappeared somewhere upstairs.

The man who had given his *hanten* coat to me remained alone, while smoking. When I finished my meal, he turned to us and said:

"I am Choe, though called Yamamoto here. I'm from Hwanghae-dō Prefecture."

This led Kim to say to him:

"I'm sorry. I should have introduced myself first...."

This also led me to say to him:

"Sorry. I am younger than you. So let me introduce myself first. .... I am also from Hwanghe-dō Prefecture; my family name is Ri, though the enforced change of names (from Korean names to Japanese names) has brought me a Japanese name 慶州 (Keishū). As for my age, I have just become eighteen today (according to the traditional Japanese reckoning of one year old at birth, with one year added at every New Year). In May last year, I was sent to Sumitomo Coal Mine at Tokusue as a drafted worker, and today I left there for the first time, and when we happened to be on that bridge, wondering which way to go, we happened to meet you all..... I'm pleased to have met you all."

I was glad I was able to introduce myself much better than I had expected.

Mr. Yamamoto responded to me, saying: "Why, you are from the same prefecture as I am. I'll be happy to have a good talk with you."

Then Kim said:

"Let me introduce myself all over again. I am from Hezhou also in Hwanghe-dō Prefecture. My family name is Kim, though the Japanese called me Kanemoto. To myself, everything is the first experience here. So I hope you'll kindly guide me along."

Like a senior to myself, his self-introduction sounded to me more to the point than mine.

Then Mr. Yamamoto said:

"Why, you two are from the same prefecture as mine. This does make me feel reassured." Then he went on: "Now it's already late at night. So that's all for tonight. Anyway, we shall have a good talk, since we have two more holidays — tomorrow and the day after tomorrow."

Then we were led upstairs. It was more spacious than I had expected. The room this side was a six-*tatami* room; the room beyond was an eight-*tatami* room with a closet built into the wall at the end of the room. By then, the farthest room had already been crowded with those in their bedding. In the room this side, four or five men were enjoying themselves in playing *hanafuda* or a Japanese-style card-playing. They, being absorbed in it, never turned to us even when we three entered the room.

At the top of the staircase, there was a landing which was also a place to remove and leave our shoes before stepping on to the *tatami* floor. There was a threshold there, but no sliding door or screen was seen. So the starewell had just led to the room to accommodate us.

I could not tell whether it was the sea or the river that we had been seeing beneath our feet on our way here. And now I was wondering if I could make sure of it by drawing that curtain hanging before the windows, As was the case with the dormitory

I had left behind, the lamp shades were covered with black cloth so that no light could be seen from outside. Mr. Yamamoto, while taking off his *getas* (Japanese wooden clogs) in a casual manner, called to those sitting around the cards of *hanafuda* (a deck of Japanese playing cards):

"Hey, Kanayama-*san,* we have got two workers. So take them among you, will you?"

Then there came an answer from one of them:

"Oh, have we? I hope you'll do a good job with them."

This led Mr. Yamamoto to go to the inner room and take out some bedding and throw it beside the *hanafuda* players, and said, turning to us:

"Now you had better go to bed after making your bedding so you may get rid of your fatigue."

After all those experiences we had had that evening as well as that day, and probably because we had had a full belly, we had been feeling unusually sleepy. This decided us to do as we were suggested, and after having offered a simple greeting to them: "We hope you'll be kindly guiding us along," we hurried into our bed.

As it happened, however, I could hardly go to sleep — as I was again caught by that helpless sadness I had been feeling during supper: we are all human beings, living in the same world, and still what is it that has brought us so many differences between us? What is it that has brought about such things as invasion and war? Closely examined, it seems to have come from the desires we human beings cannot do without. If we were able to live in such total freedom from passion or desire, as was advocated by the Buddha, what a happy and comfortable life we should be leading! As it is, our life today is simply kept dark and devoid of any freedom; keeping alive is all we are barely able to manage. What is the merit of living such a miserable life? Especially we Koreans today seem to have been possessed by the star of adverse fortune....."

This also reminded me of the fact that: I had never looked up at the stars in the sky during the past six months..... Even though totally exhausted, I could not get to sleep.....

This led me to sit up, and turned to look back at those who were playing a deck of Japanese playing cards (with 12 suits of 4 cards, each suit representing a month of the year signified by a flower). Then I had an eye contact with one of those sitting in a circle — the one named Kanayama, who asked me:

"What's the matter? Are we making too much noise?"

I shook my head and said:

"No. I think it's because I am in a bed strange to me."

Then Mr. Yamamoto I had mentioned before — who had been looking into what was happening in the game from an opening of the ring that surrounded the game — said to me: "Just wait. I'll bring you a medicine."

He went downstairs and came back soon with a porcelain bowl in his hand, and said:

"Now, my young man, just take a good gulp of this, and you'll soon be asleep."

That was that unrefined *sake* they had been drinking at the theater. I received that bowl and saw Kim next to me, and found him remaining as still as ever, though it was unknown whether he was asleep or pretending to be unconcerned. This led me to say "Thank you" to Mr. Yamamoto and emptied the bowl at one gulp.

"You are a drinker, aren't you? Another cup?" said he.

"No, thank you," said I. "I've had quite enough. I'll soon be asleep. Thank you."

"I've been a drinker, too. When you cannot go to sleep, this will make a good medicine for you."

Saying so, he pushed the empty bowl toward the timber frame at the entrance to the room, before moving forward to join the circle playing *hanafuda*. I pulled up the top layer of the bedding to the top of my head, so that I might not be talked to by anyone any more.

● A New Name Given to Me

I had never drunk before going to bed, but this drinking did lead me to lose consciousness even before falling asleep. When I woke up in the morning, I found neither Kim who ought to have been asleep in the bedding next to me nor anyone who had been playing *hanafuda* nor those sleeping in the next room. I was the only person having collapsed in bed. The black curtain I saw last night had been drawn, and the sunshine was coming in to a dazzling extent. Now I found myself totally refreshed.

Until yesterday (even on the morning of the New Year's Day), we had been made to wake up by the sound of the handle of the pick ax being hit along the corridor. And now, only a single day later, I found myself where I could get up by my own free will. This is what a man should be, and how a man should live. Now I felt like crying out with joy, even though I was keeping myself busy in putting on my clothes before going downstairs.

Some were at table, while others, having already finished breakfast, were chattering among themselves. Even before I finished saying "Good morning, everyone!" someone made fun of me, saying:

"Oh, Prince! .… Everyone, bring yourselves on your knees! On your knees!"

Kim, holding his bowl in his hand, stood up and beckoned me to come up to him. When I came up, he said in a low voice: "I tried to wake you up, but you didn't wake up."

I, remaining silent, took a china bowl out of the bamboo basket, and served ample rice in the bowl and the *miso* soup in the other bowl for myself before I began to take my breakfast.

When I put into my mouth the boiled rice so much so that my chopsticks had appeared overweighted, there came a woman's voice, saying:

"Is *he* the stray boy you were talking about last night? Why, he is still young. He'll make us even livelier, won't he?"

Looking toward where the voice had come from, or at the depth of the kitchen, where the kitchen stoves were placed, I saw a round-faced woman, short in stature and mature in age, was speaking to us at the top of her voice.

This woman, named Azume, was the wife of the boss with a square-cropped head. Now, she kindly brought me the special dishes she had prepared for the boss — salted cod roe spiced with red pepper and boiled *shiitake* mushroom with *kamaboko* (white fish meat made into seasoned paste, steamed and typically formed into semi-cylindrical shape, whose top is tinted pink). Someone seeing what was happening to me, teased the boss, saying:

"The young lord has arrived and Azume has at once fallen in love with him. Why, the boss has nothing on his plate!"

I still remember very well how the boss was treating it as a joke, saying:

"Say anything you like, but don't be so envious of *him!*"

While taking the meal, I casually counted the number of the people there and found there were as many as a dozen or more people, including ourselves. When they finished their meal in such a lively noise, someone among those who had been playing the *hanafuda* game the night before suggested that: they should resume the same game, and this led almost all of them to go upstairs, leaving all those empty glasses behind just as they were. Looking down at them, Mr. Yamamoto was seated in an impassive manner, with Kim and myself seated beside him.

When Azume started clearing things away, Mr. Yamamoto went to call the boss in front of his room: "Boss, here is Yamamoto." This led the paper door to slide open, and there appeared a man with a square-cropped head, saying:

"Oh?"

This led us to introduce ourselves to the boss, who kindly gave us a very simple instruction:

"Now your safety has been guaranteed. So you need not worry. And after having the New Year holidays till the 3rd, I hope you'll begin to work from the 4th together with all those around you."

Mr. Yamamoto, who was about to go upstairs, said to us:

"We are having fine weather today. So you had better go out to see how this neighborhood looks like."

This led us to go out, as we were suggested to.

Totally unlike the day before, we were having a day as fine as fine could be. Everything facing east — including the doors and walls of the row of houses — had been kept warm, thus making us forget the fact that we were in midwinter. All the houses along the street had their front decorated with the Rising-Sun flags and the navy flags both large and small in total mixture. Almost all the houses had one third of their front walls from the bottom painted deep-black, while the rest of them had been painted black at random, as if having been left to the fancy of the local rascals. Naturally, those walls had originally been gracefully whitewashed. But now, they had been badly smeared with a broom dipped in black water so that they might not be made the attack targets by the enemy planes!

The name of this part of Karatsu City was Ōshima, meaning "The Large Island." The bridge we had crossed the night before was built over the sea, and we were now staying on an island named Ōshima. I recalled how I spent the *Bon* Holiday in summer, unable to go out, leaning against the wooden wall. But here, the earthen wall had been given the final coating with mortar — the authentic one. When I leaned against it, its coldness, despite the sunshine flooding all over there, went through my spine.

As for Kim, he had probably brought himself upstairs and integrated himself into those who were playing the game. Thus, I remained alone out of doors, looking up at the sky on the second day of the New Year — the eighteenth New Year in my life. Now I was breathing in the air of freedom, which I had found much better than that of the coal mine. This led me to worship what Karatsu — our first destination — was.

I could not tell what would become of us from the 4th day on, but thinking that: we could remain as free and liberated as we were until the next day or the 3rd day of the New Year, I felt as if I were staying in a different world. Still I remained conscious of my being on my way to somewhere farther and farther away from our pursuers, so I still remained unable to set myself free from my wariness. While worrying about this and that, feeling coldness on my back, I noticed Azume, the boss' wife, beckoning to me at the entrance to the house, while calling out to me:

"*An-chan* (Young man)*! An-chan!*"

"Yes, I'm here. What can I do for you?" said I.

When I came up to her, she said:

"Just try these on."

After placing on the table a pair of trousers dark orange in color and a khaki jacket with a stand-up collar, she disappeared into her room.

Feeling ashamed as if I had been asked to be dressed in a more seasonable way, I took off my white summer suits and put on the ones offered to me. After having casually folded what I had taken off, I looked at myself in a seasonable clothing only to be astonished at myself appearing totally different from what I used to be! Without hiding the pleasure I was feeling then, I called to Azume behind the paper door in the next room:

"Azume, I'm ready!"

Then the door opened and there appeared an unexpected face of the boss with a square-cropped head.

"*Un,* well…. that appears all right. Just hang on in it for a while," said he before he closed the paper door.

I had no time to give him even a single word of thanks.

I was feeling happy then, as if I had returned to what I used to be — a member of the general public, instead of being such a specific person as was called "a drafted worker." This led me to run upstairs, feeling my light-footedness for the first time in a long time. Now I felt cheered up, saying to myself in happy excitement: "I am no longer a slave working in the coal mine, but one of those ten million of free people!"

When I had run up to the second floor to stand at the landing, which was concurrently the timber frame at the part of the corridor through which we stepped into the room proper, the animated sound of my footsteps attracted the attention of those who were in the room, and there rose an exclamation:

"Oh, you, a young man, you've made a young master!"

This led me to feel as if I were made a head-liner! Kim, who had been among them, was smiling, but his glazed look in his eyes remained impressive to me. When our eyes met, I wondered if I had gone too far. Then there followed something for me to be unable to tell whether it was teasing or admiration. All this while, Kim remained silent.

That night, Mr. Yamamoto I mentioned before, and Mr. Kanayama who was fond of playing *Hana-fuda* (a little over thirty, his large head close-cropped, and his eyes glaring) came to see us and said to us:

"I have something to tell you, Mr. Kim and Mr. Ri, who came to join us last night, holding a piece of paper with you."

When we responded to him, taking a formal attitude, Mr. Kanayama said:

"Well, from tomorrow on, Mr. Kim shall be called Kanemitsu, 27 years of age. Keep these in mind, will you? Because these will make your new identity from tomorrow on."

Then he went on to say, turning to me:

"Now, you will be called Kanamura, 20 years old. Did you understand me? At present, you, two, have no pass-book for rice. So I am going to register at the office, employing these new names and new ages of yours. Keep these in mind. Or you will find yourselves in an awkward situation. Have you understood me?"

Saying so, he made sure of the new situation offered to us. To our roommates, too, we were once again introduced by the new names of ours — Kanemitsu and Kanamura. That was, on January 2nd in the 20th year of Showa (1945), I was made a man called Kanamura, two years older than I really was. That was how we, the runaways, came to assume our different identities.

On the night of the following day (the 3rd day in the New Year) we had a pair of new rubber-soled socks distributed to us. When the day dawned the next day, our work was to resume. What sort of work would be waiting for us? I was filled with anxiety and uneasiness. Looking back on what I had done that day in bed, I noticed that: I had not exchanged even a single word with Kim — my companion in our runaway trip.

This made me call out to him: "Kim-*san*," only to receive his answer: "Un?" So I gave my brief comment on what had happened to us that day:

"We have been lucky, haven't we?"

This also led him to say: "Un."

So I went on:

"We've had good New Year Holidays, haven't we? I wonder what sort of work is waiting for us?"

All the answer I got was nothing but "Un" again. This made me feel as if I had no way to approach him. That was an insipid conversation, to my disappointment.

Forty years have passed since then. Still I can recall what it was like on that occasion. As it turned out, our relationship was growing less and less intimate, and I had no way to stop it, saying to myself: "This was the last thing I had ever expected...."

Still, it was certain that we had been exceptionally fortunate among all those runaways from the coal mines in this country. In fact, our running away turned out to be a great success! From the night of the New Year's Day through the New Year Holidays that followed it, we were to be blessed not only with such gorgeous meals as could never be imaginable at that coal miners' dormitory but also with the prospect of our immense freedom in the future!

Be that as it might, it remained immensely puzzling to me that: here we had ample rice to feed us all, while in the coal mine — even though in the same prefecture — we had been badly short of rice. On the third night of our flight from the coal mine, I was falling asleep with this insoluble question in my mind.

I KEEP SURVIVING

● At an Unloading Port

When I woke up because of the noise in and around the room, all of my fellow workers — who were also my fellow sleepers in the same floor — had already been in their work uniform, busily preparing for the work from that day on — each in his own way according to his own free will.

In the midst of our breakfast, the boss with a square-cropped head called out to our leaders:

"Kanayama, Yamamoto, I hope you'll do a good job."

Then he called out to me, too: "You, a newcomer, do your best!"

Compared with Mr. Kim, had I appeared less dependable?

Before the clock showed half past seven, all of us left for our job site.

We crossed that memorable bridge upon which we had happened to meet these compatriots of ours. We walked on and on, until I found myself, to my astonishment, at that guardhouse, where we had been made to break out in a cold sweat — on the night of the New Year's Day!

Our job site was a quay which stood farther ahead. When we passed the guardhouse, we were made to undergo a body search, but this time it was just a formality and this difference made me feel rather extraordinary. According to what I was told, about one hundred workers were at work here, and this meant our Yasuyama

Group was one tenth of them all.

At one corner there, our Yasuyama Group had our own shed for tools. While we were stationed there, a soldier in uniform came to explain what we should do that day. Our first task that year was to land the cargo of soybeans from China, before keeping it in the storehouse. What was called *Ayumi-ita* (stepping board) — ca.30cm wide, ca.7–8m long and ca.5cm thick — was put across between the quay wall and the ship, and we were expected to land the cargo by means of that board. When we got accustomed to it, we were able to come and go by giving ourselves to the pitching of that supple board. But to myself then, it seemed to be a sort of tightrope feat I should never be able to perform.

When things were ready and when the bag filled with beans was placed on my shoulder, all I could do was to keep myself standing steady.

"Why, the young man, are you all right?"

Hearing these words behind, I brought myself on the stepping board and made four or five steps forward, but unable to keep pace with the swinging of the board under my feet, I soon found myself falling into the sea three or four meters below — together with the bag of soybeans! While the heavy bag was thudding into the sea, I, having bent myself backward, came floating up to the surface of the sea. Since my childhood, I had been accustomed to the water so much so that I might be called "a son of water," and this had kept me free from fear of water, but the coldness of the water in the winter sea was really freezing, indeed!

When I put out my head from the surface of the sea, there came ropes thrown both from the ship and from the quay. The one I grasped in my desperate groping had come from the quay. When pulled out, I was quivering all over with my teeth chattering. Already someone had made a bonfire, and when I was carried up to the fire, I felt as if I had known the warmth of fire for the first time in my life. This incident had caused the break of the unloading, and the work, which was to be over within that date, was prolonged to the noon of the following day.

Around the fire, there were many people gathering to see what was happening to me, thus making a great noise around, even though I myself would have rather liked to be left alone. Honestly speaking, I had not been quite sure of my ability to perform such a feat as that, but I had let my pride as a man go first only to reveal what I really was. Indeed, I then had to feel deadly ashamed of myself. To make the matter worse, I heard my comrade, Kim — of all people — commenting on my ability, meaning it to be heard by me:

"He still remains far from what he believes he is."

This remark at once put the noisy people around into awkward silence, thus leaving me ashamed of myself even to such an extent as my blushing might start a fire.

Could it be his teasing? His grumbling at me? It was hard for me to tell. Those having been making a fuss around me were suddenly dampened, leaving me ashamed so much so that I got blushed as if I had started a fire on my face.

What had happened to Kim, my companion? .... I recalled his words and behaviors when we wandered into that guardhouse to be led to that bridge, and his curt response when I talked to him the night before, and now the manner of his speech in giving a comment on me .... while others were trying to take *it* as a sort of joke, he was deliberately giving such a speech as might dampen the atmosphere there. He was no longer what he used to be three days before. What had happened to him? It was incomprehensible to me.... Now I thrust my anger into myself.

Then I saw the boss with a square-cropped head coming breathlessly — with a bundle in his hand. On seeing me, he said in a flurry:

"What's happened to you, my young man!"

Someone must have informed him of what had happened to me. He had brought me my spare clothes. Seeing me safe, the boss seemed relieved and said, before he vanished somewhere: "Go to the storehouse and change your clothes at once. Now lunchtime is coming, so take lunch first of all so you may work in the afternoon." I had a heartfelt thanks to my colleagues as well as the boss himself. They were all so humane and kind to me.

When I returned to join them after having changed my clothes, they had already begun to have lunch. Our lunch was a collective one: the rice was served in a rice tub, both *nitsuke* (food boiled slowly in a concentrated *soy* broth) and pickles had been packed in their own container, and everyone was expected to serve themselves. I had never had any such style of lunch so far, and I found it quite enjoyable. Since that was the first day at work after the New Year holidays, our work was over at three in the afternoon.

At home, Azume, who had been worrying about me, asked me:

"Are you all right? Haven't you got injured?"

This made me happy — as happy as if I had been at home.

By and by, I grew accustomed to the work, while my physical condition and strength were becoming quite all right, and by the time about a month passed, I had made myself such a full-fledged worker as might be admitted by everyone here. This party called Yasuyama Group had regularly been assigned to unloading the ship. The first day saw the soybeans, followed by cement, gravel, sand and many other articles wrapped up in straw matting. What had impressed me most of all was the unloading of sugar.

The granulated sugar piled up in heaps at the bottom of the ship was scooped up with a shovel to put in a couple of bamboo baskets hung on the both sides of the shouldering pole to be carried up by the steep stairs. Then they were carried along the stepping board so that it could be piled up again on the concrete floor in the storehouse. In those days, sugar — along with rice and barley and wheat — was among the most precious foodstuffs, and it was placed under rationing. Strictly speaking, that was among the articles under the government control. Sugar, therefore, used to be something quite rare to the common people. This was something strange — as strange as the fact that we had ample white rice at our camp.

It was during the midwinter — soon after the New Year season was over. Fanned by the strong wind, it was hard for us to find the right place to release our snivel. This led those working at the bottom of the ship to release their snivel against the pile of the sugar, thus causing the sugar to turn into some rolling balls. This may sound lacking in common sense. But, what if we were to go up and down the deck every time we blew our nose? We should fail to finish our work — to land a certain amount of sugar within *that* day — as we were ordered to. Thus we had inevitably been forced *not* to spare any time even to satisfy our physiological need, whether we liked it or not. Every time I found such rolling balls, I used to pick them up to throw them into the sea. But every time I saw such false luxury, wastefulness and unsanitary conditions prevailing in this naval port, I was led to say to myself: this port could not be an exception, but all the military facilities all over this country would be seeing the same kind of scenes — to my unbearable disgust.

Even after the war was over and we, the Koreans, were set free to lead our own life, there was a period when I could not help breaking the bag of the sugar I had just bought to make sure there was *not* any dubious ball found in that sugar.

● To a Small Fishing Village in Fukuoka Prefecture

As the days went by, I had forgotten the fear I should have felt as a runaway from the coal mine. In March, when the wind was less cold, our Anshan Company moved to Tsuyazaki in Fukuoka Prefecture. We were made to hide among the loads in the truck covered with sheets — to be carried over — for more than three hours. The place we reached was a small fishing village lying along the seashore. Here we were expected to help to bring a new airport into being by scraping a hillside wide enough for it.

The construction camp brought about by clearing the pine wood was far from ordinary: the pillars and the framework were all built of bamboo, while the roof and walls were made of straw. As was expected, the floor alone was of board, but what was spread on it was not *tatami* but *mushiro* (straw mat). There was no bathroom. So it looked like something from the primitive ages. In order to take a bath, we had to visit a small public bath at the Tsuyazaki Street almost one kilometer away. This led some of us to do without taking a bath for as many as three or four days, and this caused us to have fleas and lice, thus sending us far back into the primitive age! To make the matter worse, some had bought a cow from a farmer in the neighborhood, and slaughtered it in secret in the pinewood, and buried the inedible parts somewhere around there. As they went rotten, unusual number of harmful insects and flies were brought into being to a hair-raising extent, and its filthiness was simply unimaginable! Still, I, who had fled from the coal mine, could not help staying there, because I had nowhere else to go. As the days went on, I got accustomed to the work and became friends with those in the other construction camps. The man called Yasumoto was one of them. He, three years older than I, was from Jeonra Nam Dō in Korea. He also, though having been brought to a coal mine in Nagasaki Prefecture, ran away from it and arrived here, Tsuyazaki, by way of a few other places. He seemed to have seen more of life than I, and he was good at gathering the hearsays that went around in the world. The regular information (obtained through the newspapers and the radio) had been always deceiving the people by reporting only the victory on this side. As it was, Japan's surrender was just around the corner.

Toward the end of March, when warm weather was staying, Tokyo suffered large-scale air raids, which caused the deaths of hundreds of thousands of people, according to the rumor Yasumoto had obtained. It seemed as if *the* time had come. What it meant when the capital of Japan had been brought down so badly was: Japan had revealed the limit of their power. If things went on this way, this airport on which we were made to work would not remain safe, so we — Yasumoto and I — consulting with each other, decided to leave here. I was eager to live on rather than afraid of dying. The land of my ancestors had been invaded one generation before or in my father's days. And I myself had been forced to sacrifice my youthful days as a drafted worker. How could I bear another penalty of death upon myself? This led me to pray and pray that Japan might be defeated as soon as possible.

● To Farther West

The news of "the Great Air Raid upon Tokyo" seemed to have disturbed the mind of the people, thus to drive them into even greater anxiety. Not long after that, I and Yasumoto decided to leave Tsuyazaki. When I revealed our plan to Kim, who had always remained my companion since we ran away from the coal mine, he said just as curtly as ever: "I cannot say anything now you have decided *it*." On the other hand, Mr. Yamamoto, who came from the same province as I did, gave me a kind message, saying:

"So you are going to fly! How I envy you! Anyway, as long as you remain "Kanamura" as you have been called here, I'll take it on myself to guarantee what you are."

Azume kindly equipped me with rice balls. This time — though this time alone so far — I was able to make a departure free from any pressure or annoyance. When asked: "Where are you going?" I simply said: "Anywhere my legs take me." As it was, we had decided our destination.

From the foot of Mt. Miyaji, we walked to Fukuma. Then we, with the morning sunlight behind us, headed straight to the west. At noon, we entered Wajiro, a seaside town. In the shade of a tree on the side of a main road, we took big mouthfuls of the rice ball Azume had prepared for us, while gazing at the horizon.

"Beyond that horizon, I have my homeland and my home….."

This thought made me feel as if I were being choked.

"What is it that makes me — such a small being as I am — feel so hard to keep living....?"

I could not help feeling bitter against the making of this world.

The next town we entered was Kashii. I remember having washed my face with the gushing water I found in a *Shinto* shrine. I gulped it down with the bamboo dipper until my stomach was full.

From Kashii onward, we followed not the highway but a side road or a country road — unpaved and graveled — where the small stones had been assembled in three lines — in the center and on both sides. The yellow flowers of dandelions reminded me of the old familiar road I used to follow at home. Looking back upon myself, whose only concern was keeping myself alive, I felt envious of those dandelions which seemed to be standing somewhere higher than myself, even though they were the flowers of the mere wild grass. Comparing those towns and villages, which appeared poor and sooty — exhausted with the war-making, while frightened by the enemies — the fields and mountains we were seeing on our way did help us feel relaxed with their gentle waves of greenery. This made me feel like reciting: "Different nations have different minds. Still, the nature remains the same, all the same."

We were able to reach Tatara, our destination, a little before the evening. That was a village in the basin surrounded by the mountain ridges or it was simply an out-of-the-way place. This led me to get worried about whether or not we were able to obtain any job there. Fortunately, however, there were three construction camps there, and we were easily accepted at the first camp we had jumped in — Hoshiyama & Company — to our great relief.

Unlike the straw hut at Tsuyazaki, the earthen walls here still retained the fresh scent of the walls, suggesting the cleanliness of the newly-built hut, while the location thoughtfully chosen had kept it well-ventilated, to our great relief and satisfaction. Fourteen or fifteen of us were to sleep in a couple of eight-*tatami* rooms — a proper size for us all.

● **The Young Men's School in Tatara**

We were expected to help them in bringing the air-raid shelters into being. We were told that: there was an army post somewhere in this village and the air-raid shelters were expected to accommodate those in that post as well as the villagers. Half way up the hill, they were digging several tunnels — each about 10m long, 1.5m wide, 1.8m high — and a waiting room at the deepest end about three *tatami* mats wide. When we joined them, each tunnel still remained three meters long. That was the only efforts they had made to defend themselves from the enemy planes that would fly over to assault them.

Here in Tatara, I felt for the first time as if I had got rid of my brand mark as a runaway from the coal mine. I felt as if I had won the freedom on my own. Still I remained a man named Kanamura, and this had kept me sad and bitter — in a feeling indescribable even to myself.

One day in May — when the carp streamers (*koi-noboris* in Japanese: the families with their sons fly these carp streamers to assure their success and good health on and around May the 5th) were seen high above the roofs here and there waving in the wind — a party of village officials and soldiers came to collect members to receive the military training at what was called Young People's Training School. As a matter of course, I, who had been considered a certain Kanamura, born in the second year of Showa (1927), to be eligible for military service, got myself into such a plight as to enter that school!

At home, when I finished the primary school (whose final year was the fourth), I had wished to enter a higher-level school, but this wish of mine was blown off, because of our poverty and the war that was badly disturbing our life.

On May 1, 1945, I attended the Young Men's School in Tatara for the first time. The classroom prepared for us was what had been converted from what used to be a storehouse of a primary school. My classmates from the neighboring towns or counties were about twenty in number. The Young Men's School, whose naming had made me associate with something like a school, turned out totally different from what I had expected. It was short-termed, and its aim was to give us an intensive military training so that we might be of any help in active combat!

It was before I was born that my homeland, Korea, was invaded by Japan, and when it was colonized, we had to suffer an enforced change of names from a Korean to a Japanese one, as had never been heard of even in the history of the world. This occurred when I was still an infant. My family named Li had come from Gyeong-ju Prefecture, a place of natural beauty. My father, wishing that his family at present and in future might not forget where they had come from, decided that their family name should be Gyeong-ju (慶州). This explains why I was drafted by the name of 慶州興燮 — Gyeong-ju Funsebi. But no sooner had I been made to enter the coal mine than I was called by the number I was given there, and this name of mine had never been employed until I ran away seven months later. Still there followed the period when I had to live under the false names while moving from Karatsu, Tsuyazaki, and Tatara. Naturally, my date of birth was also a false one. But my position at that time had forced me to retain it, and *that* was to lead me to enter the Young Men's School at Tatara.

What they called "training" at this school was to provide me with the most unforgettable experiences in my life. The training or what was formally called "the military drills" were wide-ranging: how to use guns and swords, how to crawl in the field or the mountain, how to cross the river while being heavily equipped with arms and the like, how to build an encampment with sand bags, how to respond to the enemy's attacks from the trenches we had dug, and so on, and so on. These still remained more or less reasonable.

As for the way the soldier-trainers denounced us was something unbearable. What still remains most clearly in my memory was a variety of abuses we had to be hurled at:

"A single horse is more useful to the Empire than ten of you!"

"Can't you tell why I am training you like this? It's because your lives are so made as to be dedicated to the Japanese Emperor!"

"Before you dedicate your lives to the Emperor, you had better be gone dead by putting your head into that ditch!"

These denunciations were always followed by a series of atrocious drills of kicking the shins with the combat boots and of pushing to knead the pit of our stomach with the sword in the sheath.

These might have been different stories to the Japanese, but to myself as a Korean, my having attended that Young Men's School resulted in having carved my anti-Japanese spirit into my mind even more deeply.

About the time when this three-week training was over, we were called in a room one by one and each of us was recommended to offer ourselves as a volunteer soldier. In my own case, however, I was being forced to be a soldier rather than being recommended to be. As for myself, however, I had never had any intention to make myself either an applicant or a regular. It was the last thing I should do to sacrifice myself any more for the benefit of Japan! This kept me simply saying "no," whatever I might be said.

"Can't you understand me when I am recommending you to

be so loyal not only for the benefit of the Empire but also for the benefit of your own self? You fool!"

To my relief, never again was I called into that room.

On the night of May 21st, I kept thinking in bed with the certificate of my completion in the military training at the Young Men's School at my bedside. This certificate meant that: I had already registered myself as a member of the Japanese Army. As long as I was trying hiding my identity as a runaway from the coal mine, I should have to be hung around by "Kanamura" as my false identity, while "Kanamura" had to be dogged by this certificate of the completion of the military training at the Young Men's School. There was no way to cut out those undesired identifications. This led me to determine to run away once again, saying to myself that: if I kept running away unstintingly, my whereabouts would become more and more ambiguous and even if my draft call was issued, that would help me gain time — even for an hour.... That was all I could think of.

● My Third Flight

On the day that followed, I took a day off for the reason of my fatigue, and left Tatara early in the morning, with only the clothes I had on, and in my inner pocket I had kept only the certificate of my completion in the military training issued by the Young People's School in Tatara. On this same date one year before, I was staying at the bottom of a ferry steamer that connected Busan in Korea and

Shimonoseki in Japan. And now, one year later, I was on my way to somewhere unknown even to myself — only to make myself free from any military service. I had neither destination nor expectation to reach anywhere; all I might be able to depend upon seemed to be my own destiny.

Indeed, that was a reckless journey. Still I had found myself even more relaxed when compared with that restlessness I was feeling at that runaway trip from the coal mine. Now I was heading westward for the highway without feeling any hesitation to do so.

Considering the topography of the Japanese Islands, I had concluded that: the northwestern side was the closest to my native country of Korea on the Peninsula. This led me to walk back along the same road between Tsuyazaki and Tatara; at Kashii, I followed the highway westward, and around the midday, I came to the foot of a bridge painted black all over to a weird extent. I still remember the name of 名島橋 (Najima-bashi) carved into a prop of its parapet. Looking down, I found the water below remaining unknown whether it was flowing or not, just like the water I had once looked down at at the Ōshima Bridge in Karatsu. This led me to find that the sea was quite nearby.

On my way, I came across several old people and women, and to my heartfelt relief, all of them were exchanging polite bows to each other. This sight made me happy and comfortable to find that: the people still remained unchanged in their decency and moderation, however reckless and corrupt their government had been. In fact, this sight seemed to have calmed down my anti-Japanese sentiment that had driven me into a rage. This led me to say to myself all over again: whatever inconveniences or irregularities we might have to face in our daily life, I should like to keep myself such a person as is able to retain his good sense and moderation.

At the end of this bridge or Najima-bashi, I saw the road running through a pinewood. To my amazement, each of those ancient pine trees in this wood had its trunk sharply scarred in the shape of V with an empty can hung beneath it. Looking into the can, I saw a small amount of resin collected in it. The shortage of oil had led the Japanese to make such a desperate but miserable effort in keeping the war going on. What had decided me to leave Tsuyazaki was the wholesale air raids Tōkyō had suffered, and by this time, the B29s — the superfortresses — were often seen to come flying to make atrocious bombings here in Kyūshū, too. Even though it was too late, we could not help being surprised at the latent potential of the U.S., while lamenting the helplessness on the Japanese side.

This led me to think that: the Japanese people in general, who had kept flattering those politicians who had been making sport of the matter of grave national concern, were about to be punished. Charity and kindnesses are indispensable to save the people and their society, but the misjudged flatteries would lead to nothing but the national ruin and the loss of their own selves without leaving anything worthy behind. To my mind, once one was born as a human being, one must keep holding one's own identity. As for myself, I had been desperate, trying to live up to my own identity. It was neither God nor Buddha that has brought us warfare, but we, human beings themselves, have brought about one war after another. If we were to fail to take a right step, we should be led to fall into somewhere dark and miserable. Having perceived *this fact* was the one and only reward I had received from this journey I was making then.

● What I Remember about the Pine Juice

As for that unusual road that went through that pine forest, my memory is not so clear, but it was more than 1km. In later years, I was to find that: it was the Hakozaki Highway in Hakata. All of a sudden, there appeared — beside that forestry road — a huge statue of a Buddhist priest soaring high against the sky. Its base stone taller than that statue was settled at the top of the polished stone steps. One could reach the base of the pedestal — the round base — wide enough to allow three or four grownups to walk around side by side. I saw there an old woman walking round and round, holding a Buddhist rosary on her fingers, while muttering something in the manner of a single-minded prayer. In the shade of that Buddhist statue, I saw an infant seated on its bottom — with its legs thrown out, its eyes goggling. It was unusually emaciated, with the edges of its eyes darkened, its belly swollen up to an unusual extent. Anyone could tell it was suffering from malnutrition (or starvation).

As mentioned before, I was born as a son of a farmer, and even though we were poor, we had never been driven into starvation. That morning, too, I was in such a situation as to be able to eat my fill so that I might remain properly fortified during the day's journey. Since the sun was just above our head, it was about lunchtime. The old woman, leaving that enfant alone, had simply been addicted to walking around the base stone. Even though I was about to pass them, I felt something like guilty consciousness and turned back only to find that I had had nothing to offer the little one.

The sight of that infant reminded me of what I used to do long ago at home. We, a naughty band of boys, used to dig out the root of Japanese ivy to nibble it, or to pluck up the new shoots of brambles to eat them after peeling their outer layer of the skin, or to pluck up the tip of the branch of the young pine tree and peel it in the way of holding a scroll between our teeth, so we might enjoy the taste of its astringent sweetness.

Now in this pine forest, which seemed to have kept away any other kind of trees, all I could do was to find out a comparatively younger pine tree, to pluck the tip of one of its branches and break it into two before I went to stand in front of the infant, to peel its skin in the way we peel a banana, put one between my teeth, and made the other hold in the little one's hand. Regardless of the child's response, I just put my teeth into the skin of the branch, pulled it right and then left — in a way of playing the harmonica

— as I used to do when a child.

Since it was toward the end of May, all the trees and other plants had retained enough water tasting sweet as well as astringent — making me feel as if I had returned to my childhood days for the first time in a long time. In my childhood, because of our poverty and the war we were suffering, we could seldom chance on anything sweet, and this used to make us find anything sweet available from among anything found in our daily life. The sight of that child, though a foreigner and a stranger to myself, led me to feel helplessly piteous for him (or her).

After a while, the child on the base stone began to imitate me and seemed to have found its taste acceptable and its eyes did regain their liveliness, until it broke into a smile, to my relief! Then I found myself being choked into helpless tears. That was the saddest and the most unforgettable scene I have ever had in my life.

● I was Employed at Itatsuki Air Port

I hurried on my way with such sentiments as these in my bosom. It was early afternoon, when the sun in the midair had slightly got tilted. By and by, I entered the town of Hakata, and along the street with a tramway in the center, I came to the front of Hakata Station. The station building was of the old Western style — just as the building I saw at the landing place at Shimonoseki, when I first stepped on the land of Japan. And here again, I was impressed by the sight of the building, whose walls and pillars had all been painted black, as if done so in desperation. As long as the sight of the buildings was concerned, Hakata still remained a city, but its traffic was inactive, and I could not help feeling the decline of its downtown.

After crossing the railroad coming from Hakata Station, I walked on for a while before I entered a village called Takeshita. The sun was tilting in the west, making me feel impatient to reach somewhere. Then, an old woman on the roadside rice paddy, who had been hoeing the soil with her back bent at an angle of 90 degrees, happened to straighten her waist to take a rest, when our eyes met and exchanged our nods, and this led me to be informed of there being an airport just on the eastern side of this village. She also added: the airport had in it not a few construction camps, where most of the workers were said to be those from the (Korean) Peninsula, to my own convenience.

I thanked her for the kind information she had given me, and headed for the airport. I arrived there about sunset. The airport, having neither wire netting nor barbed wire around, simply appeared defenseless. Still it had the gate-door with a couple of guards standing upright on both sides of the entrance. Farther away, several wooden buildings that appeared warehouses were seen standing side by side in total silence. Farther beyond, three or four ridges of construction camps were seen with several trees behind. I called on the first camp I came to and this led me to settle down there. That was Itatsuki Airport (present-day Fukuoka Airport), and my camp was Hirayama-*gumi*. It was May 23, 1945. Strangely enough, that was exactly on the same date when I had arrived at that coal mine one year before.

Here, different camps had been expected to do different kinds of work. My camp, Hirayama-*gumi,* was expected to keep the airport or its runway in good condition. The runway, looking like a large athletic field, was neither paved nor separated from the surrounding area. So the planes were expected to take off or to land according to their own convenience. The planes themselves were rarely seen to leave or land, while the planes permanently stationed here seemed to be only four or five.

It was about this time when rumor had it that: Germany as Japan's ally had surrendered to the allies of the U.S., the B.K., the Soviet Union and so on. When I heard of the surrender of Germany as the ally Japan had put the greatest trust in, I felt something expected had finally come true. I think: that was the worst situation Japan had expected, and it was taken as a serious matter.

To myself, too, these turned out to be a problem unexpectedly brought into being: I, even though a Korean, having been made a Japanese citizen, thought the time was drawing near when I must reconsider that matter of contradiction in real earnest.

Setting aside Japan as the prime mover that had created that contradiction, the U.S. and the U.K. and several other nations as Japan's enemies might have been acquainted with Japan's having invaded the other countries, but it seemed to me that they would have remained ignorant of those illegal pressures Japan was inflicting upon us or those individual Koreans driven into the bottom of its society. Thus what seemed to me to be the worst problem was: any of the nations that had won the war might treat us Koreans as Japanese — without uncovering all those hidden facts of Japan's wicked acts of oppression upon us, Koreans. This worry of mine could not help being intensified when I recalled all those phenomena in which all the Japanese had been single-mindedly dedicating themselves to their motto of "loyalty first; patriotism first," thus helplessly disabling themselves to protest against even the most unscrupulous oppression their government had been inflicting upon other nations.

It seemed to me that: Japan at that time had been driven into such a situation as would never be able to consider any such difficult situation as a Korean as an individual had been driven into. I now realize: Japan at that time had lost its morality, having forgotten its neighborly friendship, thus reducing itself to a self-complacent nation. Patriotism and love of one's own country have been commonly shared by everyone born as a member of any nation. But what had mattered then was their having been overdoing something by indulging themselves to their own power, while blinding themselves to such reckless violence as to trample down the weak and the poor. Such reckless subordination may cause us not only to step out of the right track of humanity but also to endanger the existence of the state itself. Whatever turbulent times we might live in, I think we must not lose our self-consciousness and moderation as a human being. Otherwise, our society would fall into disintegration that leads to the decline of the nation until it falls into the abyss of ruin. What Japan had inflicted upon Korea was none other than an atrocious crime committed in the total lack in morality and moderation we should have retained as human beings.

About that very time when I desperately jumped into Itatsuki Air Port, Japan had already been gasping, while leaning herself toward the abyss of national ruin. Exactly one year had passed since I stepped on the land of Japan. This led me to feel: any power cannot last long, while the passage of time is beyond our control.

One day in less than a week after my arrival here, there appeared a man to collect members to enter the young men's school. I felt an unspeakable fear of the tenacity of militarism that kept pursuing us wherever we might go. Of all hours, he presented himself at lunchtime when we were all there. In Hirayama and Company I had come to belong to, there was no one qualified for recruitment but myself. Even today, the mere reference to "the young men's school" exasperates me. What had made me carry that certificate of completion issued by that school was none other than my expectation that: it would surely be helpful in my tenure. What had made me run away from Tatara was to make myself flee from military service, and now — even before a week had passed — it turned out something to reveal my whereabouts.

● I Kept on Going Underground

When I showed the official (to collect the members to enter the young men's school) my certificate of completion issued by the young men's school at Tatara, he copied it deliberately before he left. This left me in great chagrin, because this underground escape I had made turned out to be simply useless. But I had no intention to give up my hope of keeping myself free from that Japanese authority, and this decided me to resume my going underground.

That night, I asked Chief Hirayama to meet me and told him about my having run away from the Coal Mine, and about how I came to run away from Tatara, and about my present state of mind concerning how I should protect myself from then on. According to what I had heard about him since I entered his camp, he was very caring and sympathetic toward us, and this had led me to come to depend upon him. In fact, he turned out to be such a person as to reveal his own secret, too, saying:

"My son is also eighteen or as old as you. His way of thinking is exactly yours. He is now hiding himself in the countryside in Shizuoka Prefecture."

Then Chief Hirayama advised me to make preparation for my trip before going to bed. Thus my petition turned out a great success! He, who had come from Daegu in the southern part of the Korean Peninsula, thus turned out to be one of my benefactors.

I had trusted in him. Still, I remained uneasy, and this left me hard to go to sleep. When I was shaken up by the wife of Chief Hirayama at dawn, none of my roommates had woken up. That was the first time I had ever been awakened since I ran away from the coal mine. The chief himself, having got up earlier, had been making himself attentive to my needs. He told me to come to see him in his room, after having washed my face, and when I did as I was told, I saw the special table — apparently arranged for me — simple but prepared to the utmost. I asked — as the impulse urged me — "Was there any memorial service?" Then the chief answered:

"I have expected you to say so. My wife has prepared for you — as a token of our best wishes for your journey. So eat to the full. Anyway, you'll have to depend on your feet, so it won't be to your disadvantage to fortify yourself."

When I left Tatara, I had sneaked away without carrying even a single baggage with me. But here, I was carrying a package of several rice balls when I set off, while being seen off by the boss and his wife.

This kindness I had received then could not possively be regarded as the consideration offered to someone who had been staying with them only for less than a week. So even today, I am made to believe: I had been seen off then by the Living Saviors seemingly even better than God or Buddha. Certainly, the people were talking of his kindness, but I realized then that: Mr. Hirayama was what a human being should be in the true sense of the word.

Filled with deep emotion, all I could do then was to hold his hand tight in my hands in order to express my heartfelt thanks. I never turned back to see Mr. and Mrs. Hirayama, but only bid my farewell to them with my back.

I had my journey guided by the map they had drawn for me on the back of his name card. I walked from Itatsuki to Takeshita Village, and by way of Dazaifu, I headed straight for Amagi. My destination then was Hagi in Fukuoka Prefecture. I had been told that: Hagi was situated in the border between Fukuoka Prefecture and Ōita Prefecture. From Dazaifu — dedicated to Sugawara Michizane, a famous man of literature in the ancient times — to Amagi, I walked straight along the Amagi Highway. Since it was unforked, there was no need to wonder which way to go.

Now I have forgot the names of the relay stations I passed on my way, but I still remember having heard an air-raid warnings two or three times, which used to made me hide myself under a tree I was about to pass by or among the tall grasses on the way, while trying to find out what was happening in the sky. The noise of *lulun-lulun* could be heard, but the enemy planes themselves were rarely seen. Their height was such that they appeared as tiny as flies or mosquitos even when they came into my sight.

It was only less than a month later that I came to witness how those tiny things which looked like flies or mosquitos jumped on their aims so quickly and repeated their atrocious bombings without showing any mercy. As for that experience of mine, I would like to mention it later.

I made as much haste as possible to arrive at Hagi, my destination. It was around two in the afternoon when I reached Tachiarai known as a location of an airport. I passed the camp of the airport, and ate the rice balls I had carried with me under the tree at the roadside. But as I had been advised *not* to ask anyone about the route for my destination, I could not ask anyone I met on my way even for some water, and this had led me to drink from the brook running around the airport. Having been extremely afraid of being taken as "a suspicious person," I had got extremely nervous, even while eating or trying to get some water to drink. After fortifying myself, I resumed my extremely hurried journey.

So far, I had had an experience of making a trip on my own — around the clock. It was in my early teens, when I was expected to take a medicine known as *Kuma-no-i* (*the Bear's Stomach*) to the wife of one of the brothers of my mother. My home was Kokusan in Hwanghae dō; while the destination of my trip was Suwon in Gangwon dō in the mountainous region. Her husband had died young, while their only son, (Jeyon), senior to me by three or four years, had been in poor health. The name of his disease remained unknown, and I heard he died soon after he was twenty in the 18th year of Showa (1943) — before I was taken to Japan as a drafted worker. My journey then, about 52km, was to bring some medicine to that invalid youth — passing over the mountain which had been made the prefectural border. Before I set off, my father had given me three pieces of advice:

① Avoid the stones lying on my way so I may keep my feet less tired

② Find out a proper stick before climbing up the mountain

③ In climbing down, keep pulling one supple branch after another behind me so I may not slip down.

The journey I was making then in Japan was free from any such ups and downs, but I made it a rule *not* to step on any stones I might come across on my way. This led me to be attentive to anything lying before me. As the years went by, I came to realize the merit of observing these rules in making my life's journey, too.

In less than an hour, I was to pass the town of Amagi. Even though it was called "town," it was far from what we might imagine by the word of "town." Not a single store or shop could be seen. All I saw around were the dusky rows of Japanese-style houses that used to consist of "a post town" during the pre-modern eras.

Soon after passing through Amagi, I found myself on the highway. On one side of the highway, whose level was higher than the other, I saw a stretch of farmland for a variety of vegetables — potatoes, cucumbers, egg plants, Indian corns and so on — growing in abundance in the waves of green; on the other side of the road, there were stretches of paddy fields, where rice-planting still remained unfinished. Thus both rice fields and vegetable fields were producing foods indispensable for human existence.

But in my native land on the Korean Peninsula, the farmers — even rice farmers — could not live on rice. This left us in sheer misery. The eighty percent of rice, barley, wheat, soybeans and anything regarded as staple food they had produced was taken away by the Japanese Government under the name of obligatory supply — without paying any money for what they had obtained! That was why we ate rice *only* on the New Year Holidays and on the *Bon* Holidays, as I had mentioned before.

While walking along the road, I was wondering what the situation would be like in the case of the owners of these rice fields. Then I heard, all of a sudden, an air-raid alarm start wailing from behind or from the direction of Amagi I had just left behind.

By those days, they had come to hear such an air-raid alarm three or four times a day and this had led them to get so accustomed to it that they never minded walking around the streets instead of being on a full alert. In all matters, growing accustomed is likely to lead to a danger. I myself was saying to myself: "The planes ought to have come over to attack some military facilities somewhere — they won't do any harm to a single person walking on the road."

● **The Falls of Drum Cans**

But, soon after the alarms were raised, I felt a strange

reverberation I had never felt before. The sound ought to have come from the sky, but it sounded as if coming also from the depths of the earth. It was earth-shaking and fear-instigating. Shuddering at something unexpected, I looked up at the sky. Just at that moment, I was frightened out of my wits and crawled on the nearest vegetable field at the sight of the numberless planes having filled the whole sky!

They disgorged numberless black spots which grew larger and larger as they came falling down indiscriminately upon the farms, rice paddies, fields and hills! Though seen from afar, those that had fallen on the paddy fields gave some slashes, but all remained unexploded, therefore no sound of falling was heard — and the unexpected stillness that had fallen around was felt even more weird. After having witnessed the final one having dropped beyond the mountain, I crawled out of the field of eggplants in fear and trembling. That was a moment's occurrence; no air-raid warning had been given; no Japanese plane was seen to come flying; nothing like fire engines made their appearance, either.

Looking around, I saw none but myself, and this led me to feel as if I were the only person who had witnessed *the* scenes, and this made me forget the fear I had been feeling then, and also led me to feel badly disappointed. Now in my excitement, even though I knew I must hurry on my runaway trip, I could not help making sure what it was that had thrown me into such a panic! In fear and trembling, I — crawling on hands and knees — approached the one lying closest to me. It might blow up at any moment! When it revealed its identity, I was left aghast. What had sent me to such a shudder and fear was nothing but an empty drum can! Still keeping my nerves on edge, I approached it to find it appearing as if afloat, slightly tilted, without lodging into the soft soil. It was painted blue, still appearing brand-new.

Presumably, it had contained the fuel for the planes. Seeing that they were dropped in dozens about in the same area, this seemed to have been done according to the order issued by some reliable quarters. The planes nowadays make a long-distance flight by air refueling, but at that time they had not yet attained to that stage of development, it seems. In those days, the guns employed by the Japanese side used to be single-loaders, while theirs were said to be repeaters or repeating rifles, and that very small in size. What was more, the enemy planes at that time, known as B29s, were outrageously huge in size. Even though they had possessed such highly-developed arms, their air-refueling seemed to have still remained far ahead.

In making war, ample materials and bravery are indispensable. In case of Japan, all they had was bravery, and they were badly lacking in materials. To make the matter worse, they were extremely short of labor power, too. This led them to employ us, Koreans, to fill up its shortage, but it still remained far from enough. This led them to be so unfeeling as to bring in the young people as the property and the treasure of their own country —

in order to keep on making that extremely merciless war. That merciless war, however, did not seem to last so long, considering the fact that: an increasing number of enemy planes were coming to assault Japan proper day after day. Still, all I could do then was to make effort to protect myself.

Because of this unexpected happening I came across on my way, I had taken much more time than I had expected in arriving at my destination in Haki.

The camp of Kunimoto Company I was heading for stood at a corner in the hilly section. The house built in log construction with board walls did make us feel the atmosphere of what was called "bunkhouse." What had attracted my attention was: the electric lamps there had not had any such black cloth to cover them. Just as the coal miners' dormitory I had left behind was, it was so built as to be able to go farther into the interior. On both sides of the earthen passage, there were rooms with the straw-mat flooring for the construction workers to sleep in.

The boss or Mr. Kunimoto was a man of small build, gentlemanly and quiet; when I handed him a letter of introduction from the captain of Hirayama & Company, he readily introduced himself to me: he came from Jinju in Gyeongsang Nam Do and belonged to the tribe of Jeon Zhou's Li. When young, he came to Japan, and he happened to work with Mr. Hirayama at a certain construction site, and they had kept friendly terms for more than thirty years since then. He kindly said to me: "So you can feel easy about staying here," to my great relief and gratitude for his warm humanity.

Here, too, one could eat as much white rice as one liked. This meant: white rice had always been with me since I left the coal mine. Here — at Haki — I had nothing to complain about in my daily life, but looking back upon those adventures I had to make in Japan, while evading military service, and thinking about what would become of me in the near future when Japan surrendered, I had never felt at ease.

● The Train I Took for the First Time

The Japanese, if defeated., would naturally submit to the administration of the U.S. as the victor nation. But what would become of us, Koreans, who had been made Japanese citizens? What should we do then? These were the serious questions that had kept gaining upon me.

If one were Japanese, it would be natural to obey the administration given by the victor nation, but what would become of me or anyone like myself — a Korean whose nationality was Japanese? What should I do? This was a pressing problem for myself. Those were the days when I had to face one difficulty after another in order to make myself survive rather than worry about what would become of the nation I belonged to. In Haki, too, we were engaged in bringing air-raid caves into being, as in Tatara. But here, Master Kunimoto had kindly offered me such paper work as to totalize our work progress of his company, and I had allowed myself to take advantage of his kindness, which, at least turned out to be a helping hand to me. Inwardly I remained struggling as ever, but in appearance, I had been kept carefree.

About half a month had passed since I came to Haki, when I heard Master Kunimoto talk of Hakata whose downtown had totally been burnt down. In Haki, we had not suffered any air raid, but it was about the time when we were accustomed to hearing the siren of an air-raid warning almost every day. On the day after we heard of the air raid on Hakata, I made a trip to Hakata without a moment's hesitation. I had simply wanted to confirm what was happening to the Hirayamas. Even though I had known them only for a week, they had taken care of me as if I were his own son. Now I wanted to make sure of what had become of them.

That was the first time for me to take a train by myself in Japan. It was a slow train which stopped at every station, but apparently incomparably faster than walking, and physically at ease; it seemed as if I had been entertained with a series of landscapes of towns and villages, the fields and paddies on the way. I am not quite sure, but it was a few days past June 20th. I got off at Takeshita Station or one station this side of Hakata Station. Takeshita Village seemed to have escaped danger, but there was a trace of air raid though only on the part adjacent to the airport. It was at Itatsuki Airport that I realized the atrocity the air raid had brought about. The guardhouse at the entrance I had passed only a month or so before and the wooden buildings beyond had turned into piles of scorched wood. Glancing at them, I turned to the right to reach the Hirayama & Company. On my way there — about 100m or so — I saw a couple of holes made by the bombardment, with the weed around scorched and withered. These sights made me so uneasy that I started running.

To my great relief, all the buildings of Hirayama & Company and other construction camps, which had clumps of trees behind, remained exactly as they used to be. Even though it was only a month before that we had parted, we were moved to tears at the sight of each other, grasping hands, as if we had not seen each other for dozens of years. This led me to turn my thought to my own father at home, saying to myself: "If we were able to meet again, we should be meeting each other in even greater emotions."

Now seeing Hirayama & Company kept safe, I was feeling as if I myself had been saved. At lunch time, Captain Hirayama said to me: "Go and see the downtown of Hakata; you'll see the scenes that reveal something totally different from what you've seen here at the airport. The air raid occurred three days ago — on the night of the 19th — but it has still been left as it is, because it is simply impossible to do anything with it."

I myself having come all the way to see what the air raid had left behind, it was not long before I was on my way there.

What the air raid had brought about — the futilities and

miseries — had been spreading as far as the eyes could reach. Even though the dead bodies had been removed — otherwise I would have offered my prayer to them — all the buildings, houses, thoroughfares, utility poles had been burnt to crumble, thus revealing the scenes of unprecedented miseries even after the three days had passed — with embers still sputtering here and there. How many bombs had been dropped in bringing about such miseries as this? Those tremendous sights of destruction and those miseries beyond description caused me to feel goose-pimply, while making me feel as if my guts were being cooled.....

In our childhood, when we boys had five or six of us gather together, we used to play at soldiers on the hill at the back of our village. If we did it anywhere in sight of the grownups, we used to be scolded, because they had thought: the very notion of killing others was no good, even if it took the form of playing the game. But whatever grows cannot be stopped. Even though we were children, we racked our brains. What was it that had made us do *it* even in secrecy? To my mind, it was probably a sense of superiority one might feel at the sight of someone being shot to fall. Such a sense of superiority as that, however, should be kept only in the sphere of children's play — instead of being carried over even to the world of grownups.

Carrying over such a sense of playing in our childhood as far as our manhood can be very dangerous, especially when it is something undesirable. To my mind, those Japanese who had been at the top of that imperialist society at that time had completely lost their common sense in this line. This had led them to their aggressive war only to turn their own land into ashes, These were the thoughts I came to hold at the sight of the miserable devastation Hakata had suffered.

Forty years have passed since then, but one of the scenes I still remember was: while walking around the scorched town of Hakata, I got extremely thirsty, and this led me to search for any water to drink until I found a cup of water being sold on a small desk for two primary school children. I paid 50*sen* for it and drank it from a cup for one *go* (0.18 liter), though unusually expensive even at that time. I remember cursing him, a man around forty, inwardly saying: "What makes you sell the water *here* — at the very place where many of your fellow citizens were burnt to death? What on earth was it that had saved such a despicable fellow as he from being bombed?"

While seeing such absurdities and humanities mixed in confusion, I kept asking myself about the meaning of keeping ourselves alive. The Japanese might talk of "an unbroken line of the Emperors in Japan" or of "*Kamikaze* (a divine wind)," but the war — a sort of living thing — will follow its own course of existence; at war there is no choice whether one will survive or not. I cannot think of any other word in calling that sheer madness in which Japan had made that imprudent invasion into the other countries only to escalate the war. If Japan had been so brave as to make a war, she ought to have had wisdom to renounce the war, too. Several years after Japan's surrender, my ancestral land of Korea also fought the Korean War (1950–53). Whichever side might have started or repulsed it, none other than their having made the war itself deprived both of them of their courage and wisdom, only to be left alone with inhuman belligerence, I think. If only we had employed our wisdom and reasoning power *then*, we should have been able to avoid the War fought between the peoples of the same race.

Forty years have passed since Japan was defeated in the Second World War (1945), and I might have easily been able to return home if I had wished to do so. But I myself could not allow myself to wish to return home in the north or to the Republic of Korea in the south — because of my sore spot of having remained unable to do anything for the War between the two parties of the same nation. What is called war does cast shadows on all the classes in that society and deprives them of what used to be theirs. The best period of my life had badly been exploited by Japan's militarism. What was once deprived of would never be retrieved. Neither any divinities nor the Buddha ought to have any right to deprive us of our right to live as human beings. As it happened, however, I was made to take the cruelties of the war to heart *not* once *but* even twice! I do wish no other person would be made to repeat any such misfortune as I had suffered…..

As long as human beings are existent on the earth, it seems that conflicts would not cease to exist, while invasion and disdain would not come to an end, either. These thoughts or prospects make our future appear hopeless and lonely. Those who had been burnt out of their houses in Hakata, too, ought to have been keeping their own prospects high in their own way, only to see them perish in a few hours that night. In fact, that was a field of ruins that invited certain frustration both from the invaders in disdain and from the invaded in resentment. Along with this image of pandemonium kept in my heart and mind, I returned to Haki.

● A Piece of Information I Obtained by Paying Three Hundred *Yen*

Naturally I was feeling as depressed as any other witness of the miseries in Hakata ought to have been. Still I could not remain only in blank amazement. Otherwise I should have been left nonplussed about what I should do after Japan was made to surrender, which was to occur unmistakably before long. This led me to make efforts to collect information about the timing of Japan's surrender. But what was reported by the newspaper or radio in those days curiously remained silent about Japan's set back, even though they still kept suggestive of Japan's victory even in reporting on the air raids it was suffering here and there on its islands or on the war situation abroad. All those things had driven me into helpless impatience until I came to make light of myself as a careful thinker in my own way. It was one of these days, when a wanderer who called himself Yūki, a dental technician — according to his self-introduction — came to stay with us. I had had a couple of large slits in my upper teeth to my inconvenience, and this led me to take this opportunity to fill those slits with gold-crowned teeth. This led me to come in brief contact with him three or four times, until I obtained some information considerably helpful to myself.

This led me to pay such a large sum of money as three hundred yen or all the money I had kept with me at that time, saying to myself: "If money remains money, it'll be of no use. If turned into something helpful for me to live in less inconvenience, it will turn out useful." This decision of mine, however, was to turn out a fatal one later on — only a month or so later on — when I needed one hundred *yen* for the passage to Busan or the entrance to my homeland: All the money I had kept with me then was only seventy *yen*, and *this* led me to wander in order to earn thirty *yen* to buy *that* ticket, to my life-long regret.

I am not going to attribute my fate to Japan, but I would like Japan to make up for her crime of having deprived me of those youthful days of mine, which were too precious for me to lose forever. Ironically, this shortage of money was to lead me to keep living in Japan throughout the rest of my life — dragging my lifelong resentment behind me.....

Still, that information I had obtained from that wanderer named Yūki was exciting indeed. By the time when I had been in Haki for a month, the Allied Forces mainly consisting of the U.S. and the U.K. had already landed on Iwō Jima Island; it was expected that it would not be long before Okinawa was occupied, too; then the mainland of Japan would also be occupied, probably within three months — in August or in September — and Japan would unmistakably be driven into surrender. That was exactly the same prospect I myself had made by judging from the air raids Japan had been suffering.

But the Japanese people themselves — having been kept unusually busy with what was called "home-front defense" they had been expected to perform with "loyalty and patriotism" — seemed to have no time to doubt about anything they had been told. In other words, the general public, who had easily been tamed to be cheated, was being tyrannized over, while being kept in sheer darkness.

As to those pieces of information I had obtained *then*, I kept silent with special caution, while suppressing my presentiment, and also giving special consideration as to how we should respond to the situation when Japan came to surrender. Apart from my artificial teeth, the information I had obtained on that occasion was certainly worth three hundred *yen*, but the fact that *this* had caused my life to go wrong — as will be mentioned in the final chapter — was to turn out my life-long regret.

One day, after supper in July, when a series of hot days were settling after the rainy season was over, the airport in Amagi —

where I had once been made to tremble by the sight of the black objects falling down from the sky — was air-raided. After the siren of warning was given from the downtown of Haki, there was no air-raid alarm for a while….. still there came a sound of *hyu—n don!,* followed by a strange sound of *kyu—n,* causing an unusual atmosphere around. This led us to go on to a small hill behind our construction camp. What we saw there below our eyes was a tremendous scene of the air-raid having been carried out in the fallen dusk. Numberless planes were giving an attack one after another, and that by the second! Each plane skimmed the surface of the earth, giving a ringing sound of *hyuhyu—n,* and at that moment, it dropped the bombs: the next moment, there came a double sound of *kyu—n do—n! Kyu—n* was the sound of metal friction when the plane rose sharply in order not to be influenced by the bomb-explosion of *do—n!*

For those who were being attacked, it would be a veritable hell, but as long as it was seen in the dark from a considerable distance, it remained a mere viewing of some performance, and every time sparks were shot out, a roar of excitement was being given. Hearing that roaring, I felt like having those scenes of sparkling shots witnessed by every Japanese in every corner of this country — so that each of them might make sure what would become of them if *the* war were kept on like this in a total lack of justice. Those caught in that air raid would have their bodies broken into pieces, burnt hideously to a cinder, and even if any one of them might survive it, he or she would have to be kept frightened at those terrible sights to the end of his or her life.

On the other hand, those who had stood on the side of seeing *it* on a breezy hill like ourselves or those who had never seen any such pictures of the Hell during the war would have failed to know what the war really *was*. And even to this day, that personal regret I had felt *then* still remains with me.

Apart from the generation who do not know the War, those who have known the true nature of the war have now (in the 1960's) come to be regarded as the older generation, while the number of them is growing smaller day after day. I know my own personal experiences during the wartime remain insignificant, but those who have experienced the cruelties, horrors and sorrows brought about by the war still remain numberless. But those who have known the truth — concerning what had happened to the Korean people before they were reduced to submit to such humiliation and persecution as were inflicted upon them — would not be so large in number. That was why I had prepared the facts in history, as follows, in the following section.

● What had been Done by the Government General of Korea

In 1910, Japan, which had succeeded in incapacitating the Yi Dynasty (1392-1910: 27 generations) seated in Gyeongseong (present-day Seoul), established the office for the Government-General of Korea or the invaders' government to rule over Korea on the Korean peninsula in place of the administrators of the Ri Dynasty.

What they had done first of all was to make a survey of the whole land of Korea. So far the Korean people in general — who had always been expected to live in accordance with the rule of self-sufficiency — had left the borderline of their own land rather vague or far from strict or particular. As it happened then (1910), all that belonged to the public such as mountains, forests and unoccupied land were all brought under the ownership of the Japanese Government. That was how our land on the Korean Peninsula was defrauded.

By and by, about the time when I was beginning to learn the way of the world, our names — both surnames and personal names — were forced to change into Japanese-style ones. When I was in my fourth year of elementary school, our own language — the Korean language — was prohibited for us to use and it was replaced by the Japanese language. Being defrauded of our land was the matter of the grownups, but the changes of our family names and the prohibition of our own language could not help humiliating us to a fatal extent, even though we were still children. Thus our frustration was readily turned into hatred. Japan, which called itself "the Great Empire of Japan" (1889-1945), which had succeeded in colonizing Korea on the Korean Penninsula, having lost its sense of moderation — which would be indispensable for anyone or any nation in coexisting with any other — was to repeat their acts of inhumanity.

If it had been anything material that had been swindled from us, we might have been able to endure, but the persecutions we suffered both mentally and physically can never be cured. Not a single sign of the faith in common humanity could be found anywhere. They simply remained shameless at their own barbarities, which would remain indelible whatever compensations might be offered to us. The persecutions they had kept inflicting upon us never ceased to exist throughout the three generations of ours. No justice had been brought about to stop such follies. War is cruel in both action and expression, and for us Koreans, making war against Japan on an equal footing was the last thing we could think of. Thus we had to live in oppression, persecution and submission throughout the three eras of Japan's history — *Meiji* (1868–1912), *Taisho* (1912–1926) and *Showa* (1926–1945* (1985)).

* Upon the collapse of Japan after World War II, independence was promised to Korea, but an American-Soviet agreement divided the country at the thirty-eight parallel. Friction between North and South followed upon this partitioning and led to an international war. Though the cease-fire agreement had been reached, the division between North and South remains unchanged.

—— *A DICTIONARY OF JAPANESE HISTORY*
By Joseph M. Goedertire, C.I.C.M.

To my mind, the identity of the Great Empire of Japan was a mass of cruel cowards. What had brought about a tentative conclusion to such atrocities was Japan's surrender (1945), which occurred soon after I was gazing at the merciless air raid upon Amagi Airport, as if it had nothing to do with myself. Japan at that time had been suffering not a few air-raids every day and everywhere. In the midst of unusual heat that had lasted day after day since the arrival of August, we heard of the monstrous bombardment upon Hiroshima that had burnt hundreds of thousands of people to death. Three days later, we heard of what they called *pikadon* or another A-bomb, which had wiped out Nagasaki.

We, never having heard of anything like such a monstrous bombing as might kill several hundreds of thousands of city-dwellers in a moment, simply remained unable to believe what we were being told about.

I was saying to myself: if hundreds of thousands of people had been killed and a whole city had been wiped out, the Government, however cold-hearted it might be, would not have remained so cool as *this*, especially when the radio and newspapers ought to have been eagerly reporting those unusual miseries. As it happened to us laborers here, we never received any such news, to my puzzlement, even though I had been trying hard to collect any piece of information available in spite of any cost I might pay for it.

● The Atomic Bombings upon Hiroshima and Nagasaki

Japan was the first to have disturbed the peace of the world. While making war against China, Japan had turned even the U.S. into its enemy, and its momentum had caused it to spread the ravages of war even from the Southeast Asia to the South Sea Islands.

In Europe at this period, Nazi Germany had been challenging not only to its neighboring countries but also to the Soviet Union, thus to fight at random, while performing unprecedented massacres here and there. By and by, there came the time when almost all the peoples on the earth became involved in the war. As for Japan, half a year after having declared war against the U.S., it had already been in such a critical situation as to be rolling down the cliff.

In 1943 or in the second year of Japan's conflict against the U.S., Japan — no longer able to produce the iron ore and coal, the most indispensable in carrying out the war, along with cloth and food stuffs — had to be driven into the national crisis, because of the shortage of manpower.

By that time, a motto of "Japan and Korea are one and inseparable!" had been created so that it might agitate Koreans' devotion to Japan. At this point, Japan had already been driven into a corner. Then, I should say: Japan should have honestly informed not only the Japanese but also the Koreans of her wretched conditions so that they might put into practice their motto: "Japan and Korea are one and inseparable" before they might find a way out they had badly needed. As it happened, however, the Japanese politicians who had been blinded by their ambition simply made light of the crises they were facing, and kept deceiving and trifling their own people. All pieces of announcement from the Imperial Headquarters about this period were nothing but falsity and camouflage themselves.

As it happened, however, the U.S. airplanes that had come to fly to Japan proper with great ease began to make air raid after air raid not only on the military facilities but also on the urban areas in large cities. By and by, in place of what was called B29, the carrier-based planes — small in size but quick in action — had been made the main force. By that time, they had come to destroy the cities middle-sized as well as small-sized, while some other planes were pursuing the farmers working on the rice fields or flying extremely low while managing their rifles. These facts, even if seen in the most favorable light, did suggest that it would not be long before Japan was defeated.

It was in the midst of these days — early in August, 1945 — the atomic bomb was dropped firstly in Hiroshima, and then in Nagasaki. I believe you all have already been informed of these facts, even if I may not give any further details about them. As it happened, the information given by the Imperial Headquarters *then* was simplicity itself: "A new-type bomb was dropped." Not any further information was given concerning either its tremendous power or the scenes of the hell it had brought about in this world.

As for myself in those days, because I was still on the run in fear of being caught, I could not yet openly obtain any proper information about it, and it was two or even three days later when I finally obtained the facts of miseries the atomic bombings had brought about.

In fact, no one had ever been able to imagine how Hiroshima and Nagasaki would vanish in a single moment only to expose themselves in such miseries. Those victims seemed to me the very souls of the war dead that would never be able to rest in peace. On the other hand, considering all these facts from my own footing, I could not help thinking: the War that seemed to me very long might finally come to an end — after having inflicted the divine punishment upon Japan that had committed every conceivable form of outrages. If Japan still refused to wave a white flag (a flag of surrender), its whole land would have to suffer the rain of fire as a punishment from Heaven, I used to say to myself from the bottom of my heart.

To my mind, the Heaven had employed the U.S. in exercising Its punishment on Japan. Be that as it might, I could not help wondering why *not* on Tokyo as the very base of their militarism and their militaristic administration.

A week later — on August 15 — I had been crouching on the height between Amagi and Haki in Fukuoka Prefecture in Kyushu. It was the middle day of the *Bon* Festival holidays, but we had been made to gather there according to the order issued by the military that had jurisdiction over that district. It was around ten in the morning.

There was not the slightest wind, but every time anyone moved, the dust of red earth was raised like the smoke of sulfa, making me feel as if it might inflame our skin. We were being seated with the foothills behind and a plain below our eyes. Before us, I saw some empty boxes for packing up apples — arranged to bring into being a makeshift stage, upon which a pole equipped with a microphone was seen standing.

On one side of it, I saw those who seemed to be local dignitaries — including the aged in their uniform suits with a stand-up collar — seated with a mournful air around.

We had already been informed of "the broadcast of the Emperor's announcement" from the soldier who had come to convey the order for us to gather there, but we had had no idea what it would be like, and this led us to make light of it, presuming that: what they called the Imperial Headquarters would be contemplating something evil again and now they were going to pronounce it.

Now, the first thing that had attracted my attention was a microphone, which had seldom been seen, fixed at the top of the iron pole placed at the center. This led me to say to myself: "This is *not* an ordinary announcement from the Imperial Headquarters, it seems." That iron pole which was gleaming black somehow appeared as if overpowering the whole of that plateau.

I was also saying to myself: "After that broadcasting, someone must give a talk or speech." As a matter of fact, it was even more painful for me than the digging of an air-raid cave to be made to keep waiting so long under the blazing sun — and that, for something totally impossible for us to presume.

● Mr. Nakagawa, the Only Japanese among us

Nearly an hour later, I came to notice that Mr. Nakagawa, the only Japanese in our camp, could not be seen all this while. Excepting Mr. Nakagawa, our camp — Kunimoto Camp — consisted of Koreans only, including the boss, Mr. Kunimoto. At that time, we had been digging out the air-raid caves about half way up on that hill, and around that job site, there were three camps, including ours.

Strangely enough in Japan in those days, Mr. Nakagawa was the only Japanese working among us or about one hundred Koreans — without revealing any sign of obsession about his identity. To myself, this seemed very strange, and I used to take him as a sort of eccentric.

Our camp at that time had been so made as to have no chair to sit on at table, or we were expected to eat while standing. But, Mr. Nakagawa alone used to sit on the chair in a leisurely manner and to drink up a bowlful of *doburoku* (unrefined *sake*) before taking his meal. He was a medium-sized man; his face somewhat long, neither pale nor hairy, unlike most of the Japanese men in those days; his forehead without even a single wrinkle on it had gone up to the top of his head, thus to characterize his personal appearance. But what had characterized him most of all was his being one-eyed, even though it was very hard for me to ask him what had happened to his right eye.

At one time, we happened to be seated at table side by side, and when we were left alone, I asked him — who had become happy or slightly intoxicated — what had happened to his right eye which had gone blind.

"How bold you are to have asked me such a delicate question!"

Saying so, he turned to me, sending a thrilling glare from his left eye which remained normal. This sent me a chill, but in a moment, he returned to his usual self, and said:

"All of them have a regard for my feelings. That's why no one has ever asked me what happened to this eye of mine. I've been in this camp longer than anyone else. So they treat me with a proper respect. Then, *that* has come to prevent me from talking about this eye as something special."

So saying, Mr. Nakagawa took this opportunity to talk about his own life so far: He was born in the vicinity of Nagoya — one of the large cities about the middle of the main island of Japan. His family had been working on the farm from generation to generation. He was the eldest son, followed by one sister and two brothers. They all had become full-fledged. His younger sister had once been made to offer herself to work at a factory to produce soldiers' gaiters, thus having been kept her from getting married even though she had already been thirty, to his apprehension. Both of his younger brothers had been called to active duty three years before, to be sent out to the battlefields in China. Mr. Nakagawa himself, having run away from home the year before his younger brothers were sent to the battle front, decided to keep silent. This had left him ignorant of anything happening not only to his family at home but also to his brothers abroad.

Saying so, he appeared lonely, keeping his eye on a single spot on the wall. This, having made me feel as if I had asked him of something unnecessary, led me to give him a casual response:

"Though between ourselves only, *the* war seems to bring about a variety of difficulties to everyone of us, doesn't it?"

"As for *that* war," said Mr. Nakagawa. "I myself had once been summoned and had a physical examination. Because of being one-eyed, I failed to stand to the test. This led me to "do a runner" the next day without saying anything even to my parents. Can you tell why? I was frightened. What if I remained at home? Everyone would come and tease me about my being at home, instead of entering the service. This would annoy my parents, too! This did dicide me to cast off my being Japanese. So I am *not* Japanese! Nor Korean! But talking of where I stand, I am much more fortunate than you. Because I am free from anything that may come to catch me. I shall never make anyone say anything whether I may stop being a Japanese or I may become a stateless person. On the other hand, you — most of you — are running from place to place. Frankly speaking, I am free to do anything, while most of you are being wanted. *Still,* I am feeling envious of you. Why? I am envious of you for your spiritual toughness with which you are placing a bet on yourselves. At one time, I was wondering if I might kill myself, but while I was coming and going with you at this construction camp for Koreans only, I have simply forgot any such notion as killing myself. Because I have seen you having committed yourselves to the survival of all the difficulties you must face in Japan. Yes. *That* image of yours had been imprinted in *this* eye of mine. As for the *other* eye, I had it pierced by the stump of a tree when I fell from a persimmon tree that stood at a corner of our vegetable patch. It was in autumn in the year when I entered the primary school. That turned out to be a case: As one sows, so one shall reap. And this did upset the course of my life."

"It is also said," Mr. Nakagawa went on. "What happens once will happen again. And Japan *now* is similar to my life. I think you have often seen such a password or a slogan as "The U.S. & the U.K. are beasts" or "The U.S. & the U.K. shall be exterminated" written on the banners hung across the street or on the posters on the walls. As it happens, only very few Japanese have ever seen what they look like in the U.S. or in the U.K.. Still, most of the Japanese are being made to fight against them by being made to believe they are beasts. I myself, never having been either in the U.S. or in the U.K., cannot tell what they look like. Most of the Japanese, unlike myself, are two-eyed and clear-sighted; still they remain totally lacking in foresight.... It's simply deplorable!"

Mr. Nakagawa went on:

"Could it be right to assume those we have never seen before to be 'beasts'? The Japanese today are totally lacking in their ability to judge: If they are told by any authority to turn to the left, they'll turn to the left. If they are told to turn to the right, they'll turn to the right. That's all they are able to do. There is no guarantee, therefore, that all the Japanese will have their heart pierced through by the steel spear, just as my eye had once been pierced..... But, they still think it a virtue to die or dedicate his life in order to exterminate the U.S. & the U.K., thus committing themselves to being looked up to as a hero. I myself, even though a Japanese, have *not* even a scrap of regret at leaving such Japanese behind!"

I had been watching Mr. Nakagawa's face all the time he was talking, and when he uttered his final words: "I myself, even though a Japanese, have *not* even a scrap of regret at leaving such Japanese behind!" I saw his clenched teeth let the upper muscle of his chin unusually swollen up, while the gnashing of his teeth was heard. This led me to feel as if I myself were being scolded; even though on the other hand, *that* made me feel sad, too. Mr. Nakagawa's speech lasted while he was smoking several cigarettes:

"I'm thirty-three and I'm as strong as you see. It was five years ago when I ran away from home. The next year, Japan started the war against the U.S., and now we have come to what we are now.

At home, I was a good farmer, too, and I was being recommended to get married, But, as the war fire kept spreading, I became more and more restless. Now I think it better that I had hesitated to get married. During these five years, I haven't sent even a single letter to my parents at home. Because I want to keep myself from being forced to enter the volunteer-labor corps. Now that I have decided to stop being Japanese, I shall never do anything helpful to the aggressive war we are making without any justice!"

"I think it fortunate of me to have been made one-eyed," he went on. "Otherwise I shall be sent to a battlefield somewhere far only to send many men called enemies to death. Or I myself might have been made to die a miserable death. The mere thought of it makes me feel chilly. Anyway the battlefield will be the last place for me to make myself function properly."

"Be that as it may," he went on. "Probably because I have been going along with the Korean people only, since I happened to meet Captain Kunimoto four years ago, I have come to get sick of the way Japan has adopted, since it makes me feel as if something dirty is being demonstrated. As I've said before, I have already stopped being Japanese from the bottom of my heart. Still I remain unmistakably Japanese. I have already lived to be well over thirty, and now it seems to me I have finally come to realize: how inconvenient, how fearful and sad it is for us to live in the framework of what we call a state."

Mr. Nakagawa's speech went on, keeping his mouth busy in

smoking tobacco and in drinking *doburoku* in gulps with great relish. His tone was brusqueness itself, but having avoided waste in his speech, he could make himself understood even to myself who still remained far from good at Japanese. This had kept me from giving him even a single nod, but I was simply eager to understand him.

The bowlful of *doburoku* before him had already been empty.

"Wait a minute, please!"

I said to him, and went to the Boss' corner beside the dining room, and asked for two more bowlfuls of *doburoku,* and placing one before Mr. Nakagawa, the other before myself, I said:

"I'll have a drink, too. You, too, have another drink, please. This is my treat."

Mr. Nakagawa, though in silence, held that bowl as naturally as if it was his from the beginning, and drank it, giving a sound of *gui-gui,* and said to me after having placed the empty bowl on the table:

"Your treat was especially good!"

Then he went on:

"We cannot say *it* openly, but to my mind, Japan will not keep long, as long as it remains as it is."

Mr. Nakagawa, probably because the alcohol was beginning to affect him, began to speak in a more relaxed tone of voice:

"To my mind, it is the Japanese people themselves who have turned Japan into such wide stretches of burnt ruins or have smashed it like this. No one can save it. No one can do anything for it. So you, too, must prepare yourselves for *the* time to come. It'll be too late for you to do anything when *the* time comes. As you know, both Hiroshima and Nagasaki had a new type of bomb dropped. Those bombs were several hundred times more effective than the Japanese bombs. So, both Hiroshima and Nagasaki have been blown off, I hear. What if they had been dropped on Tokyo? The mere thought of it makes us shudder, doesn't it? In the heart of Tokyo, the Emperor lives. And I've heard: someone of the Royal Family of your country — a prince or a son of a prince — has been brought over there. What if anything should have happened to anyone from the Royal Family of any other nation? We shall simply be unable to face them. Even though the big bosses of Japan *now* may not mind anything like that...., I do wish they would settle *the* matter as soon as possible. It would be too late to do anything if we had been deprived of everything. But all I can do now is just waiting, keeping my mouth shut. Nowadays, you know, the U.S. planes are flying around to do anything they like; on the other hand, not even a single plane with the mark of the Rising-Sun can be seen, probably because they cannot do anything against the U.S. It'll be useless for us to remain so obstinate. Even if we might settle *it* sooner, we should be able to find any other way to take. Then, you, Koreans, too, would be able to find your own way to follow."

Mr. Nakagawa turned his goggling eye to me, and finished his speech abruptly, saying:

"That's all I'd like to say to you now."

His talk had lasted for as long as two hours, but when he finished it, he appeared as if he had been relieved of something he had kept in his mind for a long time. To myself, too, his talk about his own life along with his comment on the war now going on and his kind concern for us Koreans were impressive as well as memorable to me, indeed!

Even after I went to bed, I remained excited, recalling what Mr. Nakagawa had told me. This kept me even more awake as the time went on. I still remember how he uttered: "It is the Japanese themselves who are turning Japan into such a wide stretch of burnt ruins. No one would be able to stop *it!*"

I had been here in Haki for about two months and a half, and so far I had remained unable to see this person named Nakagawa with a feeling of goodwill or sympathy. The reason was: now all the people in this country were making frantic efforts to keep guarding their own land, but this person named Nakagawa, even if blessed with such a strong physique and good health — though one-eyed — had allowed himself to stay at this construction camp originally for the Koreans who had run away only to be drifted into it. But now that I happened to listen to him, I felt ashamed of my own naivety with which I had totally misunderstood what Mr. Nakagawa really was. Mr. Nakagawa seemed to have ceased being Japanese, but when I recalled this and that in his speech, I could not help thinking he still remained unmistakably Japanese. For example, when he talked about the miseries brought about by the new-type of bombs (the atomic bombs), he said: "It'll be too late when everything is lost or gone. I do wish this war would be brought to an end as soon as possible," thus revealing his patriotism at heart and his wish to stop any more misery inflicted upon his own compatriots. This may sound quite natural at present, but in Japan in those days, no one was allowed to mention: "I do wish this war would be brought to an end as soon as possible," and if such a thing as this were to be mentioned — even by a slip of the tongue — one ought to have been regarded at once as a traitor to be looked down upon.

What they called the Great Empire of Japan had totally been united into her militarism, while the whole nation had been placed under the National Mobilization Law, and both the young and the old, even school children, had been pressed into volunteer labor. The whole of Japan had been turned into a sort of group, in which not only the individual emotions, opinions and even intentions were shut up into the group's control only to be confined in it. Therefore, as for the war to which the people had been expected to commit his life, they had not been allowed to give any complaint or dissatisfaction or grumbling even in a light-hearted manner.

Seemingly, Mr. Nakagawa then had revealed his complaints in such a light-hearted manner, partly because his listener was a

Korean youth who had not yet got full-fledged. Even though he had been emboldened by alcohol, he had spent considerably long time in revealing his frank grumbling to me about what was happening to Japan at that time. This led me to feel as if I had made another step toward manhood. What was more, despite his appearance, he was a man of striking personality — open-hearted and straight forward — while being equipped with many other merits I felt like making my own. In fact, I used to think: if I were allowed to spend two or three years with him as his disciple, I should be able to make myself a man in the true sense of the word.

Now, that very person — Mr. Nakagawa — could not be seen anywhere in this open ground. I had thought: Mr. Nakagawa would be able to presume what "the broadcast of the Emperor's announcement" was like — along with its inner situation — to a certain extent. That prospect of mine had led me to think he would be the first person to present himself here at this appointed place. Now, the absence of that very person I had expected to see *here* suddenly made me feel uneasy.

This led me to return to our construction camp, taking care not to be noticed by anyone of those dignitaries seated before us in an adverse V-shape. What was considered Mr. Nakagawa's private corner was at the end of the room on the left-hand side — one *tatami* and a half wide with no wall nor partition around — which was where he slept at night and where he made certain of his own existence. In this connection, my own private corner was just on the right-hand side of the first entrance door to the room. Since it was beside the wooden wall behind which was the dining room, it was the noisiest place in the room.

That was also the place I could find what would become of each of us when drunken. The one who had decided where each of us should sleep or stay in that room was naturally the boss of our camp, even though — according to the tradition of the camp — the newcomer was expected to sleep closest to the entrance door, thus to move farther and farther from the entrance as the newcomer arrived.

This was also the case with Yasuyama Camp at Ōshima in Karatsu, which we (Kim and I) had found ourselves on the night of the New Year's Day when we ran away from the coal mine. The place given to us then was also a small space closest to the entrance to the large room on the second floor.

Mr. Nakagawa had been working for this camp longer than anyone else, while I myself was a newcomer. Mr. Nakagawa, a Japanese, usually remained silent and rarely cracked jokes, and this had made him appear a model of the serious-minded. But after a drink or two at supper or at any such occasion, his speech used to turn arrogant and unrefined, even though his talk remained logical. Four or five days before, we — with no other person around — had talked as long as two hours on end, but such an occasion never occurred again. When talked to, he naturally responded, but usually he finished it a little earlier. Whatever he might do, he did it as steadily as was expected without any lingering. This seemed to have come from his temperament. This was the image of Mr. Nakagawa I had come to grasp. But sometimes I was made to feel I had not yet come to grasp what he really was. He was fond of playing *shōgi* (a Japanese board game resembling chess). He was sometimes heard to intone a *Naniwa-bushi* or a Japanese-style ballad, when he could not find anyone to play *shōgi* with. His repertoire seemed large, and every time I heard him render a *Naniwa-bishi* in a guttural drone, I found *it* a different one.

Mr. Nakagawa appeared happy-go-lucky and far from refined, but what he really was seemed to have revealed in his meticulous prescience with which he solved the problems in the game of *shogi*. Such was what had led me to know of him, but I simply could not tell what had made him disregard the order to listen to the broadcast of the Emperor's Announcement of something......

What had made me return to our construction camp was that: since it was "the broadcast of the Emperor's announcement," there ought to be many difficult words and phrases in it, and I wanted Mr. Nakagawa to hear it for me, so that he might tell me later what it was about. I had been in Japan for only fifteen months and my listening comprehension still remained barely able to understand the Japanese people around me.

Mr. Nakagawa, putting his heels on the window frame, was gazing at a point of the ceiling made of the bark of Japanese cedar.

Even when I approached him, he pretended to be unconcerned. I hesitated to talk to him, but now that I had come up here, I could not remain silent. So I spoke out:

"The noon is coming….."

He remained silent. This led me to explain what had made me come back:

"Please come and listen to the radio. I myself cannot understand Him. So please come and listen *for* me."

I appealed to him, mentioning my own puzzlement.

At first, I was doubtful about *it* as another trick of complete fabrication issued from the Imperial Headquarters, but seeing that we had received the same order *not* once *but* twice since early morning, I came to notice what was called "the Emperor's announcement" must be something so special as had never occurred before. In this camp under the boss Kunimoto, many Koreans had been in Japan for several years. None of us, however, had ever learned the Japanese language properly at school either in Korea or in Japan. This meant: none of us would be able to understand the Emperor. So I wished Mr. Nakagawa would come out and listen to "the Emperor's Announcement" so that he might make himself a commentator for us Koreans in a later hour.

But Mr. Nakagawa would not lend his ears to me, but remained simply unconcerned with me, while glaring at the clumsy ceiling above him. This left me disheartened. But since I had not yet grown so bold as Mr. Nakagawa was, I could not help returning to the open ground where we had been expected to gather.

● The Broadcast of the Emperor's Announcement of Japan's Surrender

I had been working along with the grownups, and this had qualified me to drink some *sake* among them; I was also allowed to give my opinion concerning the work we were engaged in. So I had thought I was right in coming back to bring Mr. Nakagawa to the ground. But, now that I had been ignored by him, I felt ashamed, saying to myself: "I've still remained immature…." In fact, I felt as if I had been defeated because of my having forgotten what I really was.

It had already been a little before noon, and there was a great deal of noise — *pee-pee gaa-gaa* — coming from the loud speaker fixed before us. That was the first time for me to see what a loudspeaker was like.

I had already been proud of myself for being able to follow the Japanese language as long as it was standard Japanese. So I brought myself closer to the loud speaker which had been set up before us, and bent my legs among the strangers, who were also engaged in the same work of bringing the air-raid shelters into being on the same hillside. I remained unconcerned even when glanced at with some curiosity.

While being made to wait so long in the sweltering heat, we were all grumbling, which sounded more or less like groaning. But none could be so bold as to ignore the order which had been issued by the military authority, as Mr. Nakagawa could be. As a matter of fact, everyone, including myself, was simply desperate to make oneself survive. Whatever abuse we might suffer, and whatever disdain we must receive, we had to survive them by instinct.

Having our own way even when trampled down was also something impossible to perform without extraordinary resolution. It seems to me: only when our instinct of self-preservation comes into being straight forward, that instinct begins to work as such.

Those Koreans thronging on that open space seemed to have been there *not* by that kind of instinct *but* by the momentary instinct inevitably brought into being by the control-power named order. This was what I was thinking then according to what I myself had been placed on that occasion. I was then eighteen years old. I was also saying to myself — while minding my sweat falling down my belly along the wrinkles brought about by my bending posture: "The changes of the fate of human beings are brought about by the powers of others or any authorities under which they are being placed, as in my own case."

On the other hand, I had also been captivated by the mechanism of what was called a loud speaker or what seemed to be a strange variation of the trumpet. Then, all of a sudden, a noticeably dignified soldier seated diagonally opposite to me suddenly stood up and gave an extra-loud order:

"Attention!"

All the people, including myself who had been on the verge of collapse until that moment, were thunderstruck and rose to our feet in bewilderment, only to see the one who had given us that order sit down! But no more order being given, some stooped down, following the example of the order-giver, while others kept standing, to bring about a very comical scene. I myself, following that order-giver, stooped down as I had done before. At that moment, there started the Emperor's announcement.

So far the open ground had been noisy, but at that moment, everything — including time and even heat haze — seemed to have stopped moving.

Mixed with the noise of *gaa-gaa* from the loud speaker, there came a loud voice of human speech as if coming from somewhere afar — as if from overseas — then all of a sudden, the voice fell down to such a faint voice as was barely audible. Whether in a loud voice or in a low voice, the quality of voice, as was heard through the loud speaker, was clear and audible, but as for the terms the Emperor adopted, they simply remained incomprehensible to me, however hard I might try to understand him. Since I was brought to Japan or to the coal mine at Tokusue in Saga Prefecture (in Kyushu or the southern-most main island of Japan), fifteen months had passed, and I had already been able to understand almost all the Japanese language spoken around myself. But as for that broadcasting of the Emperor's announcement of Japan's surrender simply remained far from understandable to myself. Not only the terms he had adopted but also the mechanical noise and the strange pitch in his speech simply left us unable to tell what he was talking about and what had been happening to us then — as we all agreed when we returned to our construction camp and talked about *it*.

The Emperor's announcement seemed to have lasted about twenty minutes or a little longer. Anyway, waiting for it for a couple of hours under a blazing sun was far from easy. Before the broadcasting began, the word of command or "Attentions!" was given to us, but as for when it was over, no one could tell. But unusual sight of those soldiers seated diagonally opposite to us, as well as the elderly men who seemed to be village officials — all sobbing convulsively, their head hanging low, their arms upon their eyes — easily enabled me to guess the occurrence of something extremely sad to them.

The sight of those devilish soldiers also weeping like everyone else, too, made me feel pity for them, even though I could not tell why. After a while, however, they seemed to have regained their usual self and the soldier who had been acting as the commander came up to the microphone and said:

"Let me inform you all! From this moment on, the Great Empire of Japan has allowed you freedom! From this moment onward, we shall never be concerned in your matter! That's all!"

At this moment, by this declaration, we were released from the humiliation and restraint which had been taken over from my grandfather to my father, and from my father to myself.

My father — having had his ancestral land conquered, his bitter tears having swallowed up — had his son, who was still a boy, abducted just before his eyes, so abruptly and so mercilessly as if a live tree was cut in two, but we were not allowed even to resist it, whatever humiliation and vexation we might have been feeling then and thereafter. And now, we, both of us, were allowed to live in freedom again! It was at noon on August 15, 1945.

● Pondering over Korea, my Ancestral Land

According to the history, the Conception of the Conquest of the Korean Empire or the Li Dynasty (1352-1910) was brought into being early in the Meiji era (1868-1912) in Japan, thus the Great Empire of Japan had kept contemplating conquering Korea, until 1910, when Japan's annexation of Korea was finally brought into being — spending about thirty-seven years. Japan's ambition to conquer Korea had been accumulated for as long as twenty-one years until 1894 when the Korea's Royal Palace was finally occupied. Looking back upon those days, we are able to imagine how the Korean people in those days stood against their enemy, while facing the events upon whose issue the fate of the nation had depended. It was apparent that: when the Great Empire of Japan was marching on without hiding its ambition, it could not be of any use even if the hastily-assembled militiamen came to swing up their sickles of justice.

Thus even after their royal palace was occupied, the people's resistance was kept on, and it was not until as long as sixteen years had passed that the Korean-Japanese Annexation Treaty was signed. (1910) This Treaty was practically the starting signal of Japan's colonization of Korea.

Seeing that it was 1873 when Japan's argument for invasion of Korea became a hot issue, they had kept struggling to satisfy their ambition for as long as thirty-seven full years. Even if seen in the most favorable light, this was so unscrupulous that it could never be regarded as something to be done by any human beings. In 1910, when the Korean-Japanese Annexation Treaty was signed, the Government-General of Korea was established and a man named Terauchi, if I remember right, came over to take the seat for the Governor-General. It was since this office of the Government-General was brought into being that the Koreans were forced to face the difficulties in the true sense of the word.

First of all, under the name of "the Land Survey," Japan's defrauding us Koreans of our land was openly performed, spending as long as nine years (1910-18). The result was that: we were deprived of all the forests, wastelands, river-side areas as well as unregistered farmland, and the signboards of "Keep Out" were put up there so that their authority might keep us all away. Indeed, this must have been carried out under their thoroughgoing preparedness.

So far the farming population in Korea had been living in a self-sufficiency lifestyle on the farm they themselves had opened and cultivated. But after the Land Survey, many of the farmers were deprived of their land simply because it had not been formally registered. The farmers' antipathy was such that it was finally developed into what is known as 3.1 Independence Movement (1919).*

*The movement for independence spread in Korea, and on March 1, 1919, civilians started a peaceful demonstration. The demonstration, however, was drowned in blood as 2,000 civilians were killed in what is known as "March 1 incident," or the *banzai* riot incident. The nationalist movement went underground, but the struggle of Kim Il-sung as well as the provincial government of the Republic of Korea, organized in Shanghai by Dr. Syngman Rhee (Lee Sung-man) received international support.

Upon the collapse of Japan after World War II (1945), independence was promised to Korea, but an American-Soviet agreement divided the country at the thirty-eight parallel. Friction between North and South followed upon this partitioning and led to an international war. Though the cease-fire agreement has been reached, the division between North and South remains unchanged.

—— *A DICTIONARY OF JAPANESE HISTORY*
By Joseph M. Goedertier, C.I.C.M.

● My Birthplace

I was born in 1928 or in the year of the *Dragon* according to the oriental zodiac or in the third year of Shōwa according to the eara name of Japan. In my native village, it was the traditional custom for a boy who had reached his twelfth year to make a formal visit to offer a greeting to the Village Elder or the elderly intellectual in the village at the beginning of the New Year: First of all, I gave my father's name, and my own name and the year in the terms of the Oriental zodiac along with the date of my birth before delivering my New Year's greetings to him. I think this was something like a coming-of-age ceremony Japan used to have before the Meiji Restoration (1868). The man who had received my visit then was my own uncle on my mother's side. He, who was a teacher of the Chinese classics and the Chinese poetry, was also the Doyen or the senior statesman to deal with everything important in the village.

About the time when I was four or five years old, there was a private school to teach the Chinese classics, and it was four or five years later that I came to know that the teacher there was that person or my uncle.

The father of my mother had already been dead before I was born, but the grandmother was still going strong about the time I was taken as a drafted worker. This means, therefore, my native village or Yomoru Village had been placed under the supreme command of this uncle of mine. I used to frequent this maternal grandmother's almost every day, but as for that uncle as a village dignitary, I had never visited him until the day for that traditional ceremony to mark a boy's coming of age. I had been aware that they were my relatives, but I, even a child, had been feeling rather awkward in visiting them. One of the reasons for that would have been that: they had no children in their family. My uncle, though having been married for as long as five years, remained childless and the people had regarded him as "seedless." Apart from such a rumor, it seemed to me that they had remained rather aloof or hard to approach.

It was this person — my mother's younger brother or a village dignitary — who, on May 19, 1944, having come along with the two soldiers to see us at work on the farm, handed my father the paper to order him to send me out as a drafted worker.

I was seventeen then, still remaining more or less childish, and this had led me to hate that uncle for many years to come, even though I now realize: the situation he had been placed into at that time had led him to perform his duty whether he liked it or not — according to the order of the Japanese Government, whose power over us, the Korean people, at that time was tremendous, indeed.

While I was pondering over what human beings are day after day, I had come to realize: a man as an individual might be able to remain a saint or a great man, but in the national system or in a body politic he belongs to, he cannot help being subject to it or placed within its limited enclosure.

Anyway, while hating my own uncle, and while feeling

resentment at the nastiness of the Japanese Empire, I had spent the summer and the autumn before the New Year came round. On the New Year's Day in 1945, I ran away from the coal mine possessed by the Sumitomos in Karatsu, where I had been leading such a restricted life as if being imprisoned. All that I could tell then in that strange town of Karatsu was: the east from the west; the south from the north.

And now, at noon on August 15, 1945, I heard the broadcast of the Emperor's announcement of Japan's surrender, and then a couple of declarations as its aftermath were delivered:

"The Great Empire of Japan has allowed you freedom from this moment onward!" and "From now on, we shall never be concerned in your matter!"

These declarations were what the Emperor's Announcement had brought us as its after effects. The declarations themselves might have been more or less different from place to place or from district to district. But the consciousness underlying it, I think, would have remained unanimously devoid of any humanity to show any sympathy toward those who had been made to suffer so much from Japan's militarism and colonialism both mentally and physically.

In the final analysis, the Emperor's announcement was none other than the declaration of Japan's unconditional surrender to the enemy nations. And, the moment that declaration was over, the Great Empire of Japan had been crumbled down.

And still, even at this disgraceful moment, they had retained their dignity by declaring: "The Great Empire of Japan has allowed you freedom from this moment onward!" And they had brought themselves to their extreme mercilessness by attacking us from the rear — by declaring: "From this moment onward, we shall never be concerned in your matter!"

Certainly we jumped up at the declaration given first: "Japan has allowed you freedom," but we failed to mind what was given next: "we shall never be concerned in your matter!"

So far we had been struggling to set ourselves free day after day, day and night, even at the risk of our own lives. Now that we were set free, no other information attracted our attention. What was worse, our listening ability in Japanese language still remained far from enough, while the Emperor's broadcasting was also far from clear, and the Japanese language spoken by Him was totally different from what we had been accustomed to. Then all we could depend upon was that declaration given by that Japanese soldier: "Japan has allowed you freedom!"

Only the words known to us caught our ears; the rest was simply left unnoticed or disregarded. This led us, Koreans, to be captivated by the fact that we were set free, while we remained totally unconcerned about the latter half of that declaration: "From now on, we shall never be concerned with your matter," — even though we should have taken *this* ever more seriously.

Before we came to notice the seriousness of what was happening to us, all of us Koreans had remained simply joyful, being fuddled with *doburoku* (unrefined *sake*) for as long as several hours on end.

I was born and brought up as a child of the colony, spent a boyhood while feeling the menace of Japan through the daily life of the people around me, and early in my youth, I suffered the Japanese Empire's threat and persecution which had directly fallen upon myself, thus to be transported as far as Japan to be engaged in the forced labor. So the mere phrase of "set you free" did capture my heart and never thought of reflecting upon that even more serious part of the declaration that went as follows: "From now on, we shall never be concerned in your matter!"

This had happened in the midst of the time when we were struggling for the freedom day and night — even at the cost of our own lives. Only having received the freedom sounded so much satisfying to us that we never minded any other information that followed. What was worse, I still remained barely able to understand spoken Japanese, while the sound of the broadcasting itself was helplessly poor in quality, and the language spoken by the Emperor sounded totally different from any such Japanese language as we had been hearing so far. Thus what was called "the broadcast of the Emperor's announcement of Japan's surrender" had remained totally meaningless to us. So the declaration made by that Japanese soldier — "we shall never be concerned in your matter" — was simply left unnoticed,

In other words, what we had managed to catch was only the words understandable to us; any other words unknown to us had simply been left to pass by. This led to the fact that: the Koreans then and there had simply been captivated by the fact that they were finally set free, but failed to take in that even more important pronouncement: "We shall never be concerned in your matter (or anything that might occur to you from now on)."

Until we finally became aware of the gravity of our situation, we had left ourselves simply thrown into our supreme joy of having finally won the freedom, happily allowing ourselves to remain fuddled with *doburoku* or unrefined *sake* for several hours on end until we finally sobered up.

I was born and brought up as a son of those whose land had been colonized; I spent my boyhood while being aware of the threat of the Japanese Empire, as was known by the daily life of my parents and the grownups around. About the time I grew up into a young man, I was directly made to suffer the threat and persecution inflicted by the Japanese Empire — or I was transported here in Japan for forced labor. That was why even a single notification of "you shall be free" simply enraptured us so much so that we jumped around with joy. This, I believe, was the case with all the other Koreans in Japan then.

Those who had been singing, while drinking *doburoku* (unrefined *sake*) for diversion, such Japanese popular songs as "Was it a shadow or a willow or Kantarō-*san*?....'' were now openly singing our own songs such as *Toraji, Arirang* and many other popular songs or folk songs we used to sing at home, until we finally began to dance while singing, as we used to do at home, thus to be carried away by our drunkenness and endless joy in our unrestrained revel. In fact, we had spent three generations before we won this national liberation — upon our national pride — not minding being injured to bleed, even dedicating our lives in our effort to win our liberation and freedom — now to be realized, and that in a single moment! Our pleasure was such as to be known only to those who had finally won *it!*

Everyone moved out of his bounds, having finally won his own liberty. In addition, the boss of this construction camp treated us to one *tō* (ca. 18,04 *l*) of *doburoku* (unrefined *sake,* home brew) as a congratulatory gift, and this naturally led our pleasure to surpass its climax. As for myself, I think I still remained a boy retaining his boyish face, but I behaved like a man among the full-fledged men, so the atmosphere then and there must have been creating an agitation so great so that it could usually be unimaginable. Partly because the boss — who had treated us as much as one *tō* of *sake* — was not seen around, our boisterous merrymaking went on and on.

Seeing that fourteen or fifteen of us had drunk one *tō* of *sake* in such a short time, our excitement must have been far from normal. As for myself, I had been carrying a big brass kettle filled with *doburoku* and was going around to fill every cup held by those around, and when the kettle had got light, I remember having put its spout into my mouth to drink what was left in it — only to make myself a sleepwalker!

Though I cannot tell how I was appearing or what sort of dream I was dreaming, I had totally been drunken. There was a man in tears with joy, while hitting upon the table; another man, standing upon the table, was crying: "Long live our freedom!"; the other was dancing around that table like mad; yet the other was mumbling: "I've won! All of us have won!" as if praying to *Amitabha* Buddha in a Buddhist invocation, while hitting upon the rim of the empty bowl with his chop sticks — each of us simply enjoyed drinking, singing, shouting and dancing as much as we liked in our own way, until we all passed out.

None of us asked or tried to find out what it was that had made the Imperialist Japan set us Koreans free literally in a moment; what had caused *that;* who could be the very person who had issued *that* order.

The Koreans there had got drunk with the single statement: "Japan has allowed you freedom!" rather than any amount of alcohol they had drunk then. Whatever gourmet food or whatever expensive treasure we might have been offered, we had already found that: nothing was better than freedom. In fact, we had got so excited or agitated that we had mistaken "the Emperor's announcement of Japan's surrender" for "His allowance of freedom for us Koreans" who had been seeking for *it* generation after generation. Thus it caused everyone of us to pass out as if ascending to heaven!

● **Japan's Unconditional Surrender**

What makes me write so meticulously about that memorable day — August 15, 1945 — is because of those most memorable facts, as follows:

Firstly, Japan's aggressive war — which started from its Invasion into Korea, to be followed by the Sino-Japanese War, to escalate into the Pacific War — was finally brought to an end.

Secondly, the Great Empire of Japan, which had been powerful not only in the Asian region but also in the world, made an unconditional surrender to the other side and the Imperialist Japan was disintegrated. Japan — which started to invade the Korean Peninsula according to "the argument for war with Korea"* which started early in the Meiji era (1868-1912) — had been despising, insulting, exploiting the Korean people, while forcing Japanese customs, culture and so on upon them throughout those seventy years of Japan's colonial rule, under which it had gone so far as to enslave the people there.

*The argument for the invasion of Korea, as advocated by Saigō Takamori (1827-77) during the early Meiji era. The anti-foreign and loyalist ideology of the late Edo period was adopted by the Meiji government along with the slogan "wealth and military strength" and an aggressive policy toward China and Korea. By maintaining her isolation policy, Korea intensified friction with Japan. In 1873, the argument for invasion of Korea became a hot issue, and the cabinet nearly decided in favor of war. Having lost their feudal privileges, the warriors were dissatisfied and launched an antigovernment movement. By engaging in an overseas war, the government intended to soothe the worriers' discontent. But as those who had just returned from an inspection tour in Europe and the U.S., opposed the government plan, which they considered to be premature, pro-war leaders such as Saigō, Itagaki, Etō, Soejima and Gotō resigned. Dissatisfied warriors took advantage of the weakened cabinet and started rebellions……

—— A DICTIONARY OF JAPANESE HISTORY
By Joseph M. Goedertire, C.I.C.M.

*The annexation of Korea: Following the Korean-Japanese annexation treaty of 1910, Korea became Japanese territory. Authority over Korea exercised by Japan was strengthened as a result of the revolt of the Togaku-to Party in 1894 and of the Sino-Japanese war (1894–95) and the Russo-Japanese war (1904–5). After the Russo-Japanese War, a firm policy toward Korea was adopted. In 1907, the emperor of Korea had unexpectedly sent a secret messenger to the International

Peace Conference of the Hague in Holland, with the purpose of presenting the Korean problem. This intensified oppression by Japan, forcing the Korean emperor to abdicate in favor of the crown prince. A Korean-Japanese agreement was concluded, and Japan seized authority over all military and economic matters. Korea became a protectorate. Japan's policy included taking over the leadership, administration, and protection of the country. But this policy meant the total loss of Korea's independence and resulted in her annexation. The Korean people suffered for thirty-five years under Japanese rule. Japan's domination came to an end after the Pacific War in 1945.

—— *A DICTIONARY OF JAPANESE HISTORY*
By Joseph M. Goedertire, C.I.C.M.

And now, we Koreans had finally been released from all those sufferings and tribulations that had lasted as long as seventy years!

Considering all those ambitions the Imperialist Japan had demonstrated so far, it was simply natural as well as inevitable that the Great Empire of Japan should have been brought to such a national ruin. I should say there was no room for sympathy, because they had remained totally inhumane.

They should learn that: injustice is the main cause of defeat. Japan now has made that date — August 15 — the anniversary of the end of World WarⅡ, thus giving a variety of events at various parts of the country. That would be a natural consequence of the war that had lasted as long as more than a dozen of years — causing several millions to be killed in action or to suffer from air raids. It is also known to all that Hiroshima and Nagasaki had suffered atrocious disasters brought about by the atomic bombings — the first and the greatest bombardments for mass murder the world has ever known. In order *not* to forget those disasters and *not* to repeat any such atrocities, the movements for nuclear abolition are also being carried out.

These events or movements are none other than the relics left behind by the war that had lasted for as long as fourteen or even fifteen years — during which men and women and even children were made to turn into imperialists, while the militarism was being drummed into them until all the people in Japan had been made fanatics in imperialism and militarism — which, to my mind, led to their disregard of the sacrifices Okinawa had made and to the miseries Hiroshima and Nagasaki had suffered.

As a result of all these things, what the Japanese called the Great Empire of Japan was brought to collapse. Seen from my point of view, however, it was certain that the Japanese who had survived the war did win the peace. Even though what was called the Great Empire of Japan had been made to collapse because of the war they had started, but the peace was inevitably brought to the people.

On the other hand, there was a nation whose fate was opposite to Japan's. That was Korea.

As I had mentioned before, what was called "the argument for war with Korea" had been brought into being early in the Meiji era (1868-1912). Then, by way of the incident at Kanghwa-dō Island (1875),* about twenty years later (1894) Japan occupied Korean Royal Palace, and at the same time, rushed into the Sino-Japanese War (1894-5).

*Japan tried to open diplomatic relations by means of military coercion and sent the gunboat *Un'yō* to the west coast of Korea. The action was of an intimidating nature. The Japanese gunboat was attacked at the island of Kanghwa by Korean coast guns, but the captain of the boat returned the fire and occupied the fort. Then the Japanese government sent the envoy Kuroda Kiyotaka (1840-1900) to Korea, and the following year an amity treaty was concluded. Korea had to open the port of Pusan and grant consular jurisdiction. This marked the opening of Korea and the beginning of Japanese inroads into Korean territory.

—— *A DICTIONARY OF JAPANESE HISTORY*
By Joseph M. Goedertire, C.I.C.M.

Following this process of Japan's invasion into Korea, it is revealed that: the ultimate purpose of their argument for war with Korea was to conquer the Empire of China under the Qing dynasty — along with the conquest of Korea. But, for some reason or other, the Sino-Japanese war (1894-5) came to an end about half a year or so after its start. The reason for that was because the

Korean people had kept challenging Japan eagerly. In other words, the Sino-Japanese war was no more than a plot like a temporary suspension of war until Japan made its complete conquest of Korea, it seems. As evidence for that, after Japan's occupation of the Korean Royal Palace (1894) and after the end of the Sino-Japanese War (1894–5), and the end of the Russo-Japanese War (1904–5), the Korean Prince was brought to Japan as a hostage, and after having worked out a plot, they managed to establish Government General of Korea for its colonial rule in 1910, thus to keep on swindling and demanding. In 1931, Japan again framed a plot in the northeastern part of China or in what Japan named Manshu-koku (1932–45), and this was to lead to the all-out war between China and Japan — the Sino-Japanese War (1937–45).

Nazi Germany in the West and the Great Empire of Japan in the East had been inflicting pain upon the people — treating them cruelly or slaughtering them, thus to cause the terror worldwide. As the final consequence, in 1941, Japan declared war even against the U.S. The U.S., having received the declaration of war after the surprise attack upon Pearl Harbor, got furious at Japan for having employed the vilest ruse, and this led to the formation of the allied forces of the U.S., the U.K. and France in order to fight against Japan.

This war had come to be called the Great East Asia War by the Tōjō's cabinet. In fact, Japan was to go advancing on and on even as far as Burma (present-day Myanmar), Indonesia and the Malay

Peninsula, thus extending its front. Those crazy aggressive actions will be regarded as inadmissible by anyone. In fact, these invasions after invasions by the Japanese military never ceased to inflict immense persecutions and cruelties even on the innocent civilians living there.

Thus Japan's aggressive war went on and on until it spread from China to all the countries in the Southeast Asia.

This was how Japan had spent more than seventy years at war, starting from "the argument for war with Korea," as was advocated by Saigo Takamori (1827-77) until the Great Empire of Japan must make an unconditional surrender (1945) to their shame, even though the people were allowed to live in peace at long last.

At the same time, we, the Koreans, were also released from the struggles that had lasted as long as more than seventy years, and many of my compatriots were finally able to return to their ancestral land. Those who had been taken to Japan as drafted workers like myself or the women who had been forced to leave home and work as the prostitutes for the Japanese soldiers were also set free according to the proclamation of the unconditional surrender issued by the Japanese Government on August 15, 1945.

Thus the Japanese had their state perish and obtained peace, while the Koreans regained their state and obtained their freedom. As it happened, however, we certainly regained our state, but as for our "having obtained freedom," I cannot help thinking that: we were taken in by the shrewd trick created by the Japanese

Government.

Certainly, having been set free was something indispensable for us to keep living, so to myself nothing was more pleasing than this. But the piece of information that followed was simply crafty or tricky: "From now on, we shall never be concerned with your matter!" That was — as we all agreed — we Koreans had now been thrown out of this Japanese society we had once been forced to enter!

Now, we all agreed that: we had not only been taken out of our native country, but also been thrown out of the Japanese society, when Japan was defeated and it no longer needed us! Thus we were to suffer a double punch of misfortune and mercilessness!

IV

OUR EXPECTATION TO GO HOME

● On the Morning of August 16

The day dawned on August 16. The weather was as good as the day before. I woke up to find it was almost noon. Still I was the sixth or the seventh in rising from the bed among the fifteen or sixteen of us in our camp. So far we had always been kept tense and this had prevented us from sleeping to our heart's content. But now, we had been set free, and this had been so intoxicating to us that we simply got drunk until we were sent to sleep in a profound inebriation. When we woke up, I went out to breathe in the fresh air, still feeling half asleep, but in the sunshine as blazing as ever, I remained absentminded as if I were still in a dream. If anyone so humble as myself were to have any history to hand down to my posterity, what I had experienced the day before would surely make such a one, I think.

In fact, what I had experienced the day before had still been turning round and round in my head which remained empty. Some had already left their bed; others were about to get up from then on; all remained as empty-headed as I was, but all were keeping their heart busy, saying to themselves: "We have been set free now, so we are free to do anything we like...."

So far we had been expected to take breakfast at the same time according to our daily schedule, so in the morning we were usually kept busy, but that morning, everyone was able to take a meal according to his own schedule. Mr. Nakagawa alone, however, remained unchanged, taking breakfast by himself — seated in a grand manner — as he usually was. As for myself, having disliked the attitude he had adopted the day before — when I came back to ask him to join us in listening to the Emperor's announcement — I began to eat, avoiding his company. Strangely enough, no one was talking about that welcome piece of news of the liberation we had finally obtained the day before. All were eating in total silence. I myself had found: something unspeakable was lingering in my mind. The only notion that had clearly come up to my mind was a message to my father at home in Yomoru Village far away beyond the seas and the mountains:

"Father, Your Heungseop, is alive! Yes, we've won the liberty and freedom!"

As it happened, however, we had no means of conveying any such personal emotions as I was feeling then. Japan, whose polity had brought us so much misery, now remained simply overcome by the grief brought about by the Emperor's announcement the day before. Even the military authorities that had inflicted so much menace upon us, having been thrown into consternation, remained simply incompetent in dealing with any of the aftermath of what their militarism had brought about. Their incompetency was simply apparent when seen how they had failed to take any necessary steps concerning us, drafted workers.

None of us had chosen to make ourselves drafted workers! We had been brought here in Japan for the convenience sake of the Great Empire of Japan. When the war was over, therefore, Japan ought to be responsible for bringing everything back to what it used to be. As it happened, however, Japan — when defeated — not only abandoned its responsibility but also evaded its responsibility with utmost cleverness. And, *that* was to be completed by a single declaration they had given us: "From this moment onward, we shall remain unconcerned in your matters!"

On the morning of August 16, too, we ought to have been overjoyed at having won the freedom, while gulping down a celebratory drink, giving cheers, jumping around, and what not! As it happened, however, we simply remained unable to do so, because something swirling in our mind had prevented us from doing so.

I could not help wondering what was it — that boisterous merrymaking we had enjoyed the night before. We all had totally been deprived of our heart and mind by the word "free" so much so that we could not afford to think about where we should stand from then on. Now, the next morning, we could not help wondering what was that boisterous merrymaking we had had the night before. All of us, including myself, had been so much enchanted by the word "freedom" that we could not afford to think of what would become of us from then on.

"What should we do from tomorrow on?" said a man called Yamashita, a little before sixty, from Jeonra Nam Dō, as if saying to himself. Then the man, who had always been with him at work, gave a prompt answer to him, saying:

"You should leave it to the boss."

It sounded as if he was saying to himself. Most of us in the room were hearing this question and answer, but no one said anything, as if they were all agreeing with him. As for myself, too, when unexpectedly set free and left alone with that pronouncement: "From this moment on, we shall remain unconcerned in your matter," I could not help feeling as if I had suddenly fallen into a pit, and thought: the boss would be the only person I could turn to from then on.

What was it that: Japan had brought us here as it wished, and now when the situation had changed, they simply told us to do as we wished to? I could not help saying to myself: "Oh, no! That's not fair at all!"

We should have found it much better and felt more or less thankful if we had been told: "According to the order, you shall be sent back to Korea."

Looking back, we found: Japan had kept neglecting us from the beginning to the very end! I wondered what the Japanese Government was thinking about this situation we were facing now. All of us, wishing that the Boss would manage to dispose of this matter anyhow, finished our meal, while keeping our inner agitation under control.

Even when we returned to our own place in our camp, everyone having fallen into depression, we were all feeling as if holding a wake. Whoever might have seen us then, we should not have appeared those who had just been allowed to enjoy freedom as well as liberation from then on. I, simply unable to remain as I was, went to see the boss in his room, only to find him absent, but his wife told me that he and two of his fellow bosses, who had been controlling each of the three construction camps in this area, had been talking till dawn about what they should do from then on. She sighed over his having gone out somewhere early in the morning without even taking breakfast, as he had done the day before, too. This led me to know the fact that: the bosses were also moving about with such selfless devotion, trying to find out the ways we might follow from then on.

● Mr. Nakagawa's Talk

I returned to my own camp, saying to myself: "I cannot help leaving everything to the Boss...." As it happened, however, there was something like meeting being held there. What if we had happened to have any such a day off unexpectedly? We ought to have had a cup of *sake* even in the morning so we might relax ourselves. But now, things were totally different! None appeared drunk to be red-faced, but they simply remained as humble and quiet as if being engaged in some military drill. What was even more surprising to me was: the leader of this meeting was Mr. Nakagawa, the only Japanese in our camp. Mr. Nakagawa, never minding my having come to join them, kept talking:

"This means that: Japan's Emperor made an unconditional surrender to the combined forces of the U.S., the U.K. and France. So, what *that* army officer said after that Emperor's Announcement of Japan's surrender — "We have permited you to be free" — simply means: "you have already been set free." To my mind, when he said: "We shall no longer be concerned in your matter," what he really meant was: "You have already been set free." What he really meant was: "We are no longer able to be concerned in your matter." Until yesterday's broadcast of the Emperor's announcement of Japan's surrender, you had to obey Japan's order, but at that moment when that broadcast was over, your relationship with Japan had simply become nonexistent. So you have now returned to what the Korean people used to be until thirty and several years ago. Yes! Your wish to be free has finally come true! Everything in your homeland, Korea, has now returned to what it used to be thirty-five years ago. And it has become independent! Your wish has come true! So you need not mind what that army officer said: "Japan will not be concerned in your matter!" You seem to be perplexed at that declaration made by that army officer. But you need not worry about it. I say *this*, because I believe you will be able to cope with anything; you have survived this hardest period of time or the war time in Japan. All you have to do now will be to head for your homeland. Right? Even if you may not be able to go home at once or so soon, if you think you'll be able to go home before long, you'll find it less hard to wait for *the* day. Even if you may have any reason for *not* being able to go home, you can remain here to live on without feeling any embarrassment, or compunction because what had brought you to Japan was none other than this state of Japan! True, Japan was defeated, but its responsibility of having done *it* will not vanish but remain forever. Well, what makes me worry most of all now is: whether or not the ferryboat is available. If available, the Government ought to arrange one boat after another for you. Anyway, you should head for Shimonoseki with the harbor for the ferry steamers that connect Shimonoseki ⑪ (in Japan) and Busan ⑧ (in Korea). Then, somehow or other, things will turn out all right."

What Mr. Nakagawa mentioned last — "things will turn out all right" — had already been repeated again and again in his speech. To tell the truth, *this* had already become my own motto while managing to survive for these eight months since I ran away from that coal mine.

This conception — commonly possessed by those who had to keep living without any particular aim or prospect to live for — ought to have called forth a favorable response from those who were present there.

Mr. Nakagawa went on:

"I cannot tell how many Koreans are there in this island of Kyūshū alone, but I am sure a great many Koreans will rush to the port for the ferryboats. Even though the ferryboats are available, their number will be far from large. …. Considering this and that, I think you had better leave here as soon as possible. There is one more problem I must mention: since that broadcasting of the Emperor's announcement of Japan's surrender was over, all the factories, construction sites, coal mines, and even the government offices all over this country have come to cease their function, I think. Why? Because all the government systems in this country must be reorganized into those of the victor nations. At that moment when that broadcast of the Emperor's announcement of Japan's surrender was over, your state has been released and you have won the freedom, while Japan has been sent to the situation totally different from yours. Then, what will happen? All the Japanese, including myself, have already been driven into no working or no income since yesterday. No one can tell how long such a situation as this will last. All the decisions will be made and performed by the Occupation Armies of the victorious nations. All Japan could do then would be waiting for the decisions made by them before obeying them. So from now on, the Japanese people will have to face the crucial time of non-working and non-income. Concerning this matter alone, this will turn out to be your own problem, too. The reason is: even if you may go to the port to take the ferry boat for Korea, it is only when a ferry boat is available that you can return home. What if thousands of people, or even tens of thousands of people rushed to the port? While waiting for your turn to get on board, you'll have to spend many days or even months! What if you have to wait for several months? You'll have to think about how to keep yourselves alive. I do wish all those factories and construction works would be resumed in a month or in a few months, but it is unknown until you yourselves go and find it out. What if you have to wait month after month? What will you do to keep yourselves alive? This seems to me the greatest problem you will have to face, now that you have won your liberty. Whatever we may say, we must eat as long as we are alive, and in order to eat, we must earn money. On the other hand, seeing Japan *now* so flurried after having been defeated, I don't think they can afford to consider the situations of the Korean people — thousands of or even tens of thousands of Korean people — who are wishing to return home.

The reason is: the millions of soldiers dispatched abroad will be repatriated; Besides, those who had migrated abroad — in Korea, Manchuria,* China and Southeast Asian countries — hundreds of thousands of them — must be driven back to Japan, too. So it seems to me: the Japanese government will be kept too agitated only by these two matters.

*a so-called independent state (1932–45) created by Japan in the northeastern provinces of China.

As for myself, I have grown so weary of being Japanese that I have sincerely sworn to have ceased to be Japanese. But now, it is quite certain that I am the only one Japanese *here*. Considering this fact, I could not remain unconcerned with you. I know what I might think of is quite limited, but I've dared to talk of something drastic I've kept in my mind, wishing it might be of any help to you. Thank you for your having listened to me so attentively. My speech is over. All I wish now is: you will have a good talk among yourselves, while showing your wisdom, so that all of you may return home as soon as possible — even by an hour!"

While listening to Mr. Nakagawa, I was being impressed by his great intelligence, even though he had once said his school career was no more than the six years at the primary school. What was it that had enabled him to give such cool thinking to every aspect of things before he made a forecast of everything? On the other hand, I could not help thinking: if all the Japanese were like Mr. Nakagawa, we, the Koreans, would have been saved from *the* war and *the* invasion the Japanese had inflicted upon us, the Asian peoples. I, even though still remaining a boy, did feel it necessary to have taken into my own spirit such intention and wisdom as were possessed by Mr. Nakagawa.

I had come in contact with several Japanese, since I was brought to Japan as a drafted worker about one year and a half before the War was over, but I had to find most of them were looking down upon me. One of the exceptions was Mr. Ura I had mentioned in earlier chapters, who, even if he had perceived me planning to run away from the coal mine, casually suggested me how to do *it* successfully. This helped me to make a successful runaway from the coal mine so that I could live longer than otherwise.

Another reason that makes me regard Mr. Ura as a fine Japanese was: Japan at that time, if mentioned in a word, was *darkness* itself, and one was easily called "an unpatriotic fellow" or "a traitor," and everything was operated according to the order of the armed forces. Then, what if one were to have one's own affiliated person run away — not to mention to help him flee? One would surely be thrown into the slammer!

Mr. Ura, though he had been well aware of such a risk, did choose to run *the* risk for me. I, eighteen years old then, was to learn from his example what *human courage* means.

Another person, who had exerted a great influence upon me or I should say upon my life, was Mr. Nakagawa I have already mentioned. Seen from my point of view, he appeared somehow or other self-centered and free from control. But authentic was his view of mutuality as a human being, which he seemed to have established from his own situation. Even though he was eccentric, it seemed certain to me that he had kept an extremely normal spirit and humanity as a Japanese citizen at this period of time. I still remember the criticism of Japan he had offered when we were talking face to face while drinking:

"We, the Japanese, are making a war against the U.S. and the U.K., calling them ogres & beasts, even though we have never seen or spoken to them."

At another time when he was talking of the atomic bombings, he said:

"If one of them had been dropped on Tokyo and if anything had happened to the Prince of the Royal Family of your country, we should not have had any excuse for that...."

This worry he had revealed about the Korean Prince — who had been brought to Japan as a hostage even though he was still very young — also attracted my attention.

In his talk on August 16, too, Mr. Nakagawa's thoughtfulness and consideration for us Koreans were apparent, and this did move me even to tears. We, Koreans, had been driven into the situation in which we honestly remained totally helpless and unable to tell what we should do then. So far all we should do was to follow the order given by the Japanese side, and now we were simply at a loss, totally left alone, and that all of a sudden.....

"Being allowed to be free" was welcome, indeed, but when we were "left unconcerned," we found *it* totally perplexing, as if we had been blindfolded and discarded on a desert island beyond a vast expanse of waters.

Then, none other than Mr. Nakagawa came to encourage us and instructed us what we should do. But we Koreans — a dozen or so in number — remained unable to find out a solution, mainly because of the money. We had all agreed to return home in Korea. But the ferryboat was only for Pushan. Then, the problem was how to reach home from Pushan.

None of us could walk home from Pushan. As for myself, it was to take three days and nights by train before reaching my home. The others were all from the South or Seoul at present and southward — Gangwon-dō, Gyeonggi-dō, Jeolla-dō, Chungcheong-dō or Gyeongsang-dō — all of them were too far away to go on foot. There was another problem, too. As for myself, still a boy, I remained far away from wine and women, but the others had spent most of the money they had earned on gambling — *hanafuda* or a deck of Japanese playing cards — or in a red-light district, which used to be found at any town even though it was in time of war. Thus no one had saved any money.

Until the end of the war, we had been living on the motto of "The entire population of Japan shall be united in a single motto of exterminating the U.S. & the U.K.," and none had even dreamt that the war would come to an end so soon and so suddenly at noon on August 15 (1945).

In the case of us Koreans here who had been made to live according to the order given from above, it seemed totally nonsense to save any money. So it was only natural that we had not saved any money. A few of us had even got some money in advance from the boss.

Thus our problem then was how we should adjust the matter

according to how much money we each had possessed and how far away from Pusan each of our homes was. In the final analysis, we had been afraid of committing any immorality by allowing ourselves to deviate from our brotherly love. Leaving even a single fellow courtryman behind would become our racial dishonor — such a notion as this must have been occupying our heart and mind.

Thus our argument went on and on for a few days. So far we had been fellow workers at the same construction camp, but now we had been talking as compatriots, and it was far from easy to reach any conclusion.

● Thinking about How to Go Home

Naturally we all wished to go home, but the distance we had before us was different from person to person, while the expenditure for reaching there was naturally different, too. Since we were compatriots, nothing would be better if we were all able to go home without leaving any one of us behind. As a matter of fact, however, every one of us had led his own way of life so far: some had been eager to save money for later use, while others were simply spending all the money he had earned in eating and drinking, and so on. Ideally speaking, it might have been best if we all had been able to go home together, but as a matter of fact, it turned out impossible. Among all of us, I had come from the farthest prefecture or Hwanghae-*dō*.

As for returning home together with other Koreans, I was quite ready to go on board the ship with them, but once we reached our homeland — wherever it might be — I was quite ready to go home even on foot all the way. So, I asked them *not* to count me as a member of any group of theirs.

As the days went by, both Mr. Yamasaki from Gangweon-*do* and Mr. Umimoto from Gyeonggi-*do* left their group for the same reason as I had given. This naturally led that meeting only for those from Chungcheong-*do,* Jeonra-*do,* and Gyeongsang-*do.*

We, having already been liberated, were all legally independent citizens of Korea, and still we kept calling each other by the assumed name or by the alias — without employing our real name, or even the Japanese-style names we had been given several years before. *This,* I said to myself, would surely lead us to be totally separated from one another, and this prospect had made me feel even more regrettable than anything else. Talking about our racial identity or talking about our returning home together was important, indeed, but once we returned home, we should naturally be called by our real name. Then they should inevitably be separated from each other for ever, I was afraid.

On the fourth night after the end of the war, we were given an informal talk by Mr. Kunimoto, our boss. First of all, he mentioned the broadcast of the Emperor's announcement of Japan's surrender. Then he explained what *that* meant, saying:

"The Emperor himself declared the end of the war, and Japan

had unconditionally accepted all of the articles in the Potsdam Declaration with a variety of conditions in it. What has liberated us, while making us independent, is an article that goes: "Japan shall lose all the rights it used to have in all the regions it had occupied so far." All of our sufferings so far have been rewarded, and our long-felt national wish to regain our land has been finally realized. And now, we have decided to leave here by the end of this month of August. Yes, we shall soon be on our way home!"

He went on:

"Returning home is also one of the duties we are expected to perform. In addition, now that Japan has been defeated, the national emotions must unusually be intensified. So the sooner we leave here, the better it will be not only to ourselves but also to the Japanese. As for how to return home, I'll leave it to each of you. I do hope you will be ready for your departure from here by the appointed date. I think you have already had your own meetings and had a good talk among yourselves, and now I hope you will observe all those decisions we, the chiefs, have made for you."

At the and of his speech, he said:

"Well, nowadays, you seem to have been too busy to enjoy drinking. So, this evening, I hope you'll enjoy drinking. This is on me! I do hope you will make it a happy memory for you to bring home with you!"

For the latest three days or so, all of us, probably having been mentally fatigued at the matter of our going home, had drunk much less than usual. So, we were simply happy to accept the Boss' treat! We did enjoy drinking, while making a big fuss, even though not so noisy as on the night of August 15. I myself had got so drunk as to become unsteady on my feet. Mr. Nakagawa, the Japanese, was drinking among us, while remaining completely calm. as usual. During this happy occasion, none of us gave any opinion about the talk the boss had given us at the beginning.

All of us had agreed with the conclusion the Boss had given. So far I had never drunk so much as I had to walk with a tottering gate. But, that was the first and only night when I wanted to get drunk. On the night of August 15, I drank, because I was so pleased with the freedom we were finally allowed to enjoy; I got tipsy and noisy until I drank myself unconscious. But, as for that night, I could not help feeling like drinking together, getting drunk together and talking together with all those dear old comrades of mine.

Somehow or other, I had been feeling as if that was the final opportunity for us to drink together, get drunk together and talk together. Now that it was decided that one should adopt any means available in going home, it was quite probable that some would leave here the following day. Even if I might say I should like to talk with them, the number was limited — only two from the neighboring prefectures Mr. Yamasaki from Gangweon-*dō* ③ and Mr. Umimoto from Gyeonggi-*dō* ⑭. I left the drinking party, which was still at its height, and having returned to my own quarters, I waited for them to return.

As for my own returning home, I had already made a decision: first of all, I was to go to Hakata Harbor, which had been made *the* anchorage. That was all I had been able to think of so far. I could not tell whether or not any ship was available there. I had once heard that: the number of Koreans, who had been brought to Japan as drafted workers, was several millions. Apparently, here in Kyūshū alone, several hundreds of thousands of Koreans would come to the harbor. Suppose one ship would take three hundred people on board, three boats a day would carry nine hundred people home. In ten days, nine thousand people would be carried; in one hundred days, ninety thousand people would be on board the ship. All the money I had with me then was three hundred yen. This meant: I must get on board the ship before I spent all this money, Yes, I must. "Whatever might happen, I must return home!" said I to myself. That decision alone had been made my supreme directions.

By and by, I had fallen asleep. I had been intoxicated. After all, my wish to talk with others about this matter had been blown off. So far — or when we were at work — we used to wake up each other, but since August 15, we were on holiday every day, and however long we might be in bed — till noon or even till night — none minded it and none woke us up. Anyway, I seemed to have been dead drunk…..

When I woke up. it had already been nearly at noon the following day. I washed my hands at the kitchen sink of stone at one side of the dining room, and after having taken a pinch of salt out of the lidless pot, I put it into my mouth to brush my teeth with my middle finger and went out of the rattling wooden door to find we had had another fine day. The sun had already risen nearly as high as the roof of our camp. That thatch of *hinoki* bark made me feel rather sorry to part from it. In a literary magazine, I had once read of a traveler who, while gazing on the moon high in the mid-sky, indulges himself in sentimentality; and now I was to find myself being so sentimental even while bathing in such hot sunshine in mid-summer! Indeed, that seemed a funny experience even to myself.

Then I went back into the kitchen-cum-dining room, and took a meal after having served myself the boiled rice from the rice-tub left there and the *miso*-soup which was getting cold. Since the night before, when our boss told us that: it was till the end of that month (August) that we were allowed to stay there, I had found myself having begun to feel sentimental about whatever I might be doing there.

Where had it gone — all that pent-up resentment against Japan? Fifteen months had passed since I was forced to come to Japan under the pretext of commandeering. If I had been at home, it would have been an insignificant lapse of time, but now in Japan, I was feeling as if dozens of years had passed and I had already been a grownup and even a middle-aged man before I knew it — or as if I had been living in a phantom..... So far we had been taken about and driven hard like pigs, horses or cattle, but now we were living in a situation where not a single word of complaint would be given to us by any Japanese, while we were finally able to fulfill our wish to go home! Even the mere thought of *it* did fill me with infinite pleasure, making me feel as if I were in a dream — which had now turned out a reality!

As for the money needed for the ship we would take, and all the other realities I should have to face from then on, I did not mind at all, saying to myself:

"Nothing ventured, nothing gained! Somehow or other everything will turn out all right, just as it has done so far since I was commandeered and brought to Japan — to lead a miserable life at the coal mine, to make a runaway trip at the risk of my life, while employing a variety of craftsmanship of a *ninja* (spy craft), wishing to evade any military service — everything shall go up to heaven and fly away!"

If only I could leave here and get on board the ship, I should not ask for anything. If only I returned home, I should be able to live on our own mountain, on our own farm and rice field! I'll work on them so that my father, brother and sister might live a better life; this will lead me to take a wife! Then the hardships I had to go through here would simply vanish far into the sky! This was what I was saying to myself, while taking brunch — with little appetite.

Setting aside that day, I was going to prepare for returning home on the day that followed so that I might reach the port in Hakata as soon as possible — even a single day sooner!

Since August 15 when we were set free, we had had enough time to do anything we liked, because we were no longer expected to work. This must have been the same in all the construction camps and all the other places of work all over Japan. Everyone — both Japanese and Korean — was resting himself or herself. The Japanese, having been set free from the long, long war, would have been feeling relieved as well as bitterly disappointed at their defeat.

On the other hand, we, Koreans — having retrieved our freedom, but *not* yet having received any practical guidance for returning home — had been lost in a fog and driven into such tendency as to act in an ad-hoc manner, and this had kept us spiritually far from taking any rest.

About a couple of days after the talk given by the boss of our construction camp, those from such prefectures as Gyeongsang-*do* or Jeonra-*do* or Chungcheong-*do* began to leave for Hakata in twos or threes.

In the meantime, I was able to have a talk firstly with Mr. Yamasaki from Gangweon-*do*. He was from Cheorwon — where the local farmers were engaged in slash-and-burn agriculture on the mountainside under the leadership of his family. Even to such a remote village as that, there had arrived an allotment for drafted workers, and since he was unable to appoint any other person in the same village, he chose to make himself a drafted worker. At first, he was taken to a coal mine at Yamada in Fukuoka Prefecture, and after having worked there for nearly a year, he made an escape, having seized an opportunity. He had been drafted nine months earlier than I. At home, he had his wife forty-three years old — two years younger than he — and the eldest daughter who was twenty, the second daughter seventeen, the eldest son fifteen, the third daughter eleven, and the elder son nine. So they were seven if he returned home.

Their terraced fields had been cultivated by themselves, but since they had been left unattended for a couple of years since he left home, they might have returned to the wilderness, as he was afraid. Anyway, we decided to accompany each other till we reached Busan.

Mr. Yamasaki, the father of five children, more than twenty years senior to myself, still seemed to have remained so pure of heart as was sensed even by such a boy as myself. But such purity as was retained by him had come to do him some harm; some were calling him "a screwball (turning to the left)." But now, those who had regarded him as such had already gone. When I consulted him about going home, he said: "I wonder why they were hurrying so much when they cannot tell which port we should go to," and "I have already been made to hang around and around, so I'd rather *not* stop off anywhere on my way home." He also said to me: "At home, we live in the neighboring counties, so helping each other will be good for both of us. I, too, when I was brought here, had taken the train and the ferryboat for the first time in my life. So I have been feeling uneasy, too, as you must have been."

We talked about many other things, and I found that he was very sensible and reliable — more substantial-minded than he appeared to be. So far we, the workers at this construction camp, had seldom talked to each other about anything special or important, so it was the first time for me to have had any such substantial talk with someone as a colleague of mine.

His home — Cheolweon in Gangwon-*dō* Prefecture — was about the middle of the Korean Peninsula. That was also where the Yongbong River — which runs along one side of my own village or Yomoru Village in Goksan County of Hwanghae-*dō* Prefecture — has its origin.

Now that a week had passed since the War was over, those who still remained here at this construction camp were only three: I and Mr. Yamasaki and one more from Gyeonggi-*dō* Prefecture — who was called Mr. Umimoto. Gyeonggi-*dō* Prefecture was the central area of Korea, where Japan had established the capital for its direct control of Korea; it faces the Yellow Sea (the Hwanghae) in front — with a big city called Gyeongseong (present-day Seoul) in it. Formerly, Gaeseong — just in the north of Gyeongseong — used to be the capital of Korea.

In order to reach my home in Hwanghae-*dō* Prefecture, I was to go through those cities in that capital area. That was why I had felt like offering to travel together with Mr. Umimoto, even though I had not had any particular mingling with him so far.

● Mr. Umimoto's Way of Working

Mr. Umimoto was a man of few words. He never indulged in any particular diversion; he had always remained obscure and vague. It was only several days before that I happened to learn he came from an island in the Yellow Sea, where he had naturally been a fisherman.

His breast was as swollen as might be associated with a woman's; in fact, his whole body was so muscular and tall that he was the strongest in this camp. As far as I knew, Mr. Umimoto's group had always been by far the best in the digging of the air-raid cave, while the other groups had remained so slow as if they had agreed to. I myself — having been in charge of attendance register as well as recording how each group was making progress every day — was able to tell how far the works were going on.

The boss of the camp, having administered the record I had made, reported it to the military before receiving the labor charge; so it was what was called "progress payment." Because of this system, every time an account was settled on the 15th every month, Mr. Umimoto's group used to receive the best pay in the camp. The workers in the camp being all Koreans — excepting Mr. Nakagawa — there used to appear such prejudice and vanity as had been retained among ourselves. Especially among those from Gyeongsang-*dō* Prefecture, some openly called Mr. Umimoto's group "half-Japanese" out of jealousy. The boss, who had heard of it, said to those from that prefecture:

"Don't you feel ashamed of saying such a thing behind his back? Do give a careful thinking about *it*. All of us, including myself as the boss, and all of you — including Umimoto — are working in the same situation and on the same footing. The only thing that differentiates us is: whether or not we are working with proper sincerity. True we have had our land colonized and we have been deprived of our ancestral land. But, what if we cannot do *it* properly — even the work given to us? That will turn out none other than our own disgrace. Give a careful thinking whether or not you can say this and that about someone working honestly. We are working *not* for the Japanese Empire *but* for ourselves. By doing *it* properly, we shall be able to look down upon the other party. The half-hearted persons are more likely to envy others or speak ill of others. I come from Gyeongsang-*dō* Prefecture, as you do. We should feel ashamed of ourselves by seeing Umimoto working exactly as he should, and that in total silence. Umimoto himself ought to have a grudge against Japan, just as we all do. But he has suppressed it with a proper might. That's something to need iron nerves."

I was then on my way to the toilet, but I could not help standing to listen to the boss for a while, but since I felt as if I had made myself an eavesdropper, I stopped going to the toilet and returned to where I was expected to stay.

I never revealed what I had heard then, partly because I had a weak point of having overheard the boss' advice given to those from the same prefecture as his, and partly because I somehow felt I should keep it to myself even though I could not tell why.

In less than half a month since this occurrence, the war was over. And now those from Gyeongsang Prefecture and Jeonra Prefecture were leaving the camp for their own home a few days after the War was over. Those who had spoken ill of others and those who had been spoken ill of were shaking hands with each other, exchanging their hearty wishes of "Take care!" and "Stay well!"

Now those left behind were three of us, who were from the farthest from Japan. I succeeded in talking Mr. Yamasaki into accompanying me; and we two tried to invite Mr. Umimoto to join us.

I had been able to talk to Mr. Yamasaki with comparative ease, but when I came to talk to Mr. Umimoto, I felt tense for some reason or other, probably because he was a man of "iron nerves," as the Boss had once mentioned. Having still remained more or less far from "full-fledged," I could not help feeling tense as well as nervous. What was more, he was not only muscular and tanned but also as tall as almost two meters. To make the matter worse, his face, having been covered with small, round holes, could not help appearing very forbidding. Mr. Yamasaki, whose real surname was Hwang, was from Gangweon-*do* Prefecture ③, while Mr. Umimoto, whose real surname was Bian, was from Gyeonggi-*do* Prefecture ⑭.

That was the first time for me to introduce myself formally to

Mr. Yamasaki and to Mr. Umimoto. As for what I had learned about the former, I had already mentioned. Now, Mr. Umimoto said: his father was a fisherman in a small island on the Hwang-hae (Yellow Sea). In 1875 (the 8th year of Meji), when the Japanese military first attempted to land the Korean Peninsula, they set out a gun-fighting against the Korean farmers on Ganghwa Island (P.257), and his own island was quite close to that memorable island. It had less than thirty families on it. There, he said, they used to call the Japanese *Weigui* (Japanese ogres). In my village, we used to call the Japanese *Weinom* (Japanese chaps). Different districts in Korea seem to have had different ways of calling the Japanese with irrepressible hatred for nearly eighty years — throughout the three eras of Meiji (1868-1912), Taisho (1912-1926) and Showa (1926-1989). In fact, throughout these eighty years, all the Koreans had to keep living with their heart filled with such vexation and sorrow, while being impressed by such human cruelties and foolishness on their mind. Looking back and realizing all these facts, I could not help feeling pity for the Koreans rather than the indignation against the Japanese.

Mr. Umimoto, having heard my offer to accompany him, kindly accepted it, saying: "I'll be happy to go with you." Thus we agreed that: the sooner, the better, and this decided us to leave there following the day — on August 23, which I still remember.

Now, we — Mr. Yamasaki, Mr. Umimoto and I — paid the same sum of money to buy from the boss one *shō* (ca. 1.8 liter)

of *doburoku* or unrefined *sake*, and inviting Mr. Nakagawa —
who would be left alone if we were gone — we arranged to give a
banquet that night.

● Drinking *Doburoku*

So far I had drunk with Mr. Nakagawa twice, but not with Mr.
Yamasaki nor with Mr. Umimoto. But, as we gradually got slightly
intoxicated, our conversation became lively.

At first, Mr. Nakagawa asked us:

"I'm far from good at Korean geography, but is it for any
geographical reason that you three alone are still remaining here?"

This led me to raise my hand, saying "Yes," and explained to
him:

"As you have *ken* (prefecture) in Japan, we have *dō* (prefecture)
in Korea, too, and we three come from neighboring *do*s. Those
who had already started, too, had made their own party according
to the *do* or the *gun* (county) they come from. Since all of us were
brought to Japan so unexpectedly, we all remain far from sure of
our way back. As for myself, I had never taken the train or the ship
before I was brought to Japan. So I simply could not tell even the
name of the line of our train we were made to take or where our
ship was heading for."

"That sounds as if you had been slaves," said Mr. Nakagawa.

"That's right. We had been made slaves — slave themselves"
said Mr. Umimoto, whose Japanese was not better than mine, but

he went on:

"I was fishing every day. My boat was small. That day, too, I was on my way to my work of fishing, when a truck of the Japanese Army came to pick me up and took me as far as Seoul. There were three Koreans in the truck; at Seoul we were made separate. I alone was brought to Japan. I was made to work at a coal mine. I was always hungry and could not understand the Japanese language. The coal hewer was cruel to me, calling me a fool, while hitting me and kicking me. I could not endure their cruelties, so I ran away. Then I heard the Army's construction camp was safe. I went to the Navy Base at Hiroshima and begged them to let me work there. Isn't it strange that: we were forced to come to Japan by the military, but I had to beg the military — with my palms together as if in prayer — so I might work for them? At night, I wept, covering my head with a top *futon*-quilt. Indeed, I felt sad and angry; I shall never forgive Japan even after I'm no more. Can you understand my feelings, Mr. Nakagawa?....."

Drops of tears came falling from Mr. Umimoto's eyes.

Mr. Nakagawa, who had been glaring at Mr. Umimoto with his left eye, which had kept him from being totally blind, said to him:

"I can understand you very well. We are all human beings, whether we are Korean or Chinese or English; still we held other nations in contempt, giving them a lot of pains.... It's simply deplorable! As for myself, because I had become one-eyed, I have been made to come down to go around from one construction camp after another. But now, *this* makes me feel as if I had a wider view than those who have a couple of eyes, even if it may sound strange to you. I was born to be a difficult person and rather hard to go with others. But when you say you cannot forgive Japan even when you are no more, I feel as if I could tell what is making you say: "I shall never forgive Japan, even after I am no more.""

Mr. Nakagawa went on:

"To my mind, now that you have had that unfortunate connection with Japan cut off, you'll be able to do anything you like at home, and that as much as you like — for yourself and for your own family; I believe: *that* will surely lead to the benefit of your country, too. *That* will also lead to get your back on Japan and the Japanese, thus to make them realize your pent-up resentment..... As a farewell greeting, this may sound rather wishy-washy, but since we have eaten from the same pot, I hope you'll not stir up any trouble among ourselves. This is the last evening for us to have a talk stiff and formal and to sleep under the same roof. So I hope, you will have a pleasant drink and a sound sleep — in preparation for your departure tomorrow."

This was the gist of the speech Mr. Nakagawa, a Japanese, offered to us, the three Koreans, who had still remained there. All this while, both Mr. Yamasaki and I remained silent and listened to him.

The last thing Mr. Umimoto said that night was impressive to me:

"It cannot be helped, because we are all on our way to go along the course of life. *Life* offers us varieties of things. But whatever might be said about *it*, *now* is the most important, isn't it?" said Mr. Umimoto.

"Yes, indeed!"

I responded to him before I knew it.

I now realize: this conception — "*now* is the most important" — was to be of great help throughout my life later on. This also turned out to be a great activator for me to inspire myself when I got depressed. To myself, who, after all, had to be left alone in Japan or the strangers' land, planning my life in the future was something like "dreaming in a dream." So, this single motto alone — "*Now* is the most important" — was to make me "manage to live on" even to this day — in Japan. Frankly speaking, I could not afford to think seriously about my life in the future, because I was simply kept busy in eking out a bare existence from day to day.

As for the regrets and complaints given by Mr. Umimoto, Mr. Nakagawa, a Japanese, dodged them by presenting his parting words toward the Koreans, which Mr. Umimoto received by saying: "*Now* is the most important," and this led to their mutual understanding or sharing their feelings, it seemed to me. Seeing them talking like good friends, I could not help feeling the utmost satisfaction with my own response given at the right moment. I never forget how pleasant I was that night!

It may sound exaggerated if I employ the word "respect" in

expressing my feelings toward Mr. Nakagawa, that one-eyed person, but in fact, I was feeling like making myself his disciple. As for the way how a man should live, how we should see the world we live in, or how we should cope with the changes in the situations, he had stood immensely far away from myself who had still remained immature as a man. The thought of my having to part with Mr. Nakagawa I had regarded as my hero did prevent me from falling asleep that night. The more I tried to fall asleep, the more items that had come into my life so far — the war, having been drafted, the coal mine, a variety of men and women I met after having run away from the coal mine, my father, younger brother and sister and friends at home, and even the glimmering fishes in the clear water of the River Yongbong came back into my endless memories, keeping myself unusually heated.

● My Farewell Speech

Our pleasure was unspeakably great, now that our long-time enemy had perished! Our land was miraculously retrieved to us to be an independent nation! And now, we were about to go home without any scruples!

On the other hand, I was being amazed at what was happening in my mind where a variety of memories — not only pleasant ones but also sad and miserable ones — came rushing to myself to run and run around myself as if they had turned into something endearing to me and inseparable from me!

I could not help wondering how those who had left there earlier than we, three, managed to conquer such complicated uneasiness they must have been feeling before leaving here. Until I came to notice the day was gradually dawning outside the shutters kept open with the wooden props, I remained sleepless because of that endless circle of meditation I had been thrown into throughout that short night in summer.

The day dawned. Now was the time I was to give a farewell speech to Mr. Nakagawa, which I had composed and recited again and again during that sleepless night:

Day after day, we had been thinking endearingly about our own home, simply wishing to return there. And today, our wish is about to be realized. On the other hand, Mr. Nakagawa, who has always been kind to us, will have to face not a few mortifications and sorrows as a Japanese. But please remember: we are always praying for you, believing you'll overcome all those difficulties so that you may lead a new life!"

I had composed and repeated this parting speech to offer him during that sleepless night.

Fifteen months had passed since I was brought to Japan, and I had come in contact with many Japanese, but it was only two of them that had made me feel like offering my heart-felt respect or made me wish to follow their example — because of something authentic they had kept within themselves.

One of them was Mr. Nakagawa. It was only a little more than a couple of months that I had been with him under the same roof, but I had been fascinated with and attracted by his great discernment. Now that I was to bid my last farewell to such a person as that, I did wish to offer him my heartfelt courtesy. Probably this having been perceived by him, I could see his eye filled with tears. I myself, who had given him our farewell greeting, had my eyes blurred. To my surprise, Mr. Umimoto from Gyeonggi-do, who had once said he would not be able to forgive Japan even after he was no more, was now grasping Mr. Nakagawa's hands, and would not let them go, while they were gazing at each other. For myself, who still remained young, it was totally impossible to tell what they were talking of and pledging to each other in total silence.

This sight of them did reveal the fact of us human beings: even if our races or nationalities are different, if we stand as individuals, there comes into being something that runs through each other, and this will naturally lead to our familiarity, respect and affection to each other. But, when we come to stand as different races or different nations, our abilities to understand each other, to sympathize with each other, and to help each other will become less and less active until we come to despise each other, insult each other and even use violence against each other! I do wonder what sort of mechanism of human psychology brings about such phenomena!

Now, Mr. Nakagawa, too, though remaining silent, was shaking hands with Mr. Umimoto again and again.,

As for Mr. Yamasaki from Gangweon-do, he had simply left the room by himself, when my speech was over. I myself, having been left alone, felt it awkward to stay there any longer. This led me to say to Mr. Nakagawa, as if trying to separate the two hand-shakers:

"Then, Mr. Nakagawa, I'll be going! Please, take care!"

Soon, we, three, were running down along the steep, narrow path upon the hillside without stopping — led by Mr. Yamasaki, followed by myself, and by Mr. Umimoto. On reaching the ordinary road, we all looked up toward the hill we had just left behind.

There we saw Mr. Nakagawa keeping his hand raised high — with the upper half of his body naked — standing at the edge of the open ground of red earth, where a week before — at noon on August 15 — we heard what was called the broadcast of the Emperor's announcement of Japan's surrender. We three, standing side by side, made a profound bow toward the hill, and responded to Mr. Nakagawa by raising our hand high. So far I had never felt any sorrow nor loneliness in parting with anyone, since I was always anticipating the future I was about to face from then on. But now, there was something special in this parting. Of course, I — now on my way home — was jumping at heart, but at the same time, my prospect that I should never again be able to meet

Mr. Nakagawa — someone so special to myself — made me feel unexpectedly lonely. Since our parting had occurred at the moment when I was facing the *future* of my own self and when my own native land of Korea began to give a brilliant flutter toward the future, I had been affected even more greatly by this parting of ours.

● My First Step for Returning Home

About a little more than eight months before, when I was about to run away from Sumitomo Colliery in Karatsu, I kept saying to myself: "I shall never return *here* even if it should cost my life!" But now, I was leaving *here* with my heart quite in peace — free from any trouble that might occur after my disappearance here. In fact, I was feeling even a sort of nostalgia when I thought we should never meet each other again.

Until a week before, Mr. Nakagawa, though living under the same roof, was a member of the nation that had conquered our country, and this had allowed him to have such a status and a footing as might have allowed him to despise us and treat us with cruelty, if he had wanted to. But after that broadcasting of the Emperor's announcement of Japan's surrender, any such status and authority as had been possessed by Mr. Nakagawa, were washed away in a moment as if a landslide had occurred.

As mentioned before, Mr. Nakagawa, having disparaged the authority and power given to him, had simply thrown them away without any hesitation. Most people, if they were allowed to use their power and authority, would employ them properly or push their luck too far. But Mr. Nakagawa, a man of justice in the true sense of the word, had exterminated any such pride or ambition only by himself. This had once led me to weigh up the relative merits of Mr. Nakagawa and my birthplace, and to wrestle with the problem of choice between them, but after all I could not win over the natural power that had stuck to the native place itself. I had never regretted leaving the land and the polity of Japan behind, but the person I should like to offer my heart-felt thanks to was Mr. Ura, the coal hewer at the coal mine, and the person I had still felt attached to was Mr. Nakagawa. In fact, it was with such a complicated frame of mind as this that I took my first step toward returning home.

We three, after coming down the hill, crossed the road there, and went on and on, jumping across the ridges in the fields or following the footpath between the rice fields until we found out the railroad so that we could fellow it as far as the nearest station. In those days, the train on the Amagi Line used to come and go once in a couple of hours, if I remember right.

The train we caught then arrived there nearly at 10 a.m.; it was the second train that had arrived there that day. We had been told that: the ship we should take was to leave the port of Hakata. So, I, who had once been to and from Hakata, was to serve as a guide.

It was around noon when we got off the train at Hakata Station. That was the third time that I had been in Hakata. The first time was when I ran away from Hoshiyama Construction Camp in order *not* to be made a volunteer soldier; I went through the Hakozaki Pinery to reach the Camp at Itatsuki Air Port — by way of the plaza of Hakata Station. The second time was one month later: around mid-June or two days after the great air raid upon Hakata.

Now was the third time I had presented myself there — two months later — when I was openly set free and was expecting to go home, leaving behind all those vexations I had kept so far! The station building itself remained as it used to be immediately after that air raid, but what I saw around had changed to an unbelievable extent! This led me to keep saying to myself in amazement: "What's happening?"

● The Crowds of People at Hakata Harbor

To say nothing of the waiting room in the station building, the station square had been filled with throngs of people milling around. Among them, those in the threadbare military uniform were extremely bony, their eyes powerless but restless, as if in pursuit of any game that might come across their way at any moment. This must have been attracting the eyes of the locals in Hakata, too. My companions — Hwang and Bian — were also being amazed at the sight of them.

"What are all those soldiers?" asked Bian.

All I could say was: "Well, I'm not sure."

Then I recalled what I had seen at the camp we had left behind that morning: It was soon after I came to that camp. We, who had been working on the air-raid shelter on the hillside, used to return to the camp to have lunch. One day, when we were at table noisily, the two low-ranking soldiers in a wash-worn half-sleeved shirt and a pair of knee trousers — each hanging a pair of canteens on their left shoulder — made an abrupt appearance at the entrance to the mess-room, and called out in a loud voice:

"Salute!"

When we all turned our surprised look toward them, they said:

"We have come to ask for some boiled rice. Please accept our wish! That's all!"

They remained standing at attention.

I, who had never seen any such scene before, stopped using my chopsticks and stood up. But the others, I found, had just kept feeding themselves, as if nothing had happened. Then, after a while, the mistress of the construction camp approached the soldiers and raised two pairs of canteens from their shoulders, and pressed into them the boiled rice she had scooped from the rice tub placed in front of us, before she hung them back as they had been hung before. The soldiers, who had been standing at attention, went out of sight according to the orders of "Salute!" and "About-face!"

Since then, they used to present themselves two times a week, until August 15 or the end of the War. It was simply far from understandable to me that: despite such a hard time as they were having, they had been determined to offer their lives for the sake of their Empire. Frankly speaking, this revealed their difficulty in obtaining food in those days. As a matter of fact, all over Japan in those days, there was much land lying idle. I wonder why the soldiers did not turn their eyes to producing food to be self-sufficient. It ought to have been the military that had inspired the Japanese nationals into the war. And now, the soldiers that belonged to that military were coming out to beg for some boiled rice even at an insignificant construction camp whose members were mostly Koreans! There must have been quite a complicated situation, but to myself then, that appeared something thoroughly dumbfounding rather than amazing.

In fact, most of us, the workers in the camp, remained totally indifferent to them, and that indifference must have revealed our having been dumbfounded, as I was, and our disdain that conveyed our unspoken message: "Has *that* taught you?"

The Japanese military at that time was thorough-going in obtaining their food, but it seems that they had not realized the fact that food must be produced before being obtained. It is said: "An army travels on its stomach (We cannot work on an empty stomach)," and Japan was defeated in less than three months since we began to have those beggar-soldiers come round to our camp. In fact, Japan had been engaged in the war, day in, day out, for as long as fifteen years. The war, once it breaks out, cannot be brought to an end so soon, so easily; and millions of lives were blown off in vain, even before being defeated. What was more, the extravagant war expenditure had also been made to be gone with the wind.

The Koreans' labor employed to support the Japanese at war was also lost in vain. The defeat in the war which lasted as long as fifteen years had brought about nothing but total fatigue not only to the Japanese but also to the Koreans. Those hanging around Hakata Station were none other than the soldiers on their way home after having been repatriated from the defeated war. On the other hand, we, drafted workers from overseas, were also on our way home.

At Hakata, the largest city in Kyūshū then — as it is now — they had just got off to seek for food. As it happened, however, all the downtown area — excepting in and around New Hakata Station — had been turned into a burned-out area to a thorough extent, while revealing only sporadic Western-style buildings. Obtaining anything to eat *there* seemed even more improbable than coming across a Taoist immortal at his mountain abode.

● **At the Harbor**

Glancing at those repatriated soldiers from the corner of our eyes, we walked down the main street that led to the harbor. The street itself was fairly wide, but because of the earth and sand that had blown from somewhere or what had fallen from something destroyed around, we had to choose where our next step should be taken. After having walked as long as about five hundred meters, the harbor came into view. What had caught my eye next was a part of a wall burnt black and a bent iron bar — which had been blown off from something somewhere — being exposed, while revealing some ugly surface.

What had made me decide it to have been a part of the wall of a building was a sight of what used to be a window — though only a half of it — hanging in the air. On this side of the wall left unburnt, there stood something like a pole made of concrete — though its top was broken and it was unknown whether it used to be a prop or a gatepost, there was a sooty, gold-lettered signboard that read "井筒屋 (*Izutsuya*)" buried into it.

I gazed intently at it, while imagining how that fairly famous store used to be — wondering how many storied it was or how shiny that golden-lettered signboard used to be before it suffered the air raid. I could not tell what that area was called, but the harbor could be seen from this neighborhood. The moving of the crowd of people also could be seen. At the end of that same port area, some roofs in deep black could be seen. The horizon beyond could be seen, too, though nothing was seen upon it. Only the blue expanse of vast waters was lying before us.

"I shall soon be crossing that sea!" said I to myself. "Then I shall be able to return home! And I shall be living the *same* life *as* I used to be!"

That was everything that had kept throbbing in my heart and mind. My thought had already been cleared of everything concerning our land which had been colonized, the war, the sufferings inflicted upon us, drafted workers, and so on.

This total agitation in the frame of my mind made me feel as if I had kept some secret treasure hidden in my physique. In my life so far — eighteen years — I had never been so happy as I was then! I had been agitated by the pride of my being a Korean so much so that I simply remained filled with rapture and no other emotions might find any space to get in. Until half a month before, I had been placed under the control, while being made to feel humiliated, and always keeping my own will forced out. But now, the sight of Hakata Harbor just before my eyes made me feel overwhelmingly happy and free until everything that had happened to me so far was simply faded away somewhere afar!

I had totally been controlled only by my wish to return home. It was known to everyone of us that our life from then on would change 180 degrees.

As for myself and my compatriots, who had been fated to bear the sorrows of those who had to be born to live in the colony with our mind restrained, with our language oppressed and even our physiques dragged about as if we were slaves, the burning pleasure of being able to return to our homeland in the broad daylight — without feeling any fear or hesitation — had caused the spirit of us, Koreans, to change 180 degrees!

● The Stable & the Harbor Police that had Remained Unburnt

Now we were following the wide road that led exclusively to the Harbor. The air we were breathing then smelt more complicated than that of the sea. As if having been invited by that peculiar smell, tens of thousands of Korean people had already been there. We three, too, were to bring ourselves there. We, having been heading directly for the port at the quay, just stepped into the Harbor Street, after having crossed the municipal electric railway. We walked about 500m or 600m to the quay. The road was about as wide as the first-class national highway today. This area had probably been reclaimed from the sea, and the breakwaters on both sides were built of concrete, leading as far as the quay — the right one had been made 50cm higher than the flatland. The left one was left as it was, since it had been cut through hilly terrain. Because I had stepped into it for the first time, I walked on, carefully looking on both sides.

What had jumped into our eyes first of all on our way to the quay were the stables for the horses which had been driven around with proper dignity by the soldiers and the sailors of the Japanese Empire. The stables — more than a dozen of ridges of them — were arranged side by side. On the left side, there stood the harbor police alone after having been left unburnt. That concrete building, though stained with soot and appearing deprived of its dignity, had kept the symbol of its dignity or a long staircase with nearly ten steps that led to the entrance to it. If I remember right, no other buildings were seen around, excepting the stables, the harbor police on the left and the central street leading to the port.

We three, walked straight to the port. At the end of the row of the stables, there was an oblong open space, whose end led to the waiting room at the harbor. This vacant lot, as was later known to us, used to be a training ground for the horses.

Beyond the harbor was naturally the vast expanse of the sea, and far beyond, there lay our homeland we were about to head for! Upon this corner which seemed to have been so built as to protrude on to the sea, tens of thousands of people were noisily coming and going. They, too, were Koreans expecting to go home, just as we were.

In our ordinary life at home, the occasion we were able to see many people at one time was at a marriage ceremony or a funeral, or a meeting or an assembly held at the community hall. The first time when I joined a considerable number of strangers was when I entered the primary school. The second time was when I went to an open-air market held at Goksan Village as the county capital, which was governing the many towns and villages in the county. I had been taken to this market by my father several times. That market was regularly opened — once in several months — and the grownups enjoyed visiting there. Not only selling and buying of things but also bartering was the mainstream in those days. All things imaginable — cereals, animals (cattle and horses), feathered creatures, handmade furniture, earthenware, ironware, and so on —

were being sold.

Not only those from the dozens of villages in our county but also those from the other counties used to rush to join that event. So the neighborhood as well as the market itself used to be buried with the crowds of people. But about the time the sun began to decline, they started to turn back the way they had followed in the morning. On such occasions, I did see the crowds of people several times. But this still remained as a part of my daily life.

When I was in the first year or the second year of the primary school, my father took me for an overnight trip by bus and by train all the way to an exposition being held at Gyeongseong (the capital in those days: Seoul at present). Unfortunately, however, I was too young to learn anything meaningful through this experience of mine. Among the vague memories I still retain, there were Jongro or the busiest street in the capital, and the Kyongbokyu palace where our King and His Family used to live until Waenom (Japanese) made their appearance even as far as here in our land; and at the department store run by the Japanese, I was told they were selling all kinds of commodities imaginable. Certainly they kept catching my eyes, but I failed to remember even how many storied that building was, even though I still remember how Father pointed at it, looking up at that sky-scraper. I believe I had been passing tens of thousands of people on that occasion, but I simply remained totally indifferent to them.

So I had never remained unexperienced in having anything to do with such crowds of people around, but as for the crowds of people I saw at Hakata Harbor then, they simply left me aghast. We three, having been surrounded by the people ceaselessly thronging into the harbor, seemed to have been made to move on along with the waves of people.

It was a little more than only a single year ago when I was forced into Sumitomo Karatsu Coal-Mining Company, and when I heard that as many as three hundred Koreans had been sent there as drafted workers, I was simply astonished. This did prove how ignorant and naïve I used to be.

● **Our Miscalculation about Our Going Home**

We were totally wrong when we thought we were among the last arrivals at Hakata. Because more and more Koreans came rushing here at Hakata Harbor. The crowds of people that seemed to be tens of thousands had increased into hundreds of thousands before we knew it. By the season of the cool breezing in autumn, we were to be gradually falling into a hell on earth.

This was something we three — and all the other Koreans — had never dreamt of so far. Now, our happy prospect that we should be able to go home had soon turned out to be a great miscalculation, to our immense puzzlement and disappointment.....

At noon on August 15, after that broadcast of the Emperor's announcement of Japan's surrender, that high-ranking military officer gave us a declaration: "Today, from this moment on, — the

Great Empire of Japan has allowed you to have freedom. From now on, therefore, we shall never be concerned with you!"

We, Koreans, did welcome this declaration with utmost pleasure and got drunk in immense happiness. We never noticed the great gap between their declaration to evade their responsibility and our expectation of "the freedom we were allowed to enjoy from that moment on." It was not until I saw the great crowds of my compatriots — hundreds of thousands of them — that I came to notice: *that* declaration had totally been a fake! To make the matter worse, we had simply assumed that: if only we went to Hakata, we should soon be able to get on board the ship for Korea.

Another thing we had simply assumed was: "Because we had been *brought* to Japan, we should naturally be *sent back* to Korea." But we had already been declared: "We (the Japanese side) shall never be concerned in your matter," and at that moment our expectation had turned out useless! Still, that declaration: "Japan has allowed you to be free" did remain with us, keeping us emotionally uplift. Thus our simplicity and ignorance had led us to a great miscalculation. Still, we three, while pushing our way through the crowd, walked straight to the waiting room in the harbor.

When we barely managed to approach the entrance to the waiting room, we saw a thick straw rope stretched in front of the entrance, and three or four Korean youths were crying to us:

"No more people can enter! Return, please!"

Mr. Umimoto from Gyeonggi Dō drew near to them and said:

"What do you mean? We have come here to return home. We need to take steps for *that*. Don't you know?'""

Then one of them said:

"As you see, we are distributing the number tickets so they can get on board in the order of their arrival, but so far we have distributed the tickets to only about ten thousands. As for the rest, the nearer you are to the entrance to the boat, the sooner they'll get on. So, save your place as close to the entrance to the boat as possible. Three hundred people a day are able to get on board. The passage is one hundred *yen* for one person. This line has started since the 18th. So far about two thousand have returned home. Save your place as soon as possible, please!"

Saying so, he openly revealed his reluctance to spend any more time for us. Then all we could do was to walk back, retracing our way to ....

The open space, which used to be the training ground for the horses, had already been occupied by those who had arrived earlier to grab a place by spreading out straw mats or arranging old boards or old bedding. The other side of the open place beside the Harbor Police remained unoccupied, because of its concrete floor lacking in any installation to prevent the spray dashing up from the waves at high tide. Here and there, the people were seen standing or sitting with their legs thrown out — all keeping their faces toward the wide expanse of waters.

We walked along the street with the tramway, which we had crossed only a little while before — talking about what we should do from then on. The conclusion we had reached was: even if the ships were to keep carrying us back for a month, it would be no more than ten thousand people. If things were to go on that way, it would be two or three years later that we were able to reach home. This prospect was overwhelming to me! All the money I had kept with me then was only a little more than 300 yen, and this made me tremble with apprehension!

Soon we came to the stables we had seen on our way to the port some time before, and now the people's coming in and out of them attracted our attention. Then, after our consultation, we decided to take up our position *there* in case we should have to wait for a ferryboat for a long time. The stables closer to the landing place having already been occupied, we decided on the one close to the street with the tramway or diagonally in front of the harbor police. The stables, built by combining such logs as were employed at the construction site, had formed oblong ridges, with about a dozen of stables at each ridge.

It was already well past noon, and now we fortified ourselves with the rice balls we had received when we left our camp that morning. It was about 500m away from the waiting room in the port. Since we simply could not tell when we should be able to take the ship, we thought: the first thing we should do would be to decide where to sleep at night. Even while we were eating the rice ball beside the passage for the horses, the Harbor Street had been growing more and more crowded with those heading for the port.

As for the stable, it was about 9 feet across and about 12 feet deep, and there were twelve sections. This meant there were a dozen of horses in one ridge.

There were ten such ridges, and this told us the fact: a considerable number of horses had been sent to the battlefields after having been trained here. The passageway between the ridges was as wide as two *ken* (ca. 3.6m). There were three faucets at both ends of the ridges and at the halfway point, and this alone was to offer us a blessing of the heaven.

We three had decided to make one of those stables our pad, and the problem we had faced then was what we should do with the dirty straw and horses' droppings left there. It had begun to get dark before we reached any conclusion. It was toward the end of August, but it still remained hot even at night, and it did make us feel goose-pimply to see moths and various insects rushing toward us in black clouds, probably attracted by the odor peculiar to the stables.

● **Under the Staircase of the Harbor Police**

After all, we abandoned our idea of staying up all night at what used to be the passageway for the horses, and got away from Harbor Ward and walked as far as the neighborhood of what was called New Hakata at that time. While wandering around, we found a farmer's house with several empty straw bags piled up as high as one meter at a corner of the yard. We three, standing in a row, called out twice or thrice:

"Good evening! (Is anyone in?)"

There was no answer, even though it was unknown whether or not anyone was in. Now we hadn't received any answer, but we had badly needed that straw bag. This inevitably led us each to take one of those empty straw bags, and after rolling it, we held it under our left arm and returned to the Harbor Street. Mr. Umimoto, the oldest of us, having proposed that we must return to that farmer's house on the following day "to pay for those straw bags," we all agreed to do so.

Now, we returned to the Harbor Street, but it was hard to find any proper space for us to stay at night. The open space, which used to be the training ground for the horses, had already been thickly crowded with the people. This helplessly led us to return to the stable, when I suddenly thought of staying at the front garden of the Harbor Police Station beyond the Harbor Street! When I mentioned this idea of mine, Mr. Umimoto, the eldest of us, said, "We might be kicked out of it." But I insisted on going there, saying:

"No. I believe they won't do such a thing. Even if it rained, the eaves of the building are large and wide enough to make us take shelter. To my mind, *that* will make the only place for us to stay tonight. Why not try *it* at least once?"

What had made me choose to stay at the front of the Harbor Police that night was: firstly, the heat in the daytime had lasted long even after the night fell; secondly I could not suppress my anger at their total inability to deal with or cope with all those Koreans rushing there in thousands a day — until hundreds of thousands of Koreans were being left in total lawlessness. Until only a month before, the police used to flourish their power so much so that they used to be terrified not only by Koreans but also by Japanese; but the moment the War was over, they simply seemed to me to be turned totally incompetent and intimidated like a mouse being stared at by a cat.

So what had made me spend that night just in front of the entrance to the Harbor Police — by spreading the straw bags we had inevitably pinched from somewhere — was a sort of demonstration I had performed in my own way to make a revenge against the huge authority they had been flourishing at us so far. Thus Mr. Yamasaki and Mr. Umimoto were also to be drugged into this demonstration I had started.

This was apparent by the fact that Mr. Umimoto, a former fisherman, had seated himself beside me, saying: "Well, there is no other choice…." But I myself was feeling as satisfied as satisfied could be, because *that* was my final resistance to the authority of Japan.

This was the first time for me to have got my own way since we three had formed a home-coming group. Above all, I myself, being the youngest of us all, was feeling triumphant at heart.

As the night went on, it got quieter. The crowd of people, who had been noisy at what used to be the training-field for horses, would be lying on the rush mat they had carried with them, while feeling nostalgic for their own home.

Even though it appeared lacking in order, there had been a tacit order — in getting on board the ship for home — brought about both in the waiting room and on what used to be the ground for horse-training. But when we finally found out *that* fact, it was too late.....

Now, we three — at our own encampment beside the staircase to the entrance to the police station — were sighing over the absence of order at the harbor, feeling uneasy about when we should be able to get on board the ship, talking about the shortage of money we might face and about what we should do if we were to face the fact that we must wait long before getting on board the ship, which seemed quite probable.

By and by, we became sure that: even if we were able to get on board the ship smoothly without any hitch, it would surely be delayed until the next year. Then it would naturally occur that we must keep staying in the vicinity of this harbor — by finding somewhere to shelter ourselves from the elements. This led me to assert: *that* stable would be the only place to meet *the* conditions. But Mr. Umimoto, our senior, said, shaking his head:

"It won't be too late if we wait and see for four or five days, before we decide on anything about it."

So we decided to obey him.

As for where we should stay at night, we could manage to decide, but because we had aimed *only* to get on board the ship, it simply made us extremely uneasy when we came to wonder how long we must wait before getting on board the ship. My excitement had been made even greater, partly because of my camping out for the first time.

To my mind, what had led us to such suspense as this was: firstly the ignorance on the side of us, Korean people, and secondly the end of the war which had been brought about so abruptly. All the Koreans before they reached Hakata had simply been agitated at the welcome news of their ancestral land having finally been made independent after having been released from Japan. This had sent us all too agitated to foresee the situation a step further so that we could take it into consideration. On the other hand, as for the Japanese people, what had never been dreamt of until the night before had suddenly been brought about before them only by the declaration of the end of the war — a brief one which had taken only a dozen minutes or so. The people, having been thrown into the depth of intense grievance, could hardly deal with the aftermath of the war, nor could afford to turn their eyes toward such things as the Koreans' repatriation.

These situations having affected each other, all those formalities and public order required by the Japanese side turned out to be nullified. That was, the both sides of the Koreans and the Japanese had failed to possess such a frame of mind as was needed in the situation at that time. Legally speaking, when we entered the harbor area, each of us ought to have been given a numbered ticket. As it happened, none of us received anything like such a thing even when we reached the waiting room at the port. All we could see at the entrance there was a thick straw rope to prevent us from entering, and a Korean youth who seemed to be the person standing watch directed us, pointing to the open space which used to be the horses' training ground:

"Please get a place in the queue and wait for your turn to get on board the ship!"

The harbor police was certainly there within our sight, but it had simply remained lacking in any authority to keep the growing number of people in order. So it was partly our retaliation that had led us to be so daring as to camp under the staircase that led to the entrance to the police station.

Mr. Umimoto, senior to us, said in a quiet tone of voice:

"*This* is something considerably daredevil. The end of the war means the end of what the world used to be....."

I myself was feeling just as he was, but even though I wondered what it would be like now that Korea was independent and how about Japan as a defeated nation, it simply remained unimaginable to me.

With America as the main force, nearly ten nations had formed the Allies to win the war against Japan. According to the hearsay, *the* Allies, having already advanced into Tokyo, the capital of Japan, were patrolling around the streets there.

On August 23, when we arrived here, none of such authorities as the allied forces could be seen. It was after the pale shadow of night had already fallen when we crept into the darkness under the concrete staircase that led to the entrance to the Harbor Police. For a while, we all remained silent, while the time passed and the darkness was falling. According to the lunar calendar, it would have been at the beginning of the month, and we had been deprived of even the moonlight. In the harbor square, a huge crowd of Koreans had been moving restlessly, while giving clamorous noises.

At the back of the Harbor Police, there was a sort of canal; the both sides of it were the quays which were devoid of any protection against waves. What if huge waves came rushing? The sprays dashed up from the waves seemed to come up even as far as the Harbor Road. If I remember right, the staircase leading to the entrance to the Harbor Police was gently sloping and as wide as a traffic lane and as long as seven or eight meters, and the end of the space under the staircase was as high as we were able to stand on tiptoe. Since we had seated ourselves around the center of the space, we could hardly be seen by those who climbed up or down that staircase. But if seen from sideways, we could not help being seen.

We all remained silent even though we had been there for half an hour or so. This caused me to begin to feel awkward. I was the one who had suggested we should come and stay there and walked in ahead of them. Now I was beginning to wonder if both of my companions had followed me simply because they could not help it.

Certainly, as long as we were here, we could remain free from the smell of the stable, and less annoyed by the mosquitoes and other insects. It was also cool because of the breeze from the sea. Certainly, that was a fairly good place for us to stay. But somehow or other, I found myself saying in a weak voice:

"Please forgive me."

"Well, what do you mean?"

Mr. Yamasaki, seated beside me, asked me.

"I mean I've suggested coming to stay here."

"Well," said Mr. Yamasaki. "This does make us feel a bit diffident, but we might take it as a part of our experience. Don't you think so, too?"

He turned to Mr. Umimoto, as if trying to invite his opinion. Mr. Umimoto took time before he gave his answer:

"This is the best place in this harbor; it's quiet and restful. But it's *not* the right place for us to stay *long*. It's still early evening, so in an hour or so, let's leave here and return to the stable, so we may openly stretch ourselves and put our feelings and sentiments in order, so we may change our frame of mind for the new situation we are facing now. As we have found here, this is by no means a proper place for us to have a talk or a consultation among ourselves, especially when we have something to give a proper thought on it, and when we have something to think about a little more quietly, too."

Then, when about an hour had passed, Mr. Umimoto said to us: "Then shall we go?"

He folded his straw bag into two and stood up and left there. Mr. Yamasaki followed him, saying: "Shall we go, too?" This led me to say: "Yes," and followed him, holding the straw bag folded in two under my arm.

● **Heading for the Stable**

Leaving *the* place I had chosen and proposed as somewhere for us to take, I was feeling miserable while looking up at the dark sky at night, saying to myself: "I've still remained a mere boy." It was not until then that I realized that: How meaningless and vulgar I had been in my behavior. I felt ashamed and miserable, while looking up at the dark sky, saying to myself: "I've still remained a mere boy."

On the street, I saw the people heading for the harbor in darkness — some were on their own in silence, others were speaking ill of others with their companions; most of them were carrying only one modest baggage. We three, too, could be counted among them, but our direction was different from theirs. In the daytime, we would have been able to reach that stable in a couple of minutes or so, but the darkness and the crowds of people on the street did prevent us from reaching there so soon.

Mr. Umimoto, who was walking before us, was slow in progress, even if I could not tell why. Mr. Yamasaki was following him; I myself, following them, was still wondering what was it that had made me assert to go and stay under that staircase. I recalled what I was saying to myself then: "Japan was defeated; now my homeland is an independent nation! Even the Japanese military has declared: "We shall *not* be concerned in your matter!" So you see, we are free to let out our pent-up anger as much as we like! What if your police may find us and make a row? Here we have tens of thousands of our compatriots! A single harbor police station is nothing to us!"

This was what I had had in my mind when I brought ourselves under that staircase. But I soon found both Mr. Umimoto and Mr. Yamasaki simply remained silent there. This led me to notice how thoughtless and immature I had been. Still I remained unable to ask them what had made them so silent, because I was sure what had led them into silence had lain in myself.

The conclusion I drew from their silence was that: even though Japan was defeated, the police — whose duty is to keep order within their jurisdiction by exercising their authority — remains unchanged whether their state is victorious or defeated.

When I got in under the staircase, they ought to have already noticed this logic. But, instead of preventing me from carrying out my idea, they had kept waiting until I myself came to notice my own misjudgment! Now, I apologized to them for my own indiscretion, saying:

"Sorry. I was wrong."

This did lead both Mr. Umimoto and Mr. Yamasaki to return to what they usually were. But the apology I had made then was limited to my having made them feel awkward then. So the resentment I had kept against Japan remained exactly as it had been so far.

I was able to sympathize with the Japanese people in great grief at their defeated war, and I am ready to encourage them like everyone else. But all those facts about how thoughtless and inhumane Japan used to be in dealing with our territory of Korea *and* even with us Korean people, too, cannot be erased so soon so easily.

We three went to the front of the stable we had decided to sleep in, and after having taken off the rope stretched there, we made a bed by spreading the straw mat we had made out of the straw bag. Thus we felt relieved at having had somewhere to shelter ourselves from the elements even for the time being. Here and there in this stable-street, the people were burning the dried grass to get rid of mosquitoes and other insects.

The stable we had occupied was fairly close to the street with the tramway running along the perimeter of Hakata. But the air-raid three months before had turned it into a burned-out area, and now no tramcar could be seen, even though the railway remained in vain.

What became of Mr. Ri from then on?

The answer will be found in the part of the speech he gave forty-three years later — on July 5 in 1988 — at the law Court in Ōsaka, while speaking for his compatriot, Mr. Hon Inson, as a fingerprint refuser. The point of his speech went as follows:

Later on, I found there was some official stance to supply us Koreans with a passage to our homeland, but at that time, we had *never* heard of anything like that. None had told us anything about *it*, either, and after all, we had to find out our way of keeping ourselves alive. This led me to sell fried sweet potato at a street-stall quarter in and around the harbor in Hakata. Our customers having been those who had just returned from abroad after the war was over, I soon found it impossible to keep on living in this line.

Then I started selling tobacco. I went as far as Kagoshima Prefecture, the southernmost prefecture in Kyushu in order to buy leaf tobacco, which I manufactured into cigarettes at my accommodation in Hakata. This lasted for about one year. There was much to gain in this line — one hundred *yen* for leaf tobacco turned into 300*yen.* By and by, however, the occupation forces from the U.S. brought us much tobacco and this led me to move into another business for black-market rice.

Once I was caught for it and was made to pay a fine of 30,000*yen* — a huge sum at that time, but since I had already earned much by selling tobacco, I was able to pay it in cash. As for our having been engaged in such black market as I had been, the reason was because there was *not* any other way to earn any money at that time. Then about the time of the Korean War (1950-53), there came into being many construction works on the rivers to make them clean and strong by building banks with blocks and stones. This had kept me busy for about ten years throughout 1950s. Then around 1960, I came to Ōsaka. It was not easy to find any proper work to do, and this led me to live on for about a year as a picker of unused corrugated cardboard boxes and old newspapers. Then since I became afford to it, I went to a driving school and started this business of collecting metal wastes I have been engaged in since then. This case of mine, I believe, would be the same with *all* of my compatriots in my generation living in this country.

—— July 5, 1988 at Ōsaka Provincial Court

Talking about his life so far to the students at a local college of distribution science. (December 6, 2011)

From Daughter to *Aboji*

Embracing the Way How *Aboji* Outlived
the Hardest Period of His Life

If I remember right, it was when I was in the third year of North Toyoshima Junior High School in Ikeda City, Ōsaka, Japan, that *Aboji* started writing about his life so far. It was according to my father's wish that I had entered that school. As for the elementary school, I had attended a Korean school in the vicinity of our place of residence. What we were offered there included not only Korean language and principle but also the elementary education concerning our ancestral land of Korea.

What had made my father entrust my junior high school education to that Japanese school was because I was a girl. According to his belief, the women are able to live on, keeping up with whatever ethos they might be offered. If I were a boy, he said, he would have liked to give me a thoroughgoing education on the line of his own ethnology; but because I was a girl, he thought, I should find it less inconvenient in the years to come, if I had attended a Japanese school even though it was only three years. That was why I had been sent to that municipal junior high school.

Mr. Murota in charge of my class when I was a senior there had once visited us during his visits around his pupils' homes. It was on one of such occasions that Mr. Murota kindly suggested to my father that he should recall what he had experienced so far — while making me, his daughter, write down what he had recounted while trying hard to recall.

The progress was slow, partly because our conveniences did not agree, or partly because we had failed in making ourselves understood by each other. It was not until I was about to finish the junior high school that we were finally able to bring it to a tentative end. This led him to express his wish to give up writing any more, while I myself remained unable to resist him, because I felt as if I could understand the way he was feeling then. Even though we were of the same blood, I felt there was something unable to share or unable to do anything with it even if it was shared. As a matter of fact, our ways of life as well as our surroundings had been made totally different from each other, because of that overwhelming power called War......

Seen from our standpoints — especially from Father's — such adverse situations had occurred to him again and again as they could naturally be felt by myself, too. Because of this and that, he had left the latter half of this book undone for about three years, even if Mr. Murota had never been tired of coming to encourage him to resume his writing. It was not until I was about to leave senior high school that Father finally set about writing the latter half of this book all by himself.

In the meantime, I was to leave home by getting married, leaving Father with loneliness rather than pleasure, as I felt it when we happened to be left alone for a little while immediately after the wedding ceremony was over.

At his workshop (June 13, 2011)

Even while he was preparing for this book, I believe, he had his daily life filled with unspeakable sorrows and miseries. But he had kept himself as perseverant as he could until he finally reached his goal, to my heartfelt admiration for his manliness in the true sense of the word — even though I cannot help feeling depressed by the fact that such an unusual amount of perseverance had been needed before he finally reached his goal.

Last but not least, I should like to offer my heart-felt thanks to

Mr. Murota, who had kindly kept encouraging my father until he finally reached his goal. Nowadays I have come to regard my father as a secret hero of mine, who would guide me along throughout my life.

Ri Tongsun

Mr. Ri talking with a non-fiction writer, Ms. Hisae Hirabayashi who visited his workshop on October 23, 1989

The Translator's Note

On the Reader's Column of the Asahi, one of the national newspapers in Japan, dated December 22 in 2014, I read the outline of Mr. Ri's life in Japan and his decease there on October 18 in the same year. The contributor, Mrs. Sachiko Kawaguchi, a former teacher at the same junior highschool as Mr. Ri's daughter had once attended, had naturally mentioned how the Japanese version of *The Sea Aboji Had Overcome* was published in 1987 from Ashi Shobō, but its sequal was them facing difficulties in finding another proper publisher for it.

This led me to decide to translate this life story of Mr. Ri, and by the time I began to work on it, they had found another good publisher — Kaihō Shuppan-sha. I do hope this English version of his book, too, will be of some help to prevent us from committing any such crime and follies as colonialism.

January 27, 2018

Akiko Takemoto